Analyzing Doctrine

Analyzing Doctrine

Toward a Systematic Theology

Oliver D. Crisp

BAYLOR UNIVERSITY PRESS

Cover and Book Design by Savanah N. Landerholm
Cover image: Oliver D. Crisp, "Reflected Light," oil on canvas board, 2003. Used with permission of the artist.

The Library of Congress
has cataloged this book under ISBN 978-1-4813-0986-8.

Printed in the United States of America on acid-free paper with a minimum of 30 percent recycled content.

For Ben Myers

frater alterius matris

Contents

Acknowledgments

The chapters that comprise this work were written in Los Angeles, at Fuller Theological Seminary, and in Scotland at the University of St Andrews. A number of them have also been written in connection with funding from the John Templeton Foundation for grants related to the Fuller Analytic Theology Project (2015–2018), entitled "Prayer, Love, and Human Nature: Analytic Theology for Theological Formation," and to the Institute for Analytic and Exegetical Theology at St Andrews. I am grateful for the opportunities the beneficence of the foundation have provided me. I am also very thankful to the other members of the research group at the core of the Fuller Analytic Theology Project: Rev. Dr. James Arcadi, Jesse Gentile, Steven Nemeş, Dr. J. T. Turner, Dr. Jordan Wessling, and Christopher Woznicki. They have offered feedback on almost all of the chapters of this volume. Members of the Institute for Analytic and Exegetical Theology at St Andrews provided comments on talks and conference papers given there, including earlier versions of chapters 3 and 8–10. Jared Michelson read a penultimate draft of the whole manuscript and offered a number of helpful comments. Mike Rea deserves particular thanks for drawing my attention to a conceptual problem with chapter 11 when I presented a version of the argument to a seminar in the institute. I also benefited from comments given by an audience in the Theology and Ethics Research Seminar at New College, University of Edinburgh, where a version of chapter 10 was read in the fall of 2017. Earlier versions of chapters 5 and 6 were given as the Harold O. J. Brown Lectures at

Reformed Theological Seminary, Charlotte, North Carolina, in March 2015. I am grateful to the seminary, and especially to Rev. Dr. James N. Anderson, for the invitation to give these lectures and for the hospitality I received there. An earlier version of chapter 9 was given at the Philosophy Department at York University in the United Kingdom at the invitation of Rev. Dr. David Efird and Dr. David Worsley. I am very grateful for the comments received on that occasion, and the welcome I received. Reverend Dr. Stephen Wright was very helpful in providing comments on an earlier draft of chapter 11. I am also grateful to my family for their support, and especially to my wife, Claire, for her encouragement on good days and on bad days.

Earlier versions of a number of the chapters have been previously published in professional journals and, in one case, a symposium. All have been revised for inclusion in this work, some significantly. I am grateful to the publishers of the following material for permission to reprint: "Analytic Theology as Systematic Theology," published in *Open Theology* 3 (2017): 156–66; "A Parsimonious Doctrine of Divine Simplicity," published in *Modern Theology* (2019) as part of a symposium on divine simplicity guest edited by George Kalantzis and Matthew Levering; "On Original Sin," in *International Journal of Systematic Theology* 17, no. 3 (2015): 252–66; and "The Resurrection of Christ," in *The Promise of Robert W. Jenson's Theology: Constructive Engagements*, ed. Stephen John Wright and Chris E. W. Green (Minneapolis: Fortress, 2017), 141–58 (the argument of which is now significantly augmented).

Finally, this work is dedicated to my dear friend Dr. Benjamin Myers, whom I affectionately call the Beatnik Theologian. I am sure that Jack Kerouac would approve.

Introduction

Of all disciplines theology is the fairest, the one that moves the head and heart most fully, the one that comes closest to the human reality, the one that gives the clearest perspective on the truth which every disciple seeks. It is a landscape like those of Umbria and Tuscany with views which are distant and yet clear, a work of art which is as well planned and bizarre as the cathedrals of Cologne or Milan. . . . But of all disciplines theology is also the most difficult and the most dangerous, the one in which a man is most likely to end in despair, or—and this is almost worse—in arrogance. Theology can float off into thin air or turn to stone, and worst of all it can become a caricature of itself.

Karl Barth[1]

Writing systematic theology is hard. There are several reasons for this. First, because it has the grand ambition of being *systematic* in its approach to theology, attempting to carve theology at the joints, so to speak (to borrow a term from the analytic philosophers). Such an ambition is a dangerous thing, and much that goes by the name of systematic theology is not truly systematic in nature, and/or does not carve theology at the joints—that is, does not actually get at the truth of the matter. Second, systematic theology is hard because it is *conceptually demanding*. Theology is often lampooned in secular Western culture as a subject that is intellectually bankrupt or at least flaky, a subject one step removed from alchemy or astrology. But in fact doing theology well is very challenging, for the theologian must be conversant with different literatures (biblical studies, history, philosophy, social and natural sciences, and so on) and be able to synthesize much of this material in a way that actually makes some progress on what has been previously said on

---

[1] From Eberhard Busch, *Karl Barth: His Life from Letters and Autobiographical Texts*, trans. John Bowden (London: SCM Press, 1975), 244, taken from the text of the third of a series of lectures given in French in Paris at the invitation of the Protestant Theological Faculty on the subject of Calvin's theology from April 10–12, 1934.

a given topic. That is no mean thing when the theologian must engage with a tradition that is more than two and a half thousand years old.

Bad systematic theology is much easier to execute, much as bad examples of any particular intellectual enterprise are easier to find than good examples of the same thing. Anyone can draw a stick figure on a piece of paper. But far fewer people can paint something as arresting and powerful as Picasso's black-and-white masterpiece *Guernica* (1937). Similarly, it is much easier to assemble quotations from other scholars, to cut and paste some bold assertions, and to warm over ideas that have been culled from someone like Anselm, or Barth, or Schleiermacher. It is much harder to produce constructive theology that deals with the issues Anselm, Schleiermacher, or Barth were concerned with—yet takes forward a distinct research project in one's own voice.

I often say to prospective doctoral students that one of the things that distinguishes masters-level students from doctoral-level students is that the former only have to give some clear account of the ideas of other people, whereas doctoral students must find their own voices in order to make their own contributions. I think this is related to the point about how demanding systematic theology can be. Doing constructive work is hard because world building is hard. Whether the "world" you build as a writer is fictional or factual, metaphysical or poetic, it is hard work producing a conceptual structure that hangs together in a coherent way. But like any building (whether real or imaginary), it is only as strong as the framework that undergirds it. Theology that is attempted without sufficient weight-bearing structures is theology that will fail. It will not last any more than poorly drawn pictures will last, or poorly thought out fictions will endure.

This book is an attempt at such theological conceptual world building. It is not a complete system of theology. But it is a step in that direction, an attempt to provide something like a dogmatic sketch of some of the main load-bearing structures around which a systematic theology would be built. It is related to my earlier constructive work on Christology and atonement, although the present work can be read independently of this previously published material.[2] The current project is focused on what I take to be the theological core of the Christian faith—namely, the doctrine of God, of Christ,

---

[2] See in particular Oliver D. Crisp, *Divinity and Humanity: The Incarnation Reconsidered* (Cambridge: Cambridge University Press, 2007); *God Incarnate: Explorations in Christology* (London: T&T Clark, 2009); *Revisioning Christology: Theology in the Reformed Tradition* (Aldershot: Ashgate, 2011); and *The Word Enfleshed: Exploring the Person and Work of Christ* (Grand Rapids: Baker Academic, 2016).

and of the nature of salvation. It is far from complete. But it is a beginning, perhaps the first step toward something larger and more intricate.

Like any great master, Picasso painted many studies of various aspects of *Guernica* in the years before he put all these various elements together into the finished product. In a similar way, this work is a series of studies toward the making of a larger, and as yet unwritten, synthetic project. They are interconnected and hang together as components of a larger whole that I hope will become clear as the reader proceeds. But they are also sufficiently distinct so as to be read individually as studies on a given doctrine. Nevertheless, the hope is that they have a certain integrity and coherence when placed together in this whole, giving an overview of some of the central tenets of Christian doctrine that make up the traditional loci or topics (literally, "places") of systematic theology.

Some Key Terms

Before proceeding to give an overview of the different chapters and how they fit together to form this dogmatic sketch, let me say a word about how I am using terms like "systematic," "constructive," and "dogmatic" as ways of qualifying the English noun "theology." For these are words that will recur as the book unfolds.

As the reader has probably gathered from the above remarks, I take *systematic theology* to be a particular way of doing theology. It is, I think, a term that denotes that branch of theological science or *Wissenschaft* that attempts to give an organized, integrated, and systematic account of the various doctrines of the Christian faith. There are different ways in which this can be done, as a brief glance at the history of theology will demonstrate, whether it is in question-and-answer format or in clipped scholastic sentences replete with careful distinctions, the rhythm and meter of poetry (consider Dante or Milton, whose work might be read as theological studies in particular doctrines) or the simple pellucid beauty of clean prose. In each case the author is attempting to give a *systematic* account of Christian doctrine, or at least to write with such systematic motivations in mind much as one might write a novel in a series with the broader backdrop of a particular fictional world informing the issues worked out in the story. I think systematic theology is also aimed at truth and truth-apt. These days this is a more controversial claim (as we shall see in chapter 1). Yet it is an almost universally accepted assumption in older theological works, and I follow this older tradition here. For I presume (with some important qualifications registered in the first few chapters) that theology is able to speak truthfully about the divine.

Systematic theology is also about conceptual world building—but of a particular sort. These days conceptual world building is back on the agenda for analytic philosophers after a hiatus that lasted for much of the middle third of the twentieth century. One can read recent works by philosophers trying to give a metaphysical account of the structure of the world.[3] Systematic theologians have always had that ambition, but it is an ambition informed by the Christian tradition and supremely by Scripture. In other words, and unlike the world building of metaphysicians, the world building of systematic theologians depends in important respects on judgments about *testimony*, specifically the testimony of witnesses to divine revelation, and to theological and ecclesiastical leaders of the past whose work elaborating upon this testimony has generated a tradition of interpretation and theological judgment to which modern divines must pay attention. Theological world building, then, is an effort done in conversation with a great congregation of thinkers, most of whom are dead, and some of whom claim to be witnesses to divine revelation.

On my way of thinking, *dogmatic theology* is a subfield of systematic theology. It is the sort of systematic theology that is focused on giving an account of dogma—that is, the conceptual core of the Christian faith as articulated in the great postbiblical statements of Christian faith like the great creeds and the confessions and catechisms of particular churches. Dogmatic theology, then, is systematic theology that has a particular interest in churchly theology and the ways in which the church has articulated the faith in the symbols she has produced—symbols like creeds and confessions. Often, the term "dogmatics" is used in contemporary systematic theology for all intents and purposes as a synonym for systematic theology. This is a pity. There is an important distinction to be made here, one that helps to track the way in which systematic theology may attend to certain sorts of sources in its theologizing (such as creeds, confessions, and other official church documents) or may privilege the more speculative task of theological construction. Although such distinctions are not hard and fast, they do serve a purpose.[4]

---

[3] For instance, D. M. Armstrong, *A World of States of Affairs* (Cambridge: Cambridge University Press, 1997); E. J. Lowe, *The Four Category Ontology: A Metaphysical Foundation for Natural Science* (Oxford: Oxford University Press, 2006); Ted Sider, *Writing the Book of the World* (Oxford: Oxford University Press, 2011); and Peter Unger, *All the Power in the World* (Oxford: Oxford University Press, 2005).

[4] A similar point is made in the editorial introduction to Oliver D. Crisp and Fred Sanders, eds. *The Task of Dogmatics: Explorations in Theological Method* (Grand Rapids: Zondervan Academic, 2017).

These days *constructive theology* can mean one of several things. Some theologians use the term as a way of demarcating their own projects from systematic theology that is shaped more consciously by the great tradition of past Christian thought. On this way of thinking, the difference between constructive theology and systematic theology is akin to the difference between building an extension to an existing structure and demolishing the structure to build a new edifice from scratch. That is not how the difference between systematic theology and constructive theology is understood in this volume. Instead, I use constructive theology as a way of connoting systematic theology in a constructive mode—more like the work of building the extension to the existing structure than to starting some building project afresh. A constructive theology is one that seeks to give an account of a particular doctrine or (if it is a systematic theology in the formal sense of a system of theology such as Calvin's *Institutes* or Aquinas' *Summa theologiae*) to give an account of the faith as a whole. Construction can be done on the basis of foundations laid by others, which is the point of the analogy of an extension to an existing building. Consequently, I do not see why constructive theology may not also be theology resourced by the great tradition of past theology. It may even be that one can do constructive dogmatic theology—that is, systematic theology focused on the task of churchly theology (as understood by one or more of the great symbols of the church in history)—but seek to offer a new way of looking at, or thinking about, such theology, perhaps even of moving beyond such historic statements in providing a new synthetic theological whole. I take Karl Barth's magisterial *Church Dogmatics* to be a paradigm of such work.

With these preliminary distinctions in mind, we may turn to consider the substance of the chapters that follow.

Overview of Chapters

The chapters are arranged so as to follow the sequence of topics that one would expect to find in a standard textbook of theology, beginning with methodological matters and proceeding to the doctrine of God, the Trinity, God's purpose in creation, the doctrine of sin, and the incarnation and reconciling work of Christ. Thus, the first chapter is on theological method; the second to fourth chapters are on the doctrine of God; the fifth and sixth chapters are about God's intention in creating the world and his relationship to the creation; the seventh chapter focuses on the problem of original sin, which requires the work of salvation; and the eighth to eleventh chapters consider some key issues concerning the solution to this problem of human sinfulness provided by the person and work of Christ, culminating in the doctrine of the resurrection. A shorter concluding chapter draws the different strands of these studies together into a whole, offering a single vision of Christian systematic theology written as a piece of analytic theology.

There are notable absences from this list, however. For instance, there is no separate discussion of providence; no more general account of theological anthropology; no discrete doctrine of the person and work of the Holy Spirit; no mention of the order of salvation (*ordo salutis*) that includes calling, regeneration, justification, and sanctification; no clear doctrine of atonement;[5] nothing about the four last things—death, judgment, heaven, and hell—let alone the new heavens and the new earth. But the reader will recall that the doctrinal studies in this volume are only *steps toward* a systematic theology. Even if some important topics are not addressed directly, the matters that are dealt with take their bearings from a more comprehensive theological vision, one that I trust the reader will understand from the hints given in the chapters that follow.

The first chapter is the one more methodological piece that appears in this volume. It is an apology for analytic theology as systematic theology. The thesis defended here is not that analytic theology *just is* systematic theology (though some analytic theologians have claimed this as the chapter explains). Rather, the thesis is that some analytic theology counts as systematic theology just as much as any other sort of systematic theology practiced today. A brief overview of the way in which several key contemporary practitioners of systematic theology think about their discipline yields the conclusion that there is very little consensus on the nature of systematic theology. What consensus there is, I gather together in what I call Shared Task. Then, using this consensus statement of the nature of systematic theology, I show that analytic theologians may practice analytic theology in a way that is entirely in keeping with Shared Task. This does not mean that all analytic theology is systematic theology. But it does mean that at least some analytic theology counts as systematic theology as much as any of the three exemplars of modern systematic theology canvassed in the earlier section of this chapter.

This is an important thing to establish because an oft-repeated criticism of analytic theology is that it is insufficiently *theological*, and is not systematic theology at all. But if Shared Task captures core commitments of much contemporary systematic theology—commitments shared by many

---

[5] This is outlined in *Word Enfleshed*. I have also written on the scope of salvation in *Deviant Calvinism: Broadening the Reformed Tradition* (Minneapolis: Fortress, 2014).

practitioners of analytic theology—then it is much more difficult to see why analytic theology cannot count as systematic theology in principle. This sets the scene for the studies that follow, all of which are offered as instances of systematic theology (understood along the lines of SHARED TASK) that sometimes stray into dogmatic theology (for instance, chapter 8), and in many cases are instances of constructive theology as well (for instance, chapters 3, 4–7, 9, and to some extent 10). In each case it is hoped that the virtues of analytic systematic theology will be made clear through the examination of particular theological topics and issues.

With this in mind, chapter 2 considers another vexing problem in the dialogue between contemporary practitioners of what we might call analytic systematic theology and practitioners of non–analytic systematic theology—namely, the doctrine of God. In this chapter I set out two pictures of God. The first of these is often called the *classical theistic picture*. Although this is something of a term of art, it does represent a set of theological commitments that can be found among some contemporary practitioners of systematic theology and in much historic theology as well. It is characterized by a way of thinking about the divine nature that emphasizes the significant difference between God and creation and the way in which God's life is unique. By contrast, in much contemporary analytic philosophy of religion and philosophical theology—including some analytic systematic theology—God is understood as something like a very large person. In recent times the Thomist philosopher Brian Davies has labeled such theology *theistic personalism*.[6] Having set out these two pictures of the divine nature, I then consider their relationship to the debate about theological realism and antirealism, which has to do with whether God is mind independent or merely the projection or product of human imagination. This then leads into a discussion of a via media between classical theism and theistic personalism that I call *chastened theism*. I give an overview or dogmatic sketch of this alternative as a prelude to chapters 3 and 4 that focus on the two "poles" of the Christian doctrine of God—that is, his unity and triunity, respectively.

Turning to the matter of God's unity, chapter 3 develops an account of divine simplicity. This is the notion that God is without composition. In recent systematic and philosophical theology, this doctrine has been the subject of scrutiny and criticism. Though it is a mainstay of classical theism (as the first chapter points out), it has come under heavy fire from both

---

[6] See Brian Davies, *An Introduction to the Philosophy of Religion*, 3rd ed. (1982; repr., Oxford: Oxford University Press, 2004), esp. ch. 1, "Concepts of God."

analytic philosophers and from modern theologians. In both of these constituencies the doctrine is often regarded as without sufficient theological warrant, and as confusing or even incoherent. Rather than attempting yet another defense of the traditional doctrine, this chapter focuses instead upon the task of offering a constructive account that may be a way forward in discussion of this aspect of Theology Proper (i.e., of the doctrine of God). This way forward involves setting out a model of the doctrine. A model in contemporary natural science is not the truth of the matter but a toy version of reality—a cut-down account that enables us to see something about matters that are actually much more complicated, such as a physics textbook diagram of an atom. I suggest that a productive way forward on the topic of divine simplicity is to construct a model of the doctrine that delivers much of what the classical theists want but that does not commit the theologian to the strong versions of the doctrine that are to be found in the Christian tradition, and that have drawn the ire of modern theologians and philosophers. Like a scientific model, this approximation to the doctrine is not necessarily the truth of the matter, but it is a useful fiction that can be used productively in giving an account of the divine nature that appeals to a wider audience than just classical theologians. It may also be of help in bringing divine simplicity to bear upon the dogma of the Trinity, which is something of a holy grail in contemporary dogmatic theology.

This leads to the discussion of the Trinity itself in chapter 4. The history of theology is replete with accounts of this central and defining dogma. These can be grouped into two families of views, although there are some outliers that are not clearly examples of one or another family (such as the position of Jonathan Edwards[7]). The first of these families is often called the Latin Trinity, and is associated with such thinkers as Augustine, Anselm, and Aquinas—members of the "A Team" of Christian thinkers. According to this view, the persons of the Trinity are to be understood in a rather "thin" way, in terms of the relations of origin in the Godhead. These are paternity (or being the Father); filiation (or being eternally begotten by the Father, in the case of the Son); and spiration (or being breathed out by the Father, in the case of the Holy Spirit). Everything else in God is shared between the divine persons in the divine essence. So God has one will, one center of action, and so on. The main family of views that represent an alternative to this picture is often called social Trinitarianism. On this way

---

[7] I have discussed the shape of Edwards' doctrine in Crisp, *Jonathan Edwards among the Theologians* (Grand Rapids: Eerdmans, 2016).

of thinking the distinctions in the Godhead are more pronounced. God is one in essence, but his internal life is thought to be more differentiated. Typically, social Trinitarians take this to mean that there are three wills and three centers of operation in God, consistent with the three divine persons of the Godhead. Then, in addition to these traditional families of views about the Trinity, there is the recent constitution view developed by Christian philosophers like Michael Rea, Jeff Brower, and (with important modifications) Peter van Inwagen. According to this view, the divine life is more like a statue composed of marble that is also a pillar so that there are several entities colocated in one place. There is the statue, which is composed of the marble. There is the pillar, also composed of the same slab of marble. Then there is the block of marble itself, from which the statue-pillar is hewn. We have three distinct but colocated objects in the same place—namely, the block-statue-pillar. But all three, though numerically distinct, are nevertheless composed of the same "stuff"—namely, the marble slab. Perhaps, say these philosophers, the Trinity is rather like this image. The one essence of God is like the marble shared between the persons, whereas the persons themselves are like the marble block, the statue, and the pillar, respectively. Together they "compose" the one God.

Attractive though each of these models of the Trinity are in different ways, each has significant conceptual costs. After setting out these options, I offer an alternative account. This alternative does not set out a further model of the Trinity as such. Rather, it is more like an approach to thinking about the existing models of the Trinity—a kind of metamodel or theory about the various models of the Trinity that exist. This theory is that no model of the Trinity is adequate because God is fundamentally mysterious and beyond our ken. We do not have an adequate conceptual grip on the Trinity, so rather than attempting to explain the Trinity, we might be better off acknowledging that we do not have a single account of the doctrine that makes complete sense, and that our various models of the Trinity are at best piecemeal attempts to grasp something beyond our comprehension. This position is called *Trinitarian mysterianism*.

Chapter 5 turns from the doctrine of Theology Proper to discussion of the created order. It deals with the relationship between what could be called protological issues in theology and eschatological issues. Put more simply, it deals with how the first things in the eternal purposes of God in creation are related to the last things. This is dealt with in dialogue with several accounts of the relationship between first and last things in recent systematic theology, particularly the works of Wolfhart Pannenberg, Jürgen Moltmann, and

Robert Jenson. I set out and discuss the merits and drawbacks of three theses that these non–analytic systematic theologians have proffered in this connection. The first is the Hegelian Thesis; the second is the Hellenization Thesis; and the third is the Eschatological Identity Thesis.

Chapter 6 follows on from where the previous chapter left off. It sets out one version of an "incarnation anyway" doctrine, the view according to which Christ would have become incarnate without a fall, an issue that has begun to receive more attention in the recent theological literature. This version of incarnation anyway I call the *christological union account*. It is related to the union account of atonement that I have set out in my earlier study, *The Word Enfleshed*. In this chapter I argue that far from being theologically speculative in a pejorative sense, the christological union account sheds important light upon several related issues, such as the image of God and God's ultimate end in creating the world. After setting out the doctrine in an extended narrative, I weigh up some of the principal reasons in favor of the view as well as potential objections that could be raised against it.

Chapter 7 switches tack from speculation about whether there would have been an incarnation without the fall to an account of the moral state of human beings given the fall. In my earlier work, I had endorsed a traditional Reformed account on the doctrine of original sin according to which fallen human beings have ascribed to them the sin, and guilt of the sin, of our first parents. Thus all fallen human beings possess both a corrupt moral nature, which is original sin, and the guilt that accompanies this, which is original guilt. However, further reflection on this topic, and on responses to my earlier position, has led me to change my mind. This chapter is the result. It sets out a constructive account of original sin that avoids the serious theological drawback of the doctrine of original guilt, drawing on resources from a minority report in the Reformed tradition in order to do so. I dub this account *the moderate Reformed doctrine of original sin*.[8] I also argue that an adequate understanding of original sin must be open textured enough to accommodate some version of the story of evolutionary human development. Although I do not offer an account of *how* original sin is consistent with evolutionary human development, the doctrine set out here is commensurate with several live options on this controversial theological topic.

---

[8] This chapter is closely related to two other recent forays into this area. The first is my chapter entitled "Sin," in *Christian Dogmatics: Reformed Theology for the Church Catholic*, ed. Michael Allen and Scott R. Swain (Grand Rapids: Baker Academic, 2016), 194–215. The second is my article "Retrieving Zwingli 's Doctrine of Original Sin," *Journal of Reformed Theology* 10, no. 4 (2016): 1–21.

Having set out reasons for thinking that an incarnation is required for God's unitive purpose in creation, and having considered the doctrine of original sin, chapter 8 turns to a solution to the problem of human fallen-ness in the doctrine of the person and work of Christ. We begin by focusing on the traditional doctrine of the virginal conception of Christ. In a significant recent study of the doctrine, the biblical scholar Andrew Lincoln has argued that there are good biblical and theological reasons for rejecting the traditional position in favor of the view that the generation of Christ's human nature was like that of any other mere human being, and was not the result of some miraculous divine act. In the course of laying out his argument, Lincoln makes a point of engaging my earlier work in this area, in which I defended a version of the traditional dogma of the virginal conception.

In this chapter I return to the topic in order to deal with Lincoln's revisionist account of the doctrine. Along the way I argue that the biblical and theological objections Lincoln brings against the traditional position can be rebutted by those who favor the traditional dogma. Although it is perfectly possible for God to bring about an incarnation without a virginal conception, there may be good reasons why God does bring it about in this manner, reasons having to do with indicating the importance of the one being conceived—which is a common enough biblical trope. (Consider the circumstances in which John the Baptist was conceived and born, or Isaac or Samson in the Old Testament.) So although the virginal conception is not a requirement for incarnation, it is how God has brought about the incarnation according to at least some strands of the biblical witness, and the witness of the church catholic to the apostolic teaching. For these reasons, I maintain that Christians should retain the dogma.

One fundamental issue in Christology concerns the relationship between Christ's human will and his divine will. It is fundamental because it raises the question of how it is that one person can have two wills—an issue about the very coherence of the incarnation. In chapter 9 I give a defense of the traditional catholic doctrine that Christ had two wills (dyothelitism). This has recently come under fire from some analytic philosophical theologians who favor a monothelite (or one-will) understanding of the incarnation. I set out some reasons for wanting to retain the traditional doctrine and then consider the recent argument for monothelitism given by J. P. Moreland and William Lane Craig. They provide a sophisticated and theologically nuanced case in favor of their position and against the catholic doctrine. More recently, Jordan Wessling has come to their aid in his attempt to provide reasons for thinking that appeal to the traditional catholic view over other considerations (such as the weight of biblical testimony and of reason) is not sufficient to reject monothelitism. I rebut these arguments, showing that the traditional doctrine is a plausible way of understanding the incarnation, and that there are good theological reasons for retaining the doctrine enshrined in the confessional tradition of the catholic creeds rather than abandoning them for something like a neomonothelite alternative.

Chapter 10 moves to the consideration of the reconciling work of Christ in terms of theosis, or divinization, and participation in the divine life—hence the chapter's title, "Salvation as Participation." There has been a renewal of interest in theosis among academic theologians, who have found evidence of the doctrine in a range of Western thinkers, including Thomas Aquinas, Martin Luther, John Calvin, John Wesley, and Jonathan Edwards. Yet there is some difference of opinion on what the conceptual core of the doctrine entails. There is also a lot of recent work in biblical studies and systematic theology that has tried to show how important language of union and participation is in giving an account of salvation in Christ. (Here one thinks of the work of biblical scholars like Douglas Campbell, Grant Macaskill, and Michael Gorman, and of theologians like Julie Canlis, Carl Mosser, Todd Billings, William B. Evans, and many others.) However, there is much less by way of explanation with respect to this language of participation and union. What do we mean when we say that believers are "partakers in the divine nature" (2 Pet 1:4) or that in salvation we are united with Christ (Rom 6; Eph 5:32)?

In this chapter I set out one account of theosis and offer several possible ways of thinking about participation in Christ. This may then provide the raw materials for a model of theosis and participation in Christ consistent with much of the recent biblical and theological literature that seeks to retrieve these notions for contemporary theology. Such notions are of considerable interest for theologians trying to give some account of how participation and union language may be related to the means by which Christ's work reconciles us to Godself. In this way the chapter points to an important issue for atonement theology.[9] The chapter culminates in an examination of a kind of limit case of participation, provided in the recent literature by Thomas P. Flint's Theory of Final Assumptions. He speculates that participation in God in the eschaton may possibly involve the redeemed being hypostatically united to God the Son. Although this is an intriguing argument, it is, I

---

[9] I develop the notion of salvation as participation more fully in the union account of atonement given in ch. 7 of *Word Enfleshed*.

think, a step too far. For it is a kind of hypertrophied account of participation in Christ that requires that the redeemed lose their personhood in order to be personally united to God the Son.

Chapter 11 is the last constructive chapter on the person and work of Christ. It deals with the resurrection of Christ in conversation with the work of Robert Jenson. It seems that Jenson was incapable of writing a dull piece of theology. This is certainly true of his work on the doctrine of the resurrection of Christ. He ties this to his own Lutheran tradition via the claim that Christ's resurrection body is *whatever makes Christ available to us in the church*. This leads him to make some very interesting observations about the empty tomb, and about the way in which the body of Christ is present in the church by means of the sacrament of the Eucharist. He also indulges in some productive theological speculation about the location of the body of Christ postresurrection. Nevertheless, not everything he says on the topic seems on target, and there are ways in which his view leaves certain matters unresolved. After giving a critical account of Jenson's view, I offer a way of repairing what seem to me to be mistakes in his account, filling in the areas where there seem to be lacunae with some help from the analytic metaphysics of Hud Hudson, in order to provide a *Jensonian* understanding of Christ's resurrection that (so it seems to me) merits further reflection by contemporary systematic theologians, and that offers one way of thinking about this important doctrine.

In the conclusion I draw together some of the threads of the foregoing studies, offering a synthetic summary statement of the theology contained in the chapters of this work as a promissory note of a more complete account that I hope in due course to be able to prepare for the reader.

I

Analytic Systematic Theology

The emergence of systematic theology as analytic theology was . . . an accident waiting to happen.

William Abraham[1]

Since the publication of the original symposium in which William Abraham's essay appeared in 2009, analytic theology has emerged as a serious intellectual enterprise that includes a monograph series, several professional journals, a recently published introductory text, and an ever-increasing number of articles, essays, monographs, and edited books that address a wide range of topics in contemporary doctrinal theology from the arcane heights of the Trinity, incarnation, and atonement to theological practices of spiritual theology, prayer, and liturgy.[2] Perhaps it was "an accident waiting to happen." But are the results really theology? Is analytic theology actually systematic theology, or is it something else? That is one of the most persistent questions

---

[1] William Abraham, "Systematic Theology as Analytic Theology," in *Analytic Theology: New Essays in the Philosophy of Theology*, ed. Oliver D. Crisp and Michael C. Rea (Oxford: Oxford University Press, 2009), 54.

[2] Examples include the titles in the Oxford Studies in Analytic Theology series published by Oxford University Press (https://global.oup.com/academic/content/series/o/oxford-studies-in-analytic-theology-osat/), the *Journal of Analytic Theology* (http://journalofanalytictheology.com/), scholarship appearing in *TheoLogica* (http://revistatheologica.com), and works like Kevin Diller, *Theology's Epistemological Dilemma: How Karl Barth and Alvin Plantinga Provide a Unified Response*, Strategic Initiatives in Evangelical Theology (Downers Grove, Ill.: IVP Academic, 2014), and Joshua R. Farris and Charles Taliaferro, eds., *The Routledge Companion to Theological Anthropology* (London: Routledge, 2015). The literature is growing rapidly; this represents an indicative sample.

that has been asked of practitioners of analytic theology by those who are non–analytic systematic theologians in the last decade. In his 2009 response to this question, "Systematic Theology as Analytic Theology," William Abraham answered in the affirmative that "analytic theology can be usefully defined as follows: . . . systematic theology attuned to the deployment of the skills, resources, and virtues of analytic philosophy. It is the articulation of the central themes of Christian teaching illuminated by the best insights of analytic philosophy."[3] That is a good place to start. He goes on to elaborate how analytic theology might approach topics of systematic theology, focusing on the doctrine of God and Anselm's vision of the divine. Nevertheless, the worry that analytic theology is really a wolf in sheep's clothing—that is, philosophy pretending to be theology—has persisted.

The same topic has been taken up and elaborated upon by Thomas McCall in his more recent book *An Invitation to Analytic Christian Theology*.[4] Like Abraham, he thinks that "theologians should be able and willing to do *analytic* theology. They should, in other words, do theology that is able and willing to employ the skills and tools of the analytic tradition [of philosophy]." What is more, McCall urges analytic theologians to do theology. He writes,

> Analytic theology—*as theology*—should be (to borrow John Webster's phrase) "theological theology." It should be grounded in Holy Scripture, informed by the Christian tradition and attentive to the potential and pressing challenges faced by God's people in the world. But there is more— analytic theology should be oriented toward its proper end, and analytic theologians should be attentive to the proper approach and posture of theology.[5]

Perhaps unsurprisingly, I am sympathetic to both Abraham and McCall, and applaud McCall's notion that analytic theology should be a properly "theological theology." Nevertheless, even here there is some indication that analytic theology is still not always regarded as proper theology, and even that some practitioners of analytic theology may not be doing genuine theology after all—hence McCall's injunction that analytic theologians do *theology*,

---

[3] Abraham, "Systematic Theology as Analytic Theology," in Crisp and Rea, *Analytic Theology*, 54–55. Compare Oliver D. Crisp, "On Analytic Theology," in Crisp and Rea, *Analytic Theology, 33–53*; and Crisp, "Analytic Theology," *Expository Times* 122, no. 10 (2011): 469–77.

[4] Thomas H. McCall, *An Invitation to Analytic Christian Theology* (Downers Grove, Ill.: IVP Academic, 2015).

[5] McCall, *Invitation to Analytic Christian Theology*, 161–62.

which I take to be a plea for practitioners of analytic theology to do genuine theology rather than ersatz theology, or philosophy dressed up as theology. Such a concern would only arise if there was some uncertainty about whether analytic theology is a species of theology.

This opening chapter is a further attempt to address the question of whether analytic theology is systematic theology. Because I think this is an important matter, and because it seems to me that there is still widespread misunderstanding about the nature and scope of analytic theology among nonanalytic practitioners of systematic theology, I venture to think that yet another attempt to address this question is worthwhile, in the hope that we may get past this largely formal matter and onto more productive material ones.

What Is Systematic Theology?

Let us begin by thinking about the nature of systematic theology. My central claim here is that *analytic theology can (and should) be practiced as a species of systematic theology*. It is such *analytic systematic theology* that this volume is interested in. This seems to me to be the central claim of McCall's invitation to analytic theology as well. But it is subtly different from that offered by Abraham. Whereas Abraham maintains that analytic theology *just is* systematic theology of a particular variety, my claim is more modest: analytic theology *may* be practiced as a form of systematic theology, and should be received as such by the systematic theology guild when it is practiced in this way. Nevertheless, this is consistent with the notion that analytic theology may not always be a species of systematic theology. To see why this may be the case, consider the fact that someone may work on natural theology with the sensibilities and ambition of a practitioner of analytic theology (and many today do so). Yet on one widely accepted way of thinking about the project of natural theology, it does not fall under the description of systematic theology because it involves reasoning about matters theological without recourse or appeal to special revelation or ecclesiastical tradition, using evidence and premises that are accessible to all reasonable human beings, irrespective of theological persuasion.

There is now overwhelming evidence for the conclusion that analytic theology is being practiced as a species of systematic theology in the published body of work being produced by practitioners of analytic theology. Nonanalytic theologians may claim that such analytic theology is not, in fact, *genuine* systematic theology. But in order to make good on this objection, the practitioner of systematic theology would have to be able to show that nothing that falls under the description of analytic theology as it is understood by its leading practitioners is within the bounds of what falls under the description of systematic theology as it is understood by its leading practitioners. The problem here is that there is no set of necessary and sufficient conditions for systematic theology, no description under which "such and such counts as systematic theology" is agreed upon by the leading members of the systematic theology guild. In fact, there is wide divergence among members of the systematic theology guild about the nature of systematic theology, and about its relationship to philosophy, the social and natural sciences, and other intellectual disciplines. Because there is such difference of view about the nature of systematic theology among members of the systematic theology guild, judging whether analytic theology falls within the bounds of systematic theology is not quite as straightforward as it might at first appear. For if there is no agreed criteria for what constitutes a particular intellectual subdiscipline like systematic theology, then judging whether a particular work counts as an instance of the particular discipline in question is a rather difficult task.

To make this point sharper, let us consider some representative examples of contemporary systematic theology. I have chosen to focus on three theologians whose work marks them out as inheritors of different approaches to the theological task in modern theology.

John Webster

Since we have already mentioned him in passing, let us begin with the late John Webster's view of the nature of systematic theology, which is currently one of the most influential. In a recent paper entitled "What Makes Theology Theological?," he writes that "an understanding of the nature of theology comprises, *inter alia*, an account of theology's object, its cognitive principles, its ends, and the virtues of its practitioners. Acts of creaturely intellect are theological to the extent that they are directed to this object, operate on the basis of these cognitive principles, pursue these ends, and are undertaken by persons in whom these virtues may be discerned."[6] Theology's object is primarily God and secondarily the works of God in creation; its cognitive principles are intellectual acts like reading and interpretation, historical inquiry, conceptual abstraction, and practical judgment.[7] In an earlier essay,

---

[6] John B. Webster, "What Makes Theology Theological?" *Journal of Analytic Theology* 3 (2015): 17.
[7] Webster, "What Makes Theology Theological?" 20.

entitled "Principles of Systematic Theology," Webster puts it like this: "The Holy Trinity is the ontological principle of Christian systematic theology. Its external or objective cognitive principle is the divine Word, by which . . . God's incommunicable self-knowledge is accommodated to the saints. The internal or subjective cognitive principle is the redeemed intelligence of the saints. Systematic theology is thus ectypal knowledge . . . and a subaltern or subordinate science. Its matter is twofold: God, and all things in God."[8]

From these different essays a fairly cohesive account emerges. According to Webster, theology ought to be about the nature of the triune God and focused upon understanding him in an appropriate, worshipful manner by means of the word of God. Then it should be about God's works in creation, understood by means of redeemed intelligence. It brings a breadth of different tools from allied disciplines like biblical studies, historical theology, and, perhaps, philosophy to bear upon the theological task. But its principles, goals, and aims are all properly theological, both in the sense of belonging to the discipline of systematic theology (rather than critical theory, or sociology, or whatever) and in the sense of being focused principally upon Theology Proper—that is, the doctrine of God.

Brian Gerrish

Let us turn to another contemporary conception of the theological task. This time we consider Brian Gerrish, himself a Reformed theologian like Webster, though of a Presbyterian rather than Anglican persuasion. In his recent one-volume systematic theology *Christian Faith: Dogmatics in Outline*, Gerrish begins with the following dogmatic thesis statement: "Christian dogmatics, as part of Christian theology, has for its subject matter the distinctively Christian way of having faith, in which elemental faith is confirmed, specified, and represented as filial trust in God the Father of Jesus Christ."[9] In his second chapter on the definition of dogmatics, the dogmatic thesis statement reads, "Christian dogmatics is distinguished from every other part of Christian theology as the theoretical, critical, and systematic discipline that seeks to establish the unity, and to test the adequacy, of the beliefs and dogmas in which Christian faith is expressed."[10] Here the focus is on religious experience rather than upon doctrine. Systematic theology, or dogmatics (the

---

[8] John B. Webster, "Principles of Systematic Theology," *International Journal of Systematic Theology* 11, no. 1 (2009): 56.

[9] B. A. Gerrish, *Christian Faith: Dogmatics in Outline* (Louisville: Westminster John Knox, 2015), 3.

[10] Gerrish, *Christian Faith*, 13.

words are apparently interchangeable for Gerrish[11]), is primarily concerned with Christian faith. Doctrine (here, beliefs and dogmas) is a second-order attempt to express or capture something of this faith, so that systematic theology (i.e., dogmatics) is tasked with testing the adequacy of these doctrines relative to the faith Christians express.

Gordon Kaufman

A third example of a contemporary systematic theologian, with a rather different understanding of the nature of systematic theology from those of Webster and Gerrish, is the Harvard theologian Gordon Kaufman. In his constructive theology *In the Face of Mystery*, he maintains that God is a symbol, a value to which we aspire in our thinking about our own lives and worldview in relation to God. We do not have any unmediated access to the divine. Our thoughts and conceptions of God are our own, not the product of some immediate revelation. Consequently,

> Theologians should attempt to construct conceptions of God, humanity, and the world appropriate for the orientation of contemporary human life. As we have been observing, these notions are (and always have been) human creations, human imaginative constructions; they are our ideas, not God's. What is needed in each new generation is an understanding of God adequate for and appropriate to human life in the world within which it finds itself, so that human devotion and loyalty, service and worship, may be directed toward God rather than to the many idols that so easily attract attention and interest.[12]

Kaufman eschews the tradition-bound biblicism of the past as an outmoded way of thinking of the constructive theological task. Instead, he regards systematic and constructive theology as disciplines concerned in each new generation with the forging of imaginative ways of thinking

---

[11] Gerrish points out that systematic theology has often been identified in Protestant curricula as the compound of apologetics, dogmatics, and theological ethics. However, this does not seem to be how he conceives of dogmatics since he thinks it is a theoretical, critical, and systematic discipline that "seeks both understanding of Christian faith and . . . reformation of the doctrines in which it is conveyed" (Gerrish, *Christian Faith*, 19.) This, he avers, distinguishes it from apologetics, historical and biblical theology, practical theology, and moral theology. So on his way of thinking, dogmatics / systematic theology has a regulative function (giving an account of Christian doctrine) as well as a constructive one (correcting mistaken doctrine and system-building).

[12] Gordon D. Kaufman, *In the Face of Mystery: A Constructive Theology* (Cambridge, Mass.: Harvard University Press, 1993), 31.

about the divine that are adequate for particular communities and people. But for Kaufman, theology is very much a human activity directed Godward. It is not about rightly discerning the meaning of some deposit of revelation bequeathed to us.

In assessing these three examples, we can see that Webster's view is similar to, though not identical with, a certain post-Barthian trajectory in contemporary theology often called "dogmatic theology." As we have already noted, Gerrish is also concerned with this task. It is just that he conceives of it in rather different terms as principally about Christian faith and only secondarily as the conceptualization of that in doctrine. This has a greater affinity to Schleiermacher and to the classical liberal tradition than to Barth. Kaufman's project is much more clearly revisionist in nature, and owes more to the sort of theological trajectory in modern theology traced by the likes of Paul Tillich. But this, too, might be thought of as a piece of systematic theology if we include within the bounds of systematic theology the task of theological construction—which I think we must. Although that may not be the whole of systematic theology, it is often thought to be a part of it, and Kaufman's position is one live option for those engaged in systematic theology as conceptual construction, or world building.

As these three cameos indicate, there is very limited agreement among these practitioners of systematic theology regarding the nature of their task. Is systematic theology principally concerned with understanding the mystery of the triune God as apprehended in Scripture? Or is it primarily about Christian faith and only secondarily about doctrine as that doctrine expresses something of the faith experienced? Perhaps it is neither of these things. Maybe systematic theology is about imaginative human construction instead—the attempt to build an intellectual tower of our own making toward God. Or is it something else, some other way of thinking about theology that we haven't even addressed?

Advocates of analytic theology might be tempted to argue ad hominem that if practitioners of systematic theology don't have clear criteria for what counts as systematic theology, then it is rather difficult for practitioners of analytic theology to know what it is that is missing from analytic theology that means it is not an instance of systematic theology. However, let us leave that to one side. Instead, it may be more fruitful to consider what these different accounts of systematic theology share in common. Despite their significant areas of difference, it looks like they all share the following (perhaps more than this, but at least this much):

SHARED TASK: Commitment to an intellectual undertaking that involves (though it may not comprise) explicating the conceptual content of the Christian tradition (with the expectation that this is normally done from a position within that tradition, as an adherent of that tradition), using particular religious texts that are part of the Christian tradition, including sacred Scripture, as well as human reason, reflection, and praxis (particularly religious practices), as sources for theological judgments.

Let us call this the *Shared Task of systematic theology*, or SHARED TASK for short. There is much more that could be said about each of the claims that make up SHARED TASK, but for now, let us assume that SHARED TASK, or something very like it, is what we might call a conceptual threshold for systematic theology. On this way of thinking, in order for an approach to theology to count as systematic theology, it must meet the conceptual threshold of SHARED TASK.

Now, recall what Abraham and McCall say about analytic theology. It is, says Abraham, "systematic theology attuned to the deployment of the skills, resources, and virtues of analytic philosophy. It is the articulation of the central themes of Christian teaching illuminated by the best insights of analytic philosophy."[13] Or again, it ought to be, according to McCall, "'theological theology.' It should be grounded in Holy Scripture, informed by the Christian tradition and attentive to the potential and pressing challenges faced by God's people in the world. But there is more—analytic theology should be oriented toward its proper end, and analytic theologians should be attentive to the proper approach and posture of theology."[14]

This brings us to the heart of the matter: Does the characterization of analytic theology presented by these two practitioners of analytic theology fall within the parameters of systematic theology that seems to be held in common by the rather different approaches to systematic theology we have just canvassed (irrespective of whether we think analytic theology just *is* systematic theology, or whether analytic theology *may be practiced as* systematic theology)? Does it meet the conceptual threshold of SHARED TASK? Let us see.

First, concerning the ways of thinking about analytic theology that Abraham and McCall set forth, is there a stated commitment to an intellectual task that normally involves (though it may not comprise) explicating the conceptual content of the Christian tradition (with the expectation that this

---

[13] Abraham, "Systematic Theology as Analytic Theology," in Crisp and Rea, *Analytic Theology*, 54–55.
[14] McCall, *Invitation to Analytic Christian Theology*, 161–62.

is a task normally done from a position within that tradition, as an adherent of that tradition)? Clearly, there is such a commitment. Analytic theology is the "articulation of the central themes of Christian teaching illuminated by the best insights of analytic philosophy"; it is "theological theology" that "should be grounded in Holy Scripture, informed by the Christian tradition" and that "should be oriented toward its proper end, and analytic theologians should be attentive to the proper approach and posture of theology."

Second, is analytic theology an approach to theology that uses particular religious texts that are part of the Christian tradition, including sacred Scripture, as well as human reason, reflection, and praxis (particularly religious practices) as sources for theological judgments? Yes, it has that intellectual ambition. Analytic theology "articulates central themes of Christian teaching illuminated by the best insights of analytic philosophy." And, as "theological theology," it should be grounded in Scripture and informed by the Christian tradition, as well as being oriented to its proper end.

In short, as it is characterized by two of its leading proponents, analytic theology falls squarely within the bounds of the common ground occupied by the different approaches to systematic theology we have considered in SHARED TASK. It does not come to the task of systematic theology in quite the same way as these other approaches to contemporary systematic theology. But the reasons why it does not come to the subject matter of theology in quite the same way is not because it fails to qualify as systematic theology. If the characterization of the common ground shared by the three different approaches to systematic theology we have considered here is on target, then practitioners of analytic theology are doing systematic theology, provided they approach their task along the lines laid out in SHARED TASK. Some practitioners of systematic theology will still worry that practitioners of analytic theology are outsiders to the guild trespassing upon theological territory. But it is difficult to see why that should be a problem if the practitioner of analytic theology is attempting to do theology in a manner that conforms to SHARED TASK since this seems to be sufficient to qualify as systematic theology—at least as it has been practiced by three of its leading contemporary proponents. In other words, analytic theology is not (or is not necessarily) ersatz theology. In fact, one could practice analytic theology in a way that shares much of the sensibility of a Webster, or a Gerrish, or a Kaufman. McCall's characterization of analytic theology has much in common with Webster in this regard, and there are practitioners of analytic theology sympathetic to Schleiermacher's project. (I have yet to meet one sympathetic to the revisionism of Kaufman, but in principle it is possible.)

Well, then, if analytic theology may be practiced in such a way that it falls within the bounds of the SHARED TASK, what about it marks it out as something different from these other ways of approaching systematic theology? Let us consider two further candidates that are attempts to refine the objection to analytic theology as systematic theology from non–analytic theology practitioners of systematic theology as a way of trying to give some content to this difference. Neither of these options is right, as far as I can see. Nevertheless, these are objections that are often discussed in connection with analytic theology, so it behooves us to consider them. Having done so, we will be in a position to say something in closing about why analytic theology is different from the other approaches to systematic theology we have considered here.

Analytic Theology and Theological Theology

Despite McCall's enthusiasm for analytic theology as a properly "theological theology," many of those who represent the sort of view expressed by John Webster will worry that SHARED TASK doesn't get at what makes analytic theology theologically suspicious. There is something more intangible at work that distinguishes analytic theology from systematic theology, something that has to do with the characterization of systematic theology as "theological theology." Let us consider this more carefully.

As we have already noted, "theological theology" is a term coined by John Webster as a way of demarcating a particular approach to systematic theology, one that is concerned not merely with theoretical matters but also with the life of the church. In his inaugural lecture as the Lady Margaret Professor of Divinity in Oxford, Webster worries that the eponymous theological theology of his lecture's title is not a practice fostered in the modern research university, which is interested in the development of the everyman educated in the human sciences or *Wissenschaften*, a generic human enterprise, not *Bildung*, the formation of individuals with particular habits of mind aimed at the true and the good.[15] Theology has lost its bearings. It has bartered its substance away in transactions with other disciplines whose integrity is not so contested in the modern university, such as biblical studies, philosophy, and the social sciences. Instead, following Colin Gunton, Webster avers that theology should "contribute from Christian sources things that would otherwise

---

[15] See John B. Webster, "Theological Theology," in *Confessing God: Essays in Christian Dogmatics II* (London: T&T Clark, 2005), 11–32.

not be said."[16] His is a vision of a Balkanized university in which different disciplines have their own modes of inquiry that may include practices that are tradition specific. In the case of theology, this means being oriented to the object of the discipline (God) who is the agent that gives us the material by means of which the subject matter of the discipline is organized—namely, Holy Writ.

This sort of theological vision owes much to the work of Karl Barth and his disciples. Theological theology on this way of thinking is a confessional practice quite distinct from the study of religion, whether that study is conceived of under the aegis of the social sciences or of philosophy. We might dub this the *theology as confessional dogmatics* approach. It presumes that any interaction with other, nontheological disciplines should be at the behest of theology, and for particular purposes that are ancillary to the central dogmatic task of unfolding the Christian faith for the life of the church.

Well, then, what is the objection to analytic theology given this view? It is difficult to say exactly. But perhaps we can put it like this: those who espouse the "theology as confessional dogmatics" approach to systematic theology think that any other approach to systematic theology—whether it is from within theology, such as the imaginative-constructive project of Kaufman, or from without theology, such as the sociology of religion or the philosophy of religion—is inadequate, theologically speaking. These other approaches are lacking something that confessional dogmatics brings to the table. These missing ingredients are confessionalism (understood as an approach to theology that is a confession of its truth) and an ecclesial focus for doing theology. But it should be clear from the foregoing that there is no reason why analytic theology cannot be practiced in this manner. In fact, as we have seen, McCall thinks this ought to be an intellectual ambition for analytic theology—that it ought to be a properly "theological theology."

Still, some will be unpersuaded by this. The real worry, they will say, is that analytic theology is just ersatz theology. It is philosophy thinly disguised as theology. For aren't many of its practitioners philosophers? And don't many of these think of analytic theology as nothing more than philosophical theology? And isn't philosophical theology precisely the philosophical assessment of theological claims, theology done from outside the pale of the theological guild and therefore not "theological theology" after all?

---

[16] Webster, "Theological Theology," 24, citing Colin E. Gunton, "The Indispensability of Theological Understanding: Theology in the University," in *Essentials of Christian Community: Essays for Daniel W. Hardy*, ed. David Ford and David L. Stamps (Edinburgh: T&T Clark, 1996), 276.

It is true that some practitioners of analytic theology think of it as on a continuum with philosophical theology, or as just a rebranding of philosophical theology.[17] But by the same token, many have argued that existentialist theology is really just a species of philosophical theology, or that Tillichian theology is just a species of philosophical theology. If practitioners of analytic theology are doing theology in conformity to SHARED TASK, and with the desire to produce confessional dogmatics—that is, theology that is for the church, done from the perspective of a particular confession for the sake of the church—then it is being done as systematic theology, not as ersatz theology or as thinly veiled philosophy. Given its origins in analytic philosophy of religion and, latterly, analytic philosophical theology, analytic theology does have an affinity with analytic philosophy, and there will inevitably be overlap between that discipline and analytic theology. But the issue cannot be the use of philosophy in theology since all theologians use philosophical ideas and very often align themselves with one or more philosophical tradition (Aristotelian, Platonic, existential, continental, hermeneutical, and so on). I take it that the worry here boils down to the suspicion that analytic theology is philosophy, not theology, or something very similar— namely, that it is rationalism. That is, the worry is that analytic theology makes theology beholden to philosophy, or enslaves theology to a particular philosophical purview. But as practitioners of analytic theology have labored to show from its inception, analytic theology is not necessarily rationalistic, and as practiced today it is almost without exception done in a manner that makes philosophy's role that of the traditional handmaiden to the queen of the sciences. There is surely nothing theologically objectionable about that.

Philosophy as Secular Theology

However, this brings us to our second objection to analytic theology, which concedes SHARED TASK but still finds reason to be suspicious of the claim that analytic theology is systematic theology. This second sort of objection pursues the "analytic theology is philosophy" line in a slightly different way. One way to get at this worry can be found in the work of the ecumenical Lutheran Robert Jenson. He is well known for his assertion that philosophy is just a secularized theology, the theology of the ancient world,

---

[17] See, e.g., Nicholas Wolterstorff's essay, "How Philosophical Theology Became Possible within the Analytic Tradition of Philosophy," in Crisp and Rea, *Analytic Theology*, 155–68; and Eleonore Stump, "The Problem of Evil: Analytic Philosophy and Narrative," in Crisp and Rea, *Analytic Theology*, 251–64.

or what he refers to as Olympian-Parmenidian religion.[18] For him, there is no such thing as philosophy. Or, more precisely, there is something *called* philosophy, but it is not a discipline distinct from theology. It is just a rival sort of theology, one that originates in the Hellenistic world and its religions. Once we see this, our desire to conform our theology to its dictates, as if philosophy were somehow capable of providing an independent, objective standard of rationality to which all other disciplines must pay lip service, should evaporate. For, according to Jenson, we shall then see that philosophy really is a rival theology. What is more, we shall see that the attempt to construct theology using philosophical tools is tantamount to borrowing ideas and sensibilities from a rival religious tradition. Rather than radical orthodoxy's penchant for out-narrating secular approaches to religion, he takes a leaf out of Karl Rahner's book and regards philosophers as anonymous theologians.

Jenson's vision of theological theology (although he doesn't use the term) is beguiling because it provides a plausible explanation of why it is that theologians so often feel the need to apply to the ideas of philosophers in order to furnish their thought with a certain intellectual credibility, or with particular notions, concepts, and arguments. But for this very reason it is also mistaken. To equate philosophy per se with a deracinated ancient theology is like saying modern scientific cosmology is just secularized astrology. Astrologers might find this appealing, for it is certainly true that there is some conceptual overlap between these two disciplines. But few outside the guild of astrologers will think that it is *the same sort of discipline* as cosmology, or that cosmology is a secularized astrology.

So if the worry is that analytic theology subordinates Christian theology to an alien and fundamentally incompatible theological tradition—that of the "secularized theology" we find in contemporary philosophy—then this is, I think, a mistaken view of analytic theology for two reasons. First, because it is a mistaken view of the nature of philosophy, as least as it is widely understood and practiced in the analytic tradition. Second, it is mistaken because analytic theology is not necessarily philosophy but theology,

---

[18] He writes, "The secular mood by which some forms of 'philosophy' contrast with Christian theology and that tempts us to taken them for a different kind of thinking is simply a character of Olympian religion itself, which pursued a divinity purged of mystery. Insofar as Western philosophy is now reduced to the pure study of logic, it is still in fact theology, Christian or Olympian-Parmenidean. Theologians of Western Christianity must indeed converse with the philosophers, but only because and insofar as both are engaged in the *same* sort of enterprise." See Robert W. Jenson, *Systematic Theology*, vol. 1, *The Triune God* (New York: Oxford University Press, 1997), 10 (emphasis in original).

when it is practiced in a way that is consistent with SHARED TASK. I think this is also a rather naive way of thinking about the enterprise of systematic theology, as if practitioners of systematic theology can carry on their task independent of any other discipline and without reference to the philosophical notions around us. Theologians have always been intellectual magpies and have borrowed philosophical ideas, even philosophical systems (just consider use of Aristotle by the Thomists!), baptizing them for the theological task. Analytic theology is doing nothing different from this.

The Role of Traditions, Texts, and Academic Socialization

This brings us, in a final section, to outline some reasons that help clarify what analytic theology is, and why it may be practiced as a species of systematic theology. Here I want to suggest that the reason why many non–analytic theological practitioners of systematic theology are suspicious of the claim that analytic theology is systematic theology (let alone the claim that there might be such a thing as analytic systematic theology) is better understood to be a difference about what we might call *intellectual cultures*, rather than a difference of intellectual discipline. For the purposes of this chapter, an intellectual culture is a rough grouping within a particular intellectual discipline, such as philosophy or theology, that identifies itself as having a distinctive approach to its subject matter and a particular methodological approach to its subject. Such intellectual cultures are something like MacIntyrian intellectual traditions, though as I am using the term, an intellectual culture is less totalizing than a MacIntyrian tradition, being more of a discernible group within a given discipline.[19] Members of a particular intellectual culture pay attention to particular texts and particular thinkers, and privilege certain intellectual virtues and approaches over others. To be a part of such an intellectual culture is to be socialized into a way of approaching a particular intellectual discipline. This applies across subjects, I think, but it certainly applies to philosophy and theology, which are the two intellectual disciplines that I know best. The three approaches to contemporary systematic theology that we began with each represent a particular intellectual

[19] Recall that Alasdair MacIntyre characterizes an intellectual tradition in these terms: "an argument extended through time in which certain fundamental agreements are defined and redefined in terms of two kinds of conflict: those with critics and enemies external to the tradition who reject all or at least key parts of those fundamental agreements, and those internal, interpretive debates through which the meaning and rationale of the fundamental agreements come to be expressed and by whose progress a tradition is constituted." Alasdair MacIntyre, *Whose Justice? Which Rationality?* (Notre Dame: University of Notre Dame Press, 1989), 12.

culture in systematic theology. Analytic theology represents another such intellectual culture, one that also represents a particular trajectory in systematic theology. Objections from other intellectual cultures to analytic theology have often at their roots been about which texts to privilege, which scholars to pay attention to, which intellectual virtues to privilege, and how practitioners of analytic theology are socialized into their particular intellectual culture (via conferences, networks, journals, and so forth).

In the early phase of analytic theology, practitioners sought to distinguish it from other approaches to theology by way of a rather "thin" understanding of analytic theology as a particular method. On this way of thinking, analytic theology does not commit its practitioner to particular substantive doctrines. It is simply a way of approaching the theological task; paying attention to the tools and sensibilities of analytic philosophy and things like clarity, simplicity, and brevity in writing; giving clear arguments for positions; uncovering the logical form of a given view; and so on. I myself have characterized analytic theology in this way. However, in more recent times, the Oxford theologian William Wood has pointed out that the issue of what I am calling intellectual cultures is at least as central as these other matters, and—more importantly—carves the difference between analytic theology and other approaches to systematic theology at the joints in a way that these other ways of thinking about what distinguishes analytic theology do not.

I think he is right. Wood observes,

> Analytic theology as currently practiced has an ambiguous character. It may be understood either formally, as any instance of theology that draws on analytic philosophy, or substantively, as a cohesive theological school that draws on analytic philosophy in defense of traditional Christian orthodoxy. Both conceptions assume that analytic philosophy furnishes "tools and methods" to the analytic theologian. Yet on the best recent accounts of analytic philosophy, analytic philosophy has no unique tools and methods.[20]

This is also true. There are no necessary and sufficient conditions for analytic philosophy, any more than there are such conditions for demarcating systematic theology or analytic theology. How should we think of analytic theology, then? According to Wood, we should think of it as "a robust and distinctive intellectual tradition,"[21] which is tantamount to what I am calling an intellectual culture.

---

[20] William Wood, "Trajectories, Traditions, and Tools in Analytic Theology," *Journal of Analytic Theology* 4 (2016): 254.

[21] Wood, "Trajectories, Traditions, and Tools in Analytic Theology," 254.

He goes on to say that it appears from the way in which analytic theology is developing that it "continues to move away from its origins in philosophy of religion and may well be evolving into a distinctive 'school' of Christian theology."[22] This is not quite right, I think. There are certainly differences among those who practice analytic theology, and differences are emerging over how analytic theology is understood. (In this regard, Wood distinguishes between what he calls "formal" approaches to analytic theology, and "substantive" approaches.) Nevertheless, it seems to me that there is good reason to think analytic theology has always been understood by many of its practitioners as a species of systematic theology. Abraham is a clear example of this. As we have seen, McCall's approach is more circumspect, allowing that analytic theology can be practiced as systematic theology (and should be). But even given this more modest approach, there is the expectation that nothing prevents the practitioner of analytic theology from doing systematic theology—even that practitioners of analytic theology will do systematic theology much of the time. However we conceive of analytic theology, whether as a species of systematic theology (i.e., analytic systematic theology) or as something that may be practiced under the description of systematic theology in SHARED TASK, analytic theology as systematic theology requires training and care. Wood is clear about that. It also requires theologians to become "bilingual," capable of reading and understanding both analytic philosophy and systematic theology. As Wood remarks, "If philosophy presents the theologian with intellectual tools, only a full member of the analytic tradition will know how to use analytic tools expertly. At the same time, only a suitably expert theologian will know how to use analytic tools to construct an edifice worth inhabiting."[23] And, as with any intellectual culture, we can point to paradigms of the sort of expertise we are concerned with, which act as exemplars for further work in the field, just as Webster, Gerrish, and Kaufman are exemplars of other contemporary approaches to systematic theology.

So, analytic theology is an intellectual culture, one of several such cultures that coexist in contemporary systematic theology. But it is not a "club." In her 2013 contribution to the *Journal of the American Academy of Religion's* round table discussion on analytic theology, Sarah Coakley avers, "Rather than hoping to find the essence of Analytic Theology in a club with certain defined rules and requirements for admission, it would seem more profitable, in the spirit of the later Ludwig Wittgenstein, to speak of us analytic

---

[22] Wood, "Trajectories, Traditions, and Tools in Analytic Theology," 259.
[23] Wood, "Trajectories, Traditions, and Tools in Analytic Theology," 264.

theologians as a 'family resemblance' group who share some, but not all, of a range of overlapping and related goals and aspirations."[24] She continues, "And if this is right, it is pointless to look for one *essentialist* definition of our project."[25]

I am sympathetic to this. Coakley is right that analytic theology was never a monolithic enterprise, even in the original volume to which she contributed. She is also right that "family resemblance" is a good way of characterizing much of what goes under the aegis of analytic theology. This is similar in some respects to the notion of an intellectual culture, since any tradition tolerates a certain amount of diversity of views within its bounds. Warming to this theme of "bounded" groups, we might even say that analytic theology is not so much a *bounded group*, where a perimeter is policed so that one is either "out" or "in." Rather, it is something more like what might be termed a *centered group*, where we can see a cluster of members that are right at the heart of the movement, and others less central, or more peripheral, with others still farther out with some connection but without being entirely identified with the movement. Analytic theology is much more like that—and that is what I think Coakley is getting at in her remarks about analytic theology not being a club.

Summary and Conclusion

Let us sum up. Following recent work by William Wood, I have reasoned that analytic theology is an intellectual culture that overlaps systematic theology and that pays attention to particular texts, figures, ideas, and intellectual virtues in the pursuit of systematic theology. It meets the threshold requirement of SHARED TASK, so we can say of analytic theology that its practitioners demonstrate commitment to an intellectual undertaking that involves (though it may not comprise) explicating the conceptual content of the Christian tradition (with the expectation that this is normally done from a position within that tradition, as an adherent of that tradition), using particular religious texts that are part of the Christian tradition, including sacred Scripture, as well as human reason, reflection, and praxis (particularly religious practices), as sources for theological judgments. Its distinctive approach to systematic theology has much in common with historic theology, particular scholastic theology (though we have not explored that relationship in

---

[24] Sarah Coakley, "On Why *Analytic Theology* Is Not a Club," *Journal of the American Academy of Religion* 81, no. 3 (2013): 602–3.

[25] Coakley, "On Why *Analytic Theology* Is Not a Club," 603 (emphasis in original).

detail here). Like dogmaticians interested in "theological theology," it can be practiced in a way that takes seriously the Christian tradition and the place of Scripture as a preeminent norming norm of Christian doctrine. If I may be permitted an aspiration, at its best analytic theology as systematic theology *is a way of doing systematic theology that utilizes the tools and methods of contemporary analytic philosophy for the purposes of constructive Christian theology, paying attention to the Christian tradition and development of doctrine.*[26] That sounds like a properly "theological theology" to me.

Let me close with an injunction. Some years ago Nicholas Wolterstorff, himself an analytic theologian (though trained in philosophy), wrote a short essay addressed to his theological colleagues and to students at Yale who intended to become theologians. It was entitled, "To Theologians: From One Who Cares about Theology but Is Not One of You."[27] In the course of that essay, he sets out a vision of the task of being a theologian with which many practitioners of systematic theology, whether analytic theology or not, can certainly resonate. I hope that however we pursue systematic theology, we will take seriously the call to the particular vocation that Wolterstorff enjoins upon us. Here is what he says:

> To my young grad students who aim to become theologians I say, with all the emphasis I can muster: *be theologians.* Do not be ersatz philosophers, do not be ersatz cultural theorists, do not be ersatz anything. Be genuine theologians. Be sure-footed in philosophy, sure-footed in cultural theory, and the like. And struggle to find a voice that can be heard, if not agreed with, not just by theologians but others as well. But then: be theologians. There will be cultural theorists around to tell us how things look from their perspective; there will be sociologists around to tell us how things look from their perspective. What we need to hear from you is how things look when seen in the light of the triune God—may his name be praised!—who creates and sustains us, who redeems us, and who will bring this frail and fallen, though yet glorious, humanity and cosmos to consummation.[28]

These are surely words to live by. Let us pursue our theologizing *sub specie aeternitatis, et ad maiorem Dei gloriam*—under the aspect of eternity, and to the greater glory of God, as well as with a desire to promote charity and understanding between the different intellectual cultures of contemporary systematic theology.

---

[26] With some adaptation, this is the notion of analytic theology used in the Oxford Studies in Analytic Theology.

[27] Nicholas Wolterstorff, "To Theologians: From One Who Cares about Theology but Is Not One of You," *Theological Education* 40, no. 2 (2005), 79–92.

[28] Wolterstorff, "To Theologians," 91–92 (emphasis in original).

2

Picturing God

To whom then will you liken God, or what likeness compare with him?
Isaiah 40:18

It is often said that a picture is worth a thousand words. The idea is that a picture can convey to a viewer in a moment what it takes many words to communicate to the same person on a page or in conversation. In Christian theology there are different views of the divine—something akin to different conceptual "pictures" of the deity. As the first step toward outlining some key ideas concerning the doctrine of God, in this chapter I want to focus in on two of these conceptual pictures in particular that have been influential and that remain the topic of ongoing discussion and debate in systematic theology. The first is often called *classical theism*. The second is usually referred to as *theistic personalism*.[1] I will argue that there is good reason to opt for a kind of via media between these two pictures. I will call this middle way *chastened theism* because it takes classical theism as the basic framework for thinking about the divine nature, and then modifies doctrinal elements within this framework in various respects in the direction of theistic personalism in

---

[1] The locus classicus for this distinction, and elaboration upon the difference between classical theism and theistic personalism, is Brian Davies, *An Introduction to the Philosophy of Religion,* 3rd ed. (1982; repr., Oxford: Oxford University Press, 2004), ch. 2. James E. Dolezal prefers to speak of "theistic mutualists" in part because of the way in which theistic personalism often goes hand in hand with a social view of the Trinity. But I am not clear that theistic personalism *implies* a social view of the Trinity. So I retain the term "theistic personalism" instead. See Dolezal, *All That Is in God: Evangelical Theology and the Challenge of Classical Christian Theism* (Grand Rapids: Reformation Heritage, 2017).

order to provide a coherent picture of God that takes seriously the historic tradition and the witness of Scripture.[2]

The argument proceeds as follows: To begin with, I shall give an account of classical theism and theistic personalism. Then, I relate these things to the issue of theological realism, theological antirealism, and theological nonrealism—that is, to the question of whether God is a mind-independent entity and creator of all things in heaven and earth whose nature can be understood by humans. This discussion is important for at least two reasons. These are (a) not all Christian theologians conceive of God as mind-independent (some are theological antirealists), and (b) not all Christian theologians think that God's nature can be grasped by humans. Some, including some classical theists, maintain that God's nature is unknowable in a very strong sense such that they are in one important sense theological nonrealists.[3] In my view, theological realism is preferable to theological antirealism and theological nonrealism, and provides theological motivation for revising classical theism in the direction of chastened theism. In a third section I outline chastened theism as a theologically realist near neighbor of classical theism and alternative to theistic personalism, offering reasons why this is a third picture of God worthy of serious consideration for systematic theologians going forward. It is on this basis that we will proceed to discuss divine simplicity and the Trinity in the succeeding chapters.

Classical Theism

Sometimes classical theism and perfect being theology are conflated, and construed as versions of theism that project or maximalize "the ideals of creaturely existence," calling the result "divine."[4] However, it may be helpful

---

[2] Upon reading this chapter, some may draw a different conclusion—namely, that chastened theism is really a thin version of classical theism rather than a distinct third option somewhere in the conceptual space between classical theism and theistic personalism. I would not object to such a characterization of my position.

[3] It is also true to say some Christian theologians deny that God is the creator of all things in heaven and earth. But that is another matter, the discussion of which would take us too far afield. Interested readers may consult William Lane Craig, *God over All: Divine Aseity and the Problem of Platonism* (Oxford: Oxford University Press, 2016); and Paul M. Gould, ed., *Beyond the Control of God? Six Views on the Problem of God and Abstract Objects* (London: Bloomsbury, 2014).

[4] This language is taken from Michael Allen's essay "Divine Attributes," in *Christian Dogmatics: Reformed Theology for the Church Catholic*, ed. Michael Allen and Scott R. Swain (Grand Rapids: Baker Academic, 2015), 64. In the context of the essay, Allen is engaging the views of Reformed theologian Bruce McCormack, especially his essay "The Actuality of

to begin by distinguishing perfect being theology, which is a method for generating a concept of God, from classical theism, which is a particular picture of God that is often generated by means of the method of perfect being theology.

As Brian Leftow has recently argued, perfect being theology predates Christianity, but was adopted as an approach to the doctrine of God by some patristic and medieval theologians.[5] Theologians still debate the merits of the "hellenization of Christianity"—that is, the way in which early Christian thinkers adopted certain Greek philosophical ideas in their theological work. Although there are still theologians who repeat Adolf von Harnack's claim that Hebraic religion was overlaid with a Greek gloss in patristic theology, which contemporary theology needs to remove to get back to a pure biblical religion,[6] careful historical work in this area has demonstrated that Harnack's claim is at the very least problematic, and most likely false. As historian Robert Louis Wilken puts it, it is more apt to speak of the Christianization of Hellenism than the hellenization of Christianity. But he is quick to point out that this did not mean the eclipse of biblical modes of thinking but their transformation in a new context. "Christian thinking," he writes, "whilst working with the patterns of thought and expression rooted in the Graeco-Roman culture, transformed them so profoundly that in the end something quite new came into being."[7]

In keeping with this way of thinking about the Christianization of Hellenism, perfect being theology can be thought of as a theological method for

---

God: Karl Barth in Conversation with Open Theism," in *Engaging the Doctrine of God: Contemporary Protestant Perspectives*, ed. Bruce L. McCormack (Grand Rapids: Baker Academic, 2008), 185–242.

[5] See Brian Leftow, "Why Perfect Being Theology?" *International Journal for Philosophy of Religion* 69 (2011): 103–18.

[6] Consider the work of Jürgen Moltmann, or Robert Jenson, or Colin Gunton. A good recent example of this trajectory in modern theology, which is indebted to all three of Moltmann, Jenson, and Gunton, can be found in Veli-Matti Kärkkäinen, *Trinity and Revelation*, vol. 2 of *Constructive Christian Theology for the Pluralistic World* (Grand Rapids: Eerdmans, 2014), ch. 12. A popular account of Harnack's views can be found in his short work, *What Is Christianity?* trans. Thomas Bailey Saunders, 2nd ed. (New York: G. P. Putnam's Sons, 1901).

[7] Robert Louis Wilken, *The Spirit of Early Christian Thought: Seeking the Face of God* (New Haven: Yale University Press, 2002), xvi–xvii. Compare Kevin Vanhoozer, who maintains that "the legacy of patristic, medieval, and post-Reformation Protestant theology is not as captive to Greek philosophy as the 'standard account' suggests. We should therefore feel free to draw upon what these theologians actually said—about divine personhood, the love of God, and divine suffering—as we navigate our way through current debates." *Remythologizing Theology: Divine Action, Passion, and Authorship*, Cambridge Studies in Christian Doctrine 18 (Cambridge: Cambridge University Press, 2010), 93.

generating a doctrine of God that was baptized by Christian theologians and modified so as to fit its new purpose. One fairly obvious way of utilizing perfect being reasoning in Christian thought is to argue as follows: God is most perfect. The most perfect must be more perfect than anything else; so God is more perfect than anything else. Whatever has a particular predicate x (a placeholder for a given divine attribute like omnipotence or omniscience) is more perfect than a thing that lacks x. So the most perfect thing will not fail to be or to exemplify x. Hence, God is or has or exemplifies or instantiates x.[8]

Perhaps surprisingly, there is some evidence of biblical resonance[9] with this sort of method. For instance, Hebrews 6:13 explains that God swore by himself when he swore to Abraham because there was nothing greater by which he could swear. Although it would be going too far to say that this represents a biblical recommendation of perfect being theology, the natural implication of this statement is surely that God is a being greater than any other; he is perfect. So if he is to swear by something when taking an oath to Abraham, he can only swear by himself because there is nothing greater by which he can swear. Other biblical passages can be interpreted in such a way as to reinforce this supposition. For instance, Isaiah has God asking the rhetorical question, "To whom will you compare me, and who is my equal?" (Isa 40:25, 46:5).[10] The response expected is surely that there is no equal to God because he is incomparable. This is not quite a premise for perfect being theology, but it is certainly consistent with such thinking. And in both 2 Samuel 22:31 and Psalm 18:30, we are told, "As for God, his way is perfect." It would be a stretch to think the concrete language of God as a shield and protector used in both these passages is equivalent to the method of conceptual abstraction and refinement used in perfect being theology. Nevertheless, the idea seems to be that God is a perfect being in some relevant sense, one who shields and protects his people. This too is commensurate with the method of perfect being theology.

So although the Bible does not provide the theologian with an ABC of perfect being theology, there are passages that (as I have put it) *resonate* with the method of perfect being theology, which may well be a reason why

---

[8] Leftow has a similar outline in "Why Perfect Being Theology?" 104. Interestingly, as he points out, this form of reasoning can be found in the work of Zeno of Elea.

[9] The term "resonance" used here has a particular valence as a term of art in contemporary biblical studies. In the present context I mean it to convey the way in which the method of perfect being theology has an affinity with biblical material or evokes certain biblical texts in particular ways.

[10] Also mentioned by Leftow, "Why Perfect Being Theology?" 106.

it was adopted by early Christian theologians in search of philosophical resources with which to understand better the theological claims of their newfound faith.

Of course, perfect being theology can be used in such a way as to generate a false picture of God. But that is true of other theological methods as well, and the misuse of a method can hardly be an argument against its right use.[11] But an important consideration in thinking about perfect being theology as a theological method is the role played by intuitions and modal judgments. As philosopher Thomas Morris puts it, the sort of perfect being theology usually called Anselmian (in honor of the medieval archbishop)

> is fueled by our value intuitions and by our modal intuitions—our intuitions concerning what is possible and impossible. But because intuitions are correctable, and because our intuitions are typically not comprehensive . . . the method of perfect being theology is not in principle cut off from creative interaction with other methods for conceiving God. And, in fact, I think it can best be seen as the primary method for integrating all other plausible methods for thinking of God.[12]

This seems right to me. Perfect being theology can play a role in generating a doctrine of God that is consonant with the biblical and postbiblical traditions, provided the right sorts of value and modal intuitions motivate the method—intuitions that arise from, and are shaped by, the Bible and the Christian tradition. Such an approach is not without potential pitfalls, but that is not a reason to discard perfect being theology, only to be careful about the manner in which it is adopted.

In the case of the work of several important historic Christian theologians, perfect being theology plays an important methodological role. The most famous example of this is, of course, Anselm of Canterbury. Anselm speaks of God as that than which none greater can be conceived. ("Et quidem credimus te esse aliquid quo nihil maius cogitari possit," as Anselm puts it at the beginning of *Proslogion* 2.[13]) But he does not stop there. He goes on to say in *Proslogion* 15 that God is something greater than can be thought—an entity that is in some fundamental sense beyond the grasp of human cognition. So, far from attempting to circumscribe the divine nature, Anselm uses

[11] I have pointed this out elsewhere. See *Divinity and Humanity*, 170–71.

[12] Thomas V. Morris, *Our Idea of God: An Introduction to Philosophical Theology* (Downers Grove, Ill.: IVP, 1991), 41.

[13] For a translation of *Proslogion*, see *Anselm: Basic Writings*, ed. and trans. Thomas Williams (Indianapolis: Hackett, 2007).

perfect being theology to articulate an account of the immensity and mystery of God. This is often overlooked in discussion of Anselm's version of perfect being theology. Another element of his reasoning that is also often passed over is the way in which it is shaped by biblical categories, even if he is not always citing biblical verses directly. Anselm's approach to theology by means of a kind of "sanctified reason" presumes a mind formed by Christian modes of thinking, primarily from Scripture and the fathers. (In this connection it is worth noting that Anselm's daily life as a Benedictine monk was saturated with Scripture—the Benedictines chant all 150 Psalms through the daily offices every week.) As Sandra Visser and Thomas Williams put it, Anselm speaks in terms of *ratio fidei*—that is, of the reason *of* faith. This "refers to the intrinsically rational character of Christian doctrines in virtue of which they form a coherent and rationally defensible system."[14] Yet today the sort of perfect being theology Anselm championed is often derided as a kind of "abstraction," or as "theology from below"[15]—that is, an attempt to project onto God what are deemed appropriate ascriptions, suitably maximalized and cleaned up so that any residual human imperfections are removed in the process. In fact, Anselm is an example of how perfect being theology may help illuminate the doctrine of God while ensuring that it does not end up making God into the image of some abstracted set of suitably maximalized human attributes, projected, as it were, onto the clouds Feuerbach-style.

For Anselm proceeds on the assumption that theology as a faith-seeking-understanding initiative assumes a posture of faith with all that entails about appeals to theological tradition. He does not simply dream up a method by means of which he can create a picture of God wholesale, and in abstraction from the Christian tradition. Thus, a truly *Anselmian* perfect being theology is one whose value intuitions and modal intuitions are shaped in important respects by Scripture and the Christian tradition such that they act as theological constraints on the sort of picture of God generated.[16]

---

[14] Sandra Visser and Thomas Williams, *Anselm*, Great Medieval Thinkers (Oxford: Oxford University Press, 2008), 14.

[15] This is Kärkkäinen's phrase in *Trinity and Revelation*, 283–84. To be clear, Kärkkäinen is not discussing Anselm's account in particular. He is more concerned with a particular approach to the doctrine of God that can be found in classical theology. But similar sentiments can be found elsewhere in modern theological criticism of Anselm. A similar line of criticism can be found in Christopher Insole, "Anthropomorphism and the Apophatic God," *Modern Theology* 17, no. 4 (2001): 475–83.

[16] In this connection it may be that not all contemporary perfect being theologians who claim to be following Anselm's method are, in fact, Anselmian in their approach. But that is another matter.

The difference can be put like this: Sometimes, perfect being theology is characterized as a way of attempting to derive a particular picture of God from certain philosophical premises independent of divine revelation. The aim is to generate a particular idea of God from whole philosophical cloth, so to speak. However, when we look at the case of Anselm, surely the paradigmatic perfect being theologian in the Christian tradition, we find that he does not approach his task in that manner at all. Rather, at the outset he assumes the truth of the Christian tradition, including the biblical witness, and reasons on that basis to a particular account of God using his "sanctified reason" as a means to that end. That is what his faith-seeking-understanding project is about. One begins from a posture of faith, presuming the intellectual deposit of the faith is true, and then reasons from there so as to understand that deposit more fully. The important thing to see here is that the Anselmian position does not attempt to ascertain the truth of the Christian tradition and it doesn't start from purely philosophical premises. Rather, it presumes the truth of the Christian tradition and uses the method of perfect being theology to draw out what is thought to be implicit within that tradition regarding the doctrine of God.

So much for the perfect being theology as a theological method for generating a Christian doctrine of God. What about classical theism? Classical theism is a term of art that encompasses a family of views, rather than a single doctrine, that clusters around a particular set of theological commitments with respect to the divine nature. It has a long pedigree, going back to patristic theology, and finding its apogee in medieval school theology and post-Reformation discussion of Theology Proper.[17] But it is not without defenders today, though one occasionally reads contemporary systematic theologians who proceed as if classical theism is dead.[18]

The cluster of concepts that comprise classical theism include the idea that God is metaphysically perfect, noncomposite or simple, metaphysically

[17] The list of Christian theologians who are classical theists is a long and distinguished one, and includes such luminaries as Augustine of Hippo, John of Damascus, Anselm of Canterbury, Peter Lombard, Thomas Aquinas, John Calvin, Francis Turretin, and many others. Recently Eleonore Stump has argued that the God of classical theism (filtered through the lens of Thomas Aquinas) is the same as the God of the Bible. See *The God of the Bible and the God of the Philosophers, The Aquinas Lecture 2016* (Milwaukee: Marquette University Press, 2016).

[18] See, e.g., the discussion in Kärkkäinen, *Trinity and Revelation*, ch. 12. To borrow a turn of phrase from Mark Twain, reports of the death of classical theism are greatly exaggerated. A recent defense of classical theism can be found in Stephen Long's tome *The Perfectly Simple Triune God: Aquinas and His Legacy* (Minneapolis: Fortress, 2016).

and psychologically independent of the created order, outside of time, incapable of being changed by anything outside of himself, and noncorporeal. God is also said to be infinite, omnipotent, omniscient, and omnipresent (among other things). Classical theists hold that God and the created order are distinct, and that the created order is created out of nothing by God and sustained in being moment by moment by his power, without which it would immediately cease to exist. In this way, creation is radically dependent on divine sustenance for its continued existence.

Finally, classical theists have a robust notion of God's otherness or transcendence. By this I mean that they tend to think that God is significantly unlike human beings, is not one being among other beings (because he is not in a class of beings), and is mysterious and unknowable in his essence. These latter claims represent a significant part of classical theism that are sometimes underreported in textbook accounts of the classical theistic position. Whatever human beings know of God (if they know anything), this position maintains they know it in a piecemeal, fragmentary, even proximate way. It is not just that, from a human epistemic vantage, much about God is inaccessible. It is also that humans are configured in such a way that they are constitutionally incapable of apprehending significant truths about the divine nature. Given the magnitude and glory of God compared with the relative poverty of human existence, this may not be terribly surprising. However, it does represent an important conceptual constraint on the classical theistic way of thinking about the divine nature, and one to which we shall return in due course.

Classical theism is consistent with *Trinitarianism,* the view that God is essentially triune. It is not commensurate with every doctrine of the Trinity, of course, but that is another matter. Suppose Trinitarianism is just the view that God is essentially triune, as expressed in the Nicene-Constantinopolitan symbol of AD 381.[19] We can state the core theological claims of Trinitarianism thus:

(T1) There is exactly one God.
(T2) There are exactly three coeternal divine persons "in" God: the Father, the Son, and the Holy Spirit.
(T3) The Father, the Son, and the Holy Spirit are not identical.
(T4) The Father, the Son, and the Holy Spirit are consubstantial.

Taken together, (T1)–(T4) constitute Trinitarianism.

---

[19] It is convenient to appeal to the Nicene-Constantinopolitan symbol even if one thinks this simply reflects the teaching of Scripture, because all catholic Christians agree that this symbol adequately expresses the doctrine of the Trinity.

Now, adherence to the constituents of Trinitarianism does not commit the theologian to a particular model of the Trinity—a particular way of understanding or interpreting the Nicene-Constantinopolitan symbol—only to the bare theological claims of Trinitarianism. These are that God is one in some very strong sense of "one" (i.e., numerical identity or at least generic sameness) yet subsists in three persons—namely, the Father, the Son, and the Holy Spirit. Some ways of construing the metaphysics of the Trinity consistent with the claims of Trinitarianism will also be consistent with classical theism; some will not. Nevertheless, classical theism is consistent with Trinitarianism—understood according to at least one metaphysical story about how to make sense of the unity and differentiation within the Godhead expressed in (T1)–(T4).

Many Christian theologians down through the ages have simply assumed that classical theism (or something very like it) is consistent with Trinitarianism, though it does not imply it.[20] This assumption is so widely understood that it is seldom explicitly stated in traditional accounts of the doctrine of God. Today, however, it is a matter that needs to be expressed so as to avoid misunderstanding. For classical theism taken as a cluster of claims about the divine nature independent of the additional claims of Trinitarianism is consistent with non-Christian conceptions of God, such as those found in some strands of Judaism (e.g., Maimonides) and some strands of Islam (e.g., the medieval Islamic *falsafas* like Averroes and Avicenna). We might say that Trinitarianism is the distinctive contribution to classical theism made by Christian theology. When Trinitarianism is added to classical theism the resulting picture of God is often thought to look something like this:

CHRISTIAN CLASSICAL THEISM: God is one simple, perfect, immutable, impassible, and infinite being who is independent of his creation, existing eternally as one entity and revealed in three persons: the Father, the Son, and the Holy Spirit. God's essence is one, yet each person is the essence. The Father is the essence. The Son is the essence. The Spirit is the essence. The Father, the Son, and the Spirit are also the essence. Nonetheless, there is only one essence and three persons. The persons are distinguished by their relations.[21]

---

[20] Some historic theologians may have thought classical theism, or something very like it, implies Trinitarianism. If they did think this, they were mistaken. In this regard my reading of classical theism is rather different from that offered by Stephen Long in *Perfectly Simple Triune God.*

[21] Adapted from Long, *Perfectly Simple Triune God,* xix.

Theistic Personalism

Like classical theism, theistic personalism is a family of related views clustered around a group of core concepts that is widely shared rather than being a single view. Unlike classical theism, theistic personalism has a more recent pedigree, being a family of views that has grown up over the past few centuries in Christian theology. Theistic personalists regard God as a person or community of persons writ large. That is, theistic personalists regard God as a person like human persons, only greater and more perfect. Typical theistic personalist claims include the following: God is in time; God has distinct states and properties as human beings do; he relates to creatures and is affected by them and their actions, and therefore changes in substantive ways; and his relationship to the created order is more complex than is the case for (most) classical theists. Some theistic personalists regard God's relationship to the world on analogy with a soul and its body, so that in some sense the world is God's "body," with which he is intimately related. (This is one way of construing the contested doctrine of panentheism.[22]) Although there are things about God that remain mysterious on this view, the nature of God is in principle knowable and comprehensible in significant ways. For instance, even if we cannot fully grasp what it is like to be omniscient, some theistic personalists are willing to allow that we can conceive of ways in which our knowledge may increase to include an understanding of all true propositions and no false propositions in a way that mirrors what they conceive of as the scope of God's knowledge.[23] Finally, many theistic personalists are of the view that God voluntarily contracts or limits himself in his relations with creation, or even that he places upon himself certain important constraints in order to create and sustain the world. Sometimes this is spoken of in the language of kenoticism: God voluntarily empties himself or sets aside certain prerogatives he has in order to create, sustain, or interact with his creatures. This is said to be a cost worth bearing in order to relate to the creatures God has fashioned.

---

[22] For a recent account of the theological history and pedigree of panentheism, see John W. Cooper, *Panentheism: The Other God of the Philosophers—From Plato to the Present* (Grand Rapids: Baker Academic, 2006). For a recent paper that worries that there is no clear definition of panentheism, see R. T. Mullins, "The Difficulty with Demarcating Panentheism," *Sophia* 55 (2016): 325–46.

[23] Famously, something like this reasoning is deployed by Richard Swinburne. See *The Coherence of Theism*, rev. ed. (1977; repr., Oxford: Oxford University Press, 1993), ch. 10.

Like classical theism, theistic personalism is consistent with Trinitari-anism. And like classical theism, theistic personalism will be commensurate with some models of the Trinity, but not all, and not necessarily the same models as are consistent with classical theism. Thus, for example, the various sorts of "social" accounts of the Trinity are good candidates for inclusion under the rubric of theistic personalism. One reason for this is that theistic personalism emphasizes the fact that God is a person, like a human person, writ large so to speak. He is a person like a human being is a person, except for the fact that God is disembodied, perfect, and without defect of any kind. It is a short, though crucial, step from this claim of theistic personalism to the notion that the divine persons of the Godhead are each centers of will and action and co-operate within the divine life by means of the intimate relations they bear one another in perichoresis. On this way of thinking the divine persons mutually interpenetrate one another so that together they share a single divine life. Exactly what such interpenetration entails is diffi-cult to say, but one plausible way of construing it is this:

WEAK PERSON PERICHORESIS: The persons of the Trinity share all their properties in a common divine essence apart from those properties that serve to individuate one of the persons of the Trinity, or express a relation between only two persons of the Trinity.[24]

If we were to sum up some of the central constituents of many theistic personalists (in some respects a more diffuse group than classical theists), we might put it like this:

THEISTIC PERSONALISM: God is strongly unified, perfect, unchanging in his charac-ter, responsive to his creatures, infinite, everlasting, and revealed in three persons: the Father, the Son, and the Holy Spirit. God is one in a generic sense, with each person being a distinct center of will and action that instantiates the divine nature. The divine persons interpenetrate one another in a way commensurate with WEAK PERSON PERICHORESIS.

Theological Realism, Theological Antirealism, and Theological Nonrealism

As I said at the outset, these two pictures of God are certainly not the only logically possible options. They are not the only live options, either. For

---

[24] I discuss this in the context of the doctrine of perichoresis in *Divinity and Humanity*, ch. 2.

instance, the deity of process theism may well be sufficiently different from the deity envisaged by theistic personalism to count as providing a distinct "picture" of the divine, although there is significant conceptual overlap between the process and theistic personalist ways of conceiving the divine.

Panentheism is another family of views about the divine nature that might be thought to be different from either classical theism or theistic personalism. But this too is not quite so obvious, in part because the conceptual shape of panentheism is so difficult to pin down, as recent work in this area has suggested. But also, there are notable panentheists who are also either classical theists in other respects (e.g., Jonathan Edwards) or theistic personalists (e.g., Jürgen Moltmann).[25]

Other *seemingly* rival pictures of the divine nature are not, on closer examination, sufficiently distinct from classical theism and theistic personalism to count as another sort of view. In this connection, consider the God of open theism. On the face of it, this appears to be yet another divine picture, one that is distinct from classical theism and theistic personalism as well as process theism. But it seems to me that open theism is more like a variant of theistic personalism, where God's knowledge is thought to be consistent with the open future of presentism.[26]

Nevertheless, all these accounts of the divine nature do share the following important characteristic: they are *theologically realist* in outlook. That is, they all assume that the deity is a mind-independent entity that is the creator of all things in heaven and earth.[27] We might say that the debate between classical theists and theistic personalists in Christian theology is a debate about how to conceive the nature of the deity understood as a mind-independent entity that is the creator of all things. Yet if some sort of anti-realist understanding of the divine is preferred to the theological realism of classical theism and theistic personalism, then a fundamentally different way of conceiving the divine comes into view. For God becomes a mind-dependent entity, the creation of human imagination, or the projection of the best human aspirations, suitably abstracted and shorn of human limitations. There are modern theologians who follow Feuerbach's lead in this regard,

---

[25] See Mullins, "Difficulty with Demarcating Panentheism."

[26] The first of these options implies that God's knowledge is limited in some way; the latter does not.

[27] Here and in subsequent chapters, reference to God as an "entity" should not be taken to imply some claim that God is in a genus, as one entity among many. It is merely a placeholder.

embracing antirealist accounts of the divine nature (e.g., the British Anglican theologian Don Cupitt).

Such a theologically antirealist approach to the divine nature should be distinguished from *theological nonrealism*, however. We have already touched upon the nonrealist option in discussing classical theism. On this way of thinking God is not mind-dependent, or the projection of human imagination. Rather, God is something beyond all human conception—a literally ineffable and incomprehensible thing. This is not theologically antirealist because this view, which is a version of strong apophaticism, stipulates that God is a mind-independent entity that is the creator of all things in heaven and earth. It is just that we cannot know anything about this entity. There is a great gulf fixed between God and his creatures such that almost anything we predicate of the divine will be a kind of projection, a sort of anthropopathism. Apophaticism is deeply rooted in the Christian tradition, of course, including strong apophaticism that maintains God is incomprehensible and ineffable in his nature.[28] However, the sort of theological nonrealism I have in mind at this juncture entails that God is beyond any human predication whatsoever. There is historic discussion of this matter. But there are also different ways in which modern theologians have alighted on this theme (not always taking direction from a patristic source; many have arrived there through reading too much Kant!). Two recent and rather differently motivated examples of this position can be found in the work of the American Harvard Divinity School professor Gordon Kaufman (whom we encountered in the previous chapter) and the Chicago Divinity School French phenomenologist and philosophical theologian Jean-Luc Marion. Kaufman writes,

> Theologians should attempt to construct conceptions of God, humanity, and the world appropriate for the orientation of contemporary human life. . . . These notions are (and always have been) human creations, human imaginative constructions; they are our ideas, not God's. What is needed in each new generation is an understanding of God adequate for and appropriate to human life in the world within which it finds itself, so that human

---

[28] An example of this can be found in the Liturgy of Saint John Chrysostom, which is one of the historic liturgies of Orthodoxy. At one point after the confession of the Nicene faith, the priest intones, "It is meet and right to hymn thee, to bless thee, to praise thee, to give thanks unto thee, and to worship thee in every place of thy dominion: for thou art God ineffable, inconceivable, invisible, incomprehensible, ever existing and eternally the same, thou and thine Only-begotten Son and thy Holy Spirit." Cited by Jonathan D. Jacobs in "The Ineffable, Inconceivable, and Incomprehensible God: Fundamentality and Apophatic Theology," in *Oxford Studies in Philosophy of Religion*, vol. 6, ed. Jonathan L. Kvanvig (Oxford: Oxford University Press, 2015), 158.

devotion and loyalty, service and worship, may be directed toward God
rather than to the many idols that so easily attract attention and interest.[29]

Compare Marion:

> Even if we were to comprehend God as such (by naming him in terms of
> his essence), we would at once be knowing not God as such, but less than
> God, because we could easily conceive an other still greater than the one we
> comprehend. For the one we comprehend would always remain less than
> and below the one we do not comprehend. Incomprehensibility therefore
> belongs to the formal definition of God, since comprehending him would
> put him on the same level as a finite mind—ours—, would submit him to
> a finite conception, and would at the same time clear the way for the higher
> possibility of an infinite conception, beyond the comprehensible.[30]

Some versions of classical theism are almost indistinguishable from such
theological nonrealism. However, many versions of classical theism are willing to concede that by means of a doctrine of analogy, human beings can
predicate some things about the divine nature even if the way in which such
things are said to exist "in" God are significantly different from the way in
which they are instantiated by humans. (For instance, it seems to me that
Christians will want to affirm Jesus of Nazareth is God Incarnate; that God
becomes human in order to bring about our reconciliation with Godself;
that God is essentially triune, essentially loving, and so on. These are all
claims about divine action and about the divine nature that predicate things
of God.) By contrast to such careful theological nonrealism, the road taken
by theological antirealists is not an avenue open to either classical theists
or theistic personalists precisely because both classical theists and theistic
personalists begin with the presumption that God exists and is a mind-
independent entity.

Chastened Theism

We may now turn to provide a dogmatic sketch of chastened theism as a
potential alternative to the two pictures of God outlined thus far. Chastened theism shares much in common with both classical theism and theistic

---

[29] Gordon D. Kaufman, *In the Face of Mystery: A Constructive Theology* (Cambridge,
Mass.: Harvard University Press, 1993), 31.

[30] Jean-Luc Marion, "In the Name: How to Avoid Speaking of 'Negative Theology,'" in
God, The Gift, and Postmodernism, ed. John D. Caputo and Michael Scanlon (Bloomington:
Indiana University Press, 1999), 36–37.

personalism. Like theistic personalism and like at least some strands of classical theism, chastened theism is theologically realist in orientation. It presumes that there is a deity and that God is a mind-independent entity, the creator of all things in heaven and earth. And it presumes that although God is deeply mysterious and ultimately beyond human ken, God nevertheless reveals Godself in Scripture, and supremely in Christ. Because of this divine revelation, we can know things about the divine nature. Although we cannot possibly ever know everything there is to know about God, the chastened theist is committed to the notion that God can be known, and reveals himself in order that he may be known. It may be that the dogmatic fund of knowledge of the divine nature is actually very modest. Even if that is true (and I am inclined to think it is), the point is that we do have a kind of conceptual core of things that are believed about the divine nature that are held because of divine revelation. Two paramount examples of this are the dogma of the Trinity and the doctrine of the incarnation. When Christ speaks, God speaks by means of his human nature. When God reveals Godself as triune, God reveals something about Godself that is (I take it) *fundamental* to the divine nature. They cannot be less than fundamental (e.g., derived properties that do not refer to something fundamental in the divine nature) without generating the kind of God-behind-God that Karl Barth worried so much about.

This is neither a trivial matter nor a theological quibble. Some strong theological nonrealist classical theists seem to think that the doctrines of divine incomprehensibility and divine ineffability mean we can know *nothing* of the divine nature. A charitable reading of this sort of claim does not mean that those who adhere to it are committed to self-referential incoherence. On the face of it, the claim that God is in principle incomprehensible and ineffable can be quickly refuted by pointing out that if that were true, then the claim that "God is in principle incomprehensible and ineffable" would itself be true of God only if it were false. Clearly *that* cannot be right. So, says the smart-aleck theologian, the claim that "God is in principle incomprehensible and ineffable" must be false.

But this is too quick. I suppose that sophisticated defenders of the claim that God is in principle incomprehensible and ineffable mean to offer some sort of second-order reflection on statements predicated of the divine nature. That is, they presume something like the following reasoning:

Step 1: First-order God talk that predicates things of the divine nature cannot refer to the divine nature literally because God is incomprehensible and

ineffable in his nature; such predicates must be metaphorically ascribed to
God instead.

Step 2: Thus predications like "God is incomprehensible and ineffable" do not
refer literally to the divine nature; they are merely metaphorical ascriptions.

This two-step reasoning makes a claim about the status of first-order
statements of theological predication. That is, it is a statement about statements of theological predication. In this case, the second-order statement
makes it clear that any first-order statement ascribing some predicate to God
must be ascribing to God something that is metaphorical in nature. It cannot be the case that such first-order theological predication actually means
to ascribe some attribute to God literally, for no attribute refers to God literally. This means that incomprehensibility and ineffability are also metaphors, because they also count as theological attributes ascribed to the divine
nature. So if ascribing attributes to the divine nature involves metaphor all
the way down, so to speak, then nothing we predicate of God is predicated
literally. Everything predicated of God's nature is metaphor, incomprehensibility and ineffability included.

We might call this *the panmetaphoricist strategy for theological nonrealism*.
Such a view is not obviously self-referentially incoherent. But it has the significant drawback of entailing that we can know nothing of substance regarding
the divine nature, not even that God exists.[31] That seems to me to be a very significant theological cost indeed, and one that appears to cut against the grain
of the biblical witness (e.g., the claim that God is love, in 1 John 4:8, which
does not on the face of it seem to be merely metaphorical in nature).

This is not the only strategy open to the theological nonrealist, however.
Another one has recently been discussed by Jonathan Jacobs. He argues that
one way to go for the theological nonrealist is to argue that divine attributes
do not pick out anything fundamental about the divine nature.[32] Instead,
they only pick out things that are derived properties. Let us call this *the no
fundamental predication strategy for theological nonrealism*. Consider an analogy with a table. The table has fundamental properties such as being composed of a cloud of particles. But it has derived properties such as being hard
to the touch, solid, and rectangular. These two sorts of properties are distinct and refer to fundamental or derived qualities of the table, respectively.

[31] For, clearly, the claim that "God exists" involves predicating something of the
divine nature. A recent and sophisticated discussion of these things can be found in Daniel
Howard-Snyder, "Panmetaphoricism," *Religious Studies* 53, no. 1 (2015): 25–49.

[32] Jacobs, "Ineffable, Inconceivable, and Incomprehensible God."

Thus, the particle-cloud arranged table-wise is not hard, solid, or rectangular, though it has these properties in a derived sense. Perhaps, suggests Jacobs, something similar is true of God with this exception: we can know nothing about the fundamental aspects of the divine nature. Thus divine attributes are predicates about nonfundamental or derived properties.

To my way of thinking, Jacobs' strategy is one of the most promising for a theological nonrealist. But it too has costs. For instance, on this view it turns out that the predicate "triunity" or the predicates "being the Father," "being the Son," and "being the Holy Spirit" are not fundamental to the divine nature. That seems to be a very significant drawback to this strategy for theological nonrealism, and one that I am not willing to bear.

Thus, I am not denying that nonrealists have theological resources with which to give some account of their views. I am denying that such accounts are theologically satisfactory. For if Christians can know nothing of the divine nature, and can predicate nothing literally of the divine nature, then we really do worship the unknown God that Paul speaks of in Acts 17. Yet Christ is reported in the Fourth Gospel as saying in reply to Philip's claim that Christ must show him the Father, "Those who have seen me have seen the Father" (John 14:9). Taken straightforwardly, this looks like a statement about how Christ's person and works reveal the Father. They reveal something that can be predicated of the Father, something really true of the Father. But if that is right, then there are indeed actions Christ performs (including speech acts) that give us insight into the divine nature, in which case strong theological nonrealism is a nonstarter.

So chastened theism is theologically realist. It presumes that there is a deity and that God reveals himself in Scripture and supremely in Christ. For this reason it is consistent with Anselm's project of *faith seeking understanding* (FSU). That is, like Anselm, chastened theists stand within the Christian tradition as people of faith and seek through careful and thorough theological analysis and reflection to come to a better understanding of the faith that has been passed on to them. Hence, like Anselm's FSU project, chastened theism is a self-consciously *traditioned* approach to Theology Proper. In other words, it is an approach to the theological task that is cognizant of the fact that any attempt to articulate a systematic account of Christian doctrine must begin from the admission that this is just one partial, flawed, incomplete, and fragile attempt to articulate the great things of the gospel. Kaufman is right when he says that all Christian systematic theology is the human attempt to articulate something about the divine nature. It is human reflection (ectypal theology) upon the divine original (archetypical theology). It is fallible; it is the product of fallen human beings. So it will need correction and revision in light of new information, new discoveries, new ways of thinking about the same issues informed by other disciplines, and so on. As a consequence of these considerations and in keeping with an Anselmian conception of the theological task as an FSU discipline, chastened theism does not seal itself off from engagement with other relevant data from other relevant disciplines (e.g., the sciences, philosophy, history, economics, and so on). Rather, it embraces such interaction and enrichment because all truth is God's truth.

But chastened theism is traditioned in another way too. This has to do with the appeal to tradition (both biblical and ecclesiastical) as ways of trying to navigate theological judgments. There will be different ways in which this is construed by chastened theists, depending on where they sit ecclesiologically, and how they and their denominations privilege and use various strands of the deposit of tradition.

Third, chastened theism is consistent with the SHARED TASK of theology, which we introduced in the previous chapter. To recap, this can be expressed as follows:

SHARED TASK: Commitment to an intellectual undertaking that involves (though it may not comprise) explicating the conceptual content of the Christian tradition (with the expectation that this is normally done from a position within that tradition, as an adherent of that tradition), using particular religious texts that are part of the Christian tradition, including sacred Scripture, as well as human reason, reflection, and praxis (particularly religious practices), as sources for theological judgments.

Finally, the material theological commitments of chastened theism place it somewhere between classical theism and theistic personalism. Rather than attempt to give an exhaustive account of the divine nature that supports this claim, let me offer two brief indicative examples. We will then elaborate upon these examples as central components of a full-orbed doctrine of God in the next two chapters.

First, let us consider divine simplicity. The chastened theist may think that God is simple in a strong sense—stronger than many theistic personalists are willing to entertain. Yet they will stop short of the Thomist claim that God is a simple pure act. God may be metaphysically simple like a soul is metaphysically simple or a subatomic particle is metaphysically simple (as we shall see in the next chapter). However, this is clearly a much weaker claim than the metaphysical package required by Thomist versions of classical theism.

A second is the dogma of the Trinity. Like classical Christian theists and theistic personalists, the chastened theist holds to Trinitarianism. But the chastened theist is unsatisfied by the classical theistic claim that divine persons are merely subsistent relations. (How does a relation—something that holds between two relata—subsist? How is this sufficient for divine personhood?) Neither is the theistic personalist penchant for treating divine persons on analogy with human persons satisfactory to the chastened theist. (Are divine persons really instances of a generic divine nature like Zeus, Poseidon, and Hades are instances of a generic divine nature? Is perichoresis really sufficient to ensure the divine persons are sufficiently united to preserve monotheism?) The chastened theist may opt for some other model of the Trinity instead of these, such as the constitution model. Alternatively, the chastened theist may be skeptical of any model of the Trinity, preferring instead a kind of Trinitarian mysterianism (i.e., the Trinity is a mystery and no account of the Trinity can adequately model it). But both of these doctrinal strategies are distinct from those adopted by classical Christian theists and theistic personalists. We shall elaborate upon the second of these strategies in chapter 4.

In sum, chastened theism is theologically realist. It is an instance of an Anselmian FSU program in theology that, like Anselm's project, is informed by the Christian tradition in important respects. It is consistent with SHARED TASK. And its material theological commitments will be distinct from both classical theism and theistic personalism in important respects, two nodal examples of which have to do with divine simplicity and the Trinity.

Conclusion

There is much more to be said on this matter. Here I have only been able to offer the beginning of an account of chastened theism as a third picture of the divine nature. Nevertheless, I hope I have done enough to whet the theological appetite for the next two chapters. For our task is not merely to pass on a tradition but also to construct ways of thinking about Christian doctrine that provide the churches today with adequate ways of thinking about the faith once for all delivered to the saints (Jude 3).

3

Divine Simplicity

Despite its name, the Doctrine of Divine Simplicity . . . is an extremely complex and difficult doctrine.

F. G. Immink[1]

We ended our discussion of picturing God in the last chapter with two examples of how chastened theism might be of use to the analytic systematic theologian when thinking about the divine nature. The first of these had to do with divine simplicity. The second of these concerned the Trinity. In this chapter we shall take up the question of divine simplicity in more detail, offering a particular model of the doctrine. Discussion of the Trinity will have to wait until chapter 4, where we will focus on the mysterious nature of the Godhead.

Introduction

The doctrine of divine simplicity has been at the center of some of the most hotly contested discussions about the divine nature in the recent philosophical-theological literature. Some philosophers and theologians have sought to defend the doctrine, but many of the most prominent treatments of the topic have been highly critical.[2] These criticisms have centered upon

---

[1] F. G. Immink, *Divine Simplicity* (Kampen: Kok, 1987).

[2] Theological accounts of the doctrine are once again appearing from the presses. The most sophisticated recent critic of traditional forms of the doctrine is Paul R. Hinlicky, *Divine Simplicity: Christ the Crisis of Metaphysics* (Grand Rapids: Baker Academic, 2016). Recent theological defenders of a more traditional doctrine include Jordan P. Barrett, *Divine Simplicity: A Biblical and Trinitarian Account*, Emerging Scholars Series (Minneapolis:

the coherence of the doctrine and its implications for the concept of God. Little of the current discussion has been focused on the relationship between divine simplicity and the Trinity, probably because it has been thought that if the doctrine is very difficult to understand, and most probably incoherent, it makes little sense to spend time trying to ascertain whether it has any utility as an ancillary to the doctrine of the Trinity. Yet in the theological tradition there appear to be a whole host of divines who think that (a) the doctrine is coherent, useful, and true, and (b) that the doctrine is a *corollary* to a robust account of the Trinity—indeed, that these two doctrines mutually reinforce one another. There is conciliar and confessional support for the doctrine in both Roman Catholic and Protestant traditions. There is also evidence that there is more than one version of the doctrine in these communions. Perhaps unsurprisingly, some of these formulations of the doctrine may be more helpful and of greater theological utility than others.

This chapter sets out a particular strategy for rehabilitating divine simplicity as a doctrine that is internally coherent *and* that may offer support to the doctrine of the Trinity (though the task of actually setting out *how* the one relates to the other will have to await another day). This involves the adoption of a cut-down model of the doctrine that merely approximates to the truth of the matter, rather than capturing the truth of the matter as such. By a "model" of divine simplicity I mean a theoretical construction that only approximates to verisimilitude, offering a simplified account of a particular data set or (in this case) cluster of theological doctrines. Ian Barbour captures something of the view I have in mind when he says,

> Models and theories are abstract symbol systems, which inadequately and selectively represent particular aspects of the world for specific purposes. This view preserves the scientist's realistic intent while recognizing that models and theories are imaginative human constructs. Models, on this reading, are to be taken seriously but not literally; they are neither literal pictures nor useful fictions but limited and inadequate ways of imagining

Fortress, 2017); Steven J. Duby, *Divine Simplicity: A Dogmatic Account* (London: T&T Clark, 2015); and Matthew Levering, *Engaging the Doctrine of Creation: Cosmos, Creatures, and the Wise and Good Creator* (Grand Rapids: Baker Academic, 2017). Perhaps the most important recent analytic-theological criticism of the doctrine is R. T. Mullins, "Simply Impossible: The Case against Divine Simplicity," *Journal of Reformed Theology* 7, no. 2 (2013): 181–203. Although I do not interact with Mullins directly in this chapter, his work is one important reason for offering the model I set forth here.

what is not observable. They make tentative ontological claims that there are entities in the world something like those postulated in the models.[3]

This also comports with an intellectual humility on the part of the theologian: it may be that we are unable to capture the truth of divine simplicity because we are incapable of understanding it as finite creatures or do not have the epistemic access to comprehend the doctrine, which is part of the mystery of the divine nature. There are plenty of examples of such models in other disciplines as well as in Christian theology. For what are the different accounts of the Trinity but models that attempt to express something of the mysterious nature of the Godhead, the complete truth of which is forever beyond human ken? Similarly, in contemporary physics Newtonian classical mechanics can still be used to generate accurate results when applied to large-scale macroscopic objects that are not traveling at very high velocities, though it is understood that classical mechanics is, strictly speaking, an approximation to the truth of the matter rather than the truth *simpliciter*. Or take an example of a similar strategy used by philosophers. Colin McGinn and several others have argued that the mind-body problem may be a difficulty humans are simply not able to resolve given our present state of evolutionary development. In other words, it may be that we are not clever enough (yet) to solve the mind-body problem. In the philosophical literature, this has been called *mysterianism* about the philosophy of mind. I am suggesting that a similar mysterianism inform our reflections on divine simplicity and its relationship to the doctrine of God. If we approach the doctrine in this manner, trying to provide a toy model that may help us make some sense of it, our efforts, though more modest, would also more likely produce results that were usable in constructive theology today.

If the theologian adopts an account of divine simplicity that seeks only to offer a model of the doctrine, it might well have greater utility, as well as greater uptake, in contemporary theology. Such a strategy is not without

---

[3] See Ian G. Barbour, *Religion and Science: Historical and Contemporary Issues* (San Francisco: HarperCollins, 1997), 115. Barbour's view is a species of critical realism, the doctrine according to which theories about the world give rise to imaginative models that can be used to test certain aspects of theories in light of experimental procedures, refining the model (and sometimes the theory) in the process. Such a view presumes that there is a world independent of the human knower that may be the proper subject of such investigation, while acknowledging that our conceptual and theoretical grasp of the world may be tentative, or in need of revision or enrichment. That seems broadly right to me. A recent and helpful treatment of the language of models in analytic theology can be found in William Wood, "Modeling Mystery," *Scientia et Fides* 4, no. 1 (2016): 39–59. We shall return to the question of theological model building in the next chapter.

cost, of course. A cut-down version of the doctrine does not have the conceptual richness of the maximal account found in some traditional versions of the doctrine and (in the version I shall outline) is not part of the Thomist pure-act account of the divine nature—which will be a significant limitation for some. However, if it is regarded as a toy model, then the theologian can utilize it in the knowledge that it only approximates to the truth of the matter, as is the case mutatis mutandis with current ways of thinking about classical mechanics, or, in some respects, like mysterianism, or even (perhaps) our models of the Trinity. As a proxy for the truth, it serves an important function in theology, in enabling theologians to articulate a model of the doctrine that is coherent and commensurate with the Trinity and consistent with metaphysical realism. This, I submit, is no small matter.

The argument proceeds in several stages. The first outlines the relationship between the Christian doctrine of divine simplicity and the notion of a theoretical model that I have in mind. Then the second section sets out three versions of divine simplicity. These comprise the minimal, the maximal, and the parsimonious. I argue that the parsimonious account, understood as a sort of variation upon the minimal doctrine, is to be preferred (for our purposes at least) to the conceptually richer maximal doctrine that is often espoused in the current philosophical-theological literature, which draws upon the medieval accounts of the doctrine. The third section offers an argument in favor of a parsimonious account of divine simplicity. I conclude with some remarks about the utility of this account for contemporary treatments of the doctrine of God.

Doctrine, Dogma, Theories, and Models

How should we understand Christian doctrines like the doctrine of divine simplicity in relation to the way of thinking about theories and models sketched in the introduction? These are complicated matters. To begin with, let us distinguish between doctrines and dogmas in Christian theology. Some modern theologians have argued that doctrines themselves are the products of imaginative theorizing about God that are metaphorical in nature. On this way of thinking, doctrines are human constructions. They are, in principle, revisable in light of new ways of thinking about God, new metaphors and models that offer better, more useful and fruitful ways of thinking about the divine. In my judgment this way of thinking is only partially right. Doctrines are human constructs; that much is true. They are our faltering, sometimes fallible articulations of the nature and purposes of God. But they are not simply conjured up by the febrile minds of theologians. They

are second-order reflections upon the first-order language of Holy Writ. For I
suppose that Scripture is the norming norm that norms all other theological
judgments this side of the grave; it is the repository of divine revelation. If
that is right, then a particular doctrine of, say, the unity of God must measure up to the truth of the matter as set forth in Scripture. It is the task of the
theologian to attempt to articulate such doctrine, in conversation with the
tradition and with other subordinate theological norms, such as creeds and
confessions. But there is a truth value to such doctrines. The importance of
doctrine is not merely pragmatic or utilitarian, as some modern theologians
suppose. What is more, doctrines are teachings about a given theological
topic held by some community of Christians or some particular denomination. That is, doctrine has an ecclesial location. It doesn't just float free of the
life of the church.[4]

Dogma is not the same as doctrine, however.[5] The difference is that
dogma is a doctrine that has attained the status of being part of the conceptual core of the faith (*de fide*). It is not merely second-order reflection upon
Scripture but has a normative status that depends upon its relationship to
the conceptual content of Scripture. Dogma has a clear definition in Roman
Catholic theology, where it is connected to the magisterium, or teaching
office of the church. Although Protestants do not have a formal role for the
magisterium, it is true to say that certain doctrines, usually those laid out in
the four great Christian symbols of the early church, have a normative status
for Protestants, too. The clearest instance of this is the doctrine of the Trinity,
the elements of which can be found in Scripture. The dogmatic shape of the
Trinity was gradually discerned by the church in the centuries after the closing of the New Testament canon and codified in the ecumenical creeds of
the church (e.g., the Nicene-Constantinopolitan Creed). Because the Trinity
is a central and defining doctrine of Christianity, there can be no Christian
faith without it. Hence, it has a normative status, relative to Scripture as the
norming norm.

It is not clear to me that the precise form of divine simplicity is dogmatically defined like this. With the Eastern Orthodox Church, I presume that

---

[4] As I put it elsewhere, doctrine is "(minimally) a comprehensive account of a particular teaching about a given theological topic held by some community of Christians, or some
particular denomination." See my "Methodological Issues in Approaching the Atonement,"
in *T&T Clark Companion to Atonement*, ed. Adam J. Johnson (London: T&T Clark, 2017),
320.

[5] Just as systematic theology is not the same as dogmatic theology, as was pointed out
in the introduction.

there are seven ecumenical councils of the church, and none of them offers a canonical definition of divine simplicity. It was articulated by the Fourth Lateran Council and again at the First Vatican Council, which state that God is "substantia seu natura simplex omnino."[6] However, these are not ecumenical councils. They are synods of the Western church (in the case of Lateran IV) and of the Roman Catholic Church (with some Eastern churches represented in the case of Vatican I).[7] Nevertheless, this is not dogmatically weightless. At the very least, the claim that God is a substance or nature that is absolutely simple should offer some ecumenical motivation to find a version of the doctrine that is theologically acceptable.

Protestant confessions also mention divine simplicity, but usually in passing and without defining it. For instance, the Westminster Confession (2.1), the subordinate norm for Presbyterians, speaks of God as "infinite in being and perfection, a most pure spirit, invisible, without body, parts, or passions." Similarly, the first of the Anglican Thirty-Nine Articles states that God is "without body, parts, or passions." The same sort of apophatic claims are made in the Lutheran Augsburg Confession, where article 1 speaks of the unity of the divine essence as being "without body, without parts" in keeping with the claims of Nicene Christianity.

Taken as a whole, then, even this cursory symbolic survey shows that the doctrine of divine simplicity is fairly deeply embedded in the Christian tradition and has some support in confessional and synodical decisions (from the thirteenth century onward), but is not dogmatically defined by an ecumenical body. For this reason it seems to me that there is reason to attempt to shore up the doctrine in keeping with its importance in the tradition, and reason to think that the precise shape of the doctrine is not agreed upon in the different branches of the Christian church. This latter point is reinforced by the fact that different classical theologians appear to hold different

---

[6] Cited in Ludwig Ott, *Fundamentals of Catholic Dogma,* 4th ed. (Rockford, Ill.: TAN Books, 1960), 31. In the same passage Ott offers the following gloss: "The expression *simplex omnino* asserts that with regard to God any kind of composition, whether physical or metaphysical, is out of the question." But it is not clear to me that the phrase *simplex omnino*— that is, simple in every respect, or in all things—requires the elimination of *every kind* of composition.

[7] Naturally, Roman Catholics will dispute this. But the fact is, regional synods of a particular branch or branches of the church do not constitute ecumenical councils. These synods are clearly nonecumenical since they did not include all the Eastern churches or, in the case of Vatican I, Protestants. (I presume that Roman Catholicism does not represent the only valid communion of the Christian church, an assumption of much contemporary ecumenical theology.)

doctrines of divine simplicity that are not necessarily compatible with one another, or with the synodical decisions of Lateran IV and Vatican I.[8] For these reasons, it seems to me that a project such as the one envisaged here is both dogmatically feasible and may offer a strategy for taking forward discussion of the doctrine that is sensitive to the ecumenical complexities it has engendered.

Three Versions of Divine Simplicity

With this in mind, let us turn to the tasks of exposition and elucidation. The doctrine of divine simplicity could be construed in different ways, and has been construed in a number of different ways in the recent literature. Consequently, our first task must be to get a clearer notion of the doctrine in view.

Let us say that, at the very least, the doctrine of divine simplicity is the view according to which the divine nature is essentially without composition. Call this the minimal conception of the doctrine of divine simplicity, or just *the minimal doctrine*. This minimal doctrine might be thought of as a corollary of perfect being theology. For God is a perfect being (Matt 5:48). He is that than which none greater can be conceived, as Anselm put it (cf. Heb 6:13-14). According to this Anselmian way of thinking, God cannot be composite because a composite being is potentially imperfect, capable of gaining or losing parts. If God is perfect, he must be incapable of such change, so he must be without parts. But on this minimal account, exactly how God is said to be noncomposite is left mysterious. Anselm of Canterbury says things that appear to support such a view in several places in the *Monologion* and *Proslogion*. For instance,

> Therefore, since that nature is in no way composite. . . . It must be that all those things are not several but one. So each of them is the same as all the others, whether all at once or individually. . . . Whatever is truly said of his essence is not understood as expressing what sort of thing or how great he is, but rather as expressing what he is. For whatever is a thing of a certain quality or quantity is something else with respect to what it is, and so it is not simple but composite.[9]

---

[8] This is a matter that is beyond the scope of this chapter. However, for discussion of several classical versions of divine simplicity that are not identical to the Thomist version often trumpeted in the contemporary literature, and that seem to allow for some differentiation within the divine nature, see Thomas H. McCall, "Trinity Doctrine, Plain and Simple," in *Advancing Trinitarian Theology: Explorations in Constructive Dogmatics*, ed. Oliver D. Crisp and Fred Sanders (Grand Rapids: Zondervan Academic, 2014), 42–59.

[9] *Monologion* 17 in *Anselm: Basic Writings*, ed. and trans. Thomas Williams (Indianapolis: Hackett, 2007). It is also not incidental to Anselm's understanding of divine simplicity

And,

> What are you, Lord, what are you? Surely you are life, you are wisdom, you
> are truth, you are goodness, you are happiness, you are eternity, and you are
> every true good. These are many things; my narrow understanding cannot see
> so many things in one glance and delight in all of them at once. How then,
> Lord, are you all these things? Are they parts of you? Or rather, is not each of
> them all that you are? For whatever is composed of parts is not completely
> one. It is in some sense a plurality and not identical with itself, and it can be
> broken up either in fact or at least in the understanding. But such characteris-
> tics are foreign to you, than whom nothing better can be thought.[10]

Suppose this minimal doctrine is right. One might nevertheless make such a
view the basis of a metaphysically thicker account of divine simplicity, sup-
plying the conceptual content of what is meant by the claim that God is
noncomposite. Such a thicker account is often given in the contemporary
philosophical literature as a kind of distillation of the exalted doctrine of
divine simplicity found in high medieval theology. Eleonore Stump provides
a helpful summary of this version of the doctrine:

> First, it is impossible that God have any spatial or temporal parts that can be
>   distinguished from one another. . . .
> Secondly, the standard distinction between an entity's essential and accidental
>   intrinsic characteristics cannot apply to God; it is impossible that God have
>   any intrinsic accidental characteristics. . . .
> Thirdly . . . it is impossible for there to be any real metaphysical distinction
>   between one essential characteristic and another in God; whatever can be
>   correctly attributed to God must in reality be identical with the unity that
>   is his essence."[11]

---

that he also says in the *Monologion* that "his life or eternity, which is nothing other than himself, is unchangeable and without parts" (*Monologion* 24); indeed, "The supreme nature never
yields a place in his simplicity for accidents that bring about change" (*Monologion* 25). He
goes on, "Is he not uniquely whatever he is, having nothing in common with his creatures?
Accordingly, if any word is ever applied to him in common with others, it must undoubtedly
be understood to have a very different signification" (*Monologion* 26).

[10] *Proslogion* 18, in *Anselm: Basic Writings*. *Proslogion* 15 underscores the apophatic
strain in Anselm's doctrine of God when he makes clear that God is actually beyond our
conception of him.

[11] Eleonore Stump, "Dante's Hell, Aquinas's Moral Theory, and the Love of God,"
Canadian Journal of Philosophy 16 (1986): 184–85.

Furthermore . . . the essence which God is is not different from his existence. Unlike all other entities, God is his own being. [God is pure being.][12]

In his much-discussed lecture criticizing divine simplicity, Alvin Plantinga points out that a large portion of the motivation for this version of the doctrine derives from what he calls the *Sovereignty-Aseity Intuition*.[13] This, very roughly, is the intuition that if God is absolutely sovereign over all he has created, and if he exists independent of all he has created, then he must be a being that does not depend on any other entity for his existence. The worry that lies behind the Sovereignty-Aseity Intuition is that a being that has parts or properties may depend on those properties for its continued existence. But this would compromise divine aseity and diminish divine sovereignty. Taken together with Stump's summary of the conceptual content of this view, this thicker account of divine simplicity is what we shall call *the maximal doctrine*.

There are versions of the doctrine that assimilate the manner of God's unity to the pure-act account of the divine nature, according to which there is no potentiality in God, and no distinction between God's being and his action, because God is wholly *in act* without remainder. Stump's fourth thesis (above) suggests this in what it says about God's existence being identical to his essence, his being "his own being" and his being "pure being." Saint Thomas Aquinas is the paradigm among medieval theologians of what we might call the pure-act account of divine simplicity. He maintains that a being with no parts at all must be an entity that has no potentiality. For only a being without potentiality can vouchsafe simplicity. If God had dispositions, say, then he would not be simple; he would have parts that are fully realized aspects of his being and merely dispositional aspects. Or, perhaps, he would have dispositional properties, which would also count against his being absolutely metaphysically simple. Saint Thomas thinks that divine simplicity best fits with the idea that God is an entity whose essence (what he is) is identical with his existence (that he is), who is entirely realized in act, and

---

[12] See Stump, "Dante's Hell," 181–98. She has a more recent and succinct treatment of some of the basic issues that she takes up in this article in "Simplicity," in *A Companion to Philosophy of Religion*, ed. Philip L. Quinn and Charles Taliaferro (Oxford: Blackwell, 1997), 250–56.

[13] See Alvin Plantinga, *Does God Have a Nature?* (Milwaukee: Marquette University Press, 1980), 43. Recently, William Lane Craig has argued that divine sovereignty and divine aseity need to be distinguished as two different conceptual issues in the doctrine of God. I think he is right about that, but we need not press that distinction here. See Craig, *God over All: Divine Aseity and the Problem of Platonism* (Oxford: Oxford University Press, 2016), ch. 4.

who has no potentiality whatsoever. Thus Saint Thomas: "If God is eternal, of necessity there is no potency in Him. The being whose substance is an admixture of potency is liable not to be by as much as it has potency; for that which can be, can not-be. But, God, being everlasting in his substance cannot not-be. In God, therefore, there is no potency of being." He goes on to say, "In every composite there must be act and potency. . . . But in God there is no potency. Therefore there is no composition in him." Moreover, "From what has been laid down we can infer that God is His essence, quiddity, or nature. . . . In God there are no accidents. There is, therefore, nothing in God outside His essence; and hence, He is His essence."[14]

It seems to me that adding the pure-act account of the divine nature to divine simplicity makes a difficult doctrine much more problematic to defend.[15] Thankfully, we need not do this. The pure-act account of the divine nature is distinct from the doctrine of divine simplicity. Though the pure-act doctrine might be thought to entail divine simplicity, divine simplicity does not necessarily imply that God is a pure act. For we could take divine simplicity to mean something like Stump's first three statements above plus the Sovereignty-Aseity Intuition, without the fourth of Stump's claims. Indeed, this is just how some theologians in the tradition appear to have understood divine simplicity (e.g., Anselm of Canterbury). But that version of the doctrine clearly does not imply the Thomist pure-act doctrine, in which case divine simplicity may be understood independent of the pure-act doctrine. Given that the pure-act doctrine makes matters much more complicated theologically speaking, it makes sense to develop a cut-down version of the

---

[14] Saint Thomas Aquinas, *Summa contra gentiles*, vol. 1, *God*, trans. and with introd. and notes by Anton Pegist. (1955; repr., Note Dame: University of Notre Dame Press, 1975), 16, 18, 21, respectively; cf. vol. 2, *Creation*, trans. and with introd. and notes by J. F. Anderson, 8–9.

[15] This is the task James E. Dolezal sets himself in his fine study of divine simplicity, *God without Parts: Divine Simplicity and the Metaphysics of God's Absoluteness* (Eugene, Ore.: Pickwick, 2011). It is the most accessible overview of the classical doctrine in print. Thomists will respond that Saint Thomas' doctrine is part of a larger metaphysical package and that gerrymandering the pure-act aspect of the package involves much more than merely removing a troubling detail from Saint Thomas' account. Granted. But my point is that this aspect of Saint Thomas' account has proven problematic in contemporary discussion of the doctrine, and that there are historic versions of the doctrine that do not require it (e.g., that of Saint Anselm) and that may therefore be less problematic (from the point of view of the contemporary discussion of the doctrine).

doctrine that works independent of this claim.[16] For this reason, it does not feature in what follows.

Even without the complication of the pure-act account, however, the maximal doctrine involves several claims that have made it odious in the sight of many contemporary philosophical theologians. The most obvious of these is Stump's third claim, that there are no real metaphysical distinctions between divine attributes. The idea is that God does not have distinct attributes because each of his attributes implies all the others. His omnipotence just is—that is, is identical to—his omniscience, his omnipresence, and so on. This is often assimilated to a further claim—namely, that all the divine attributes are identical to the divine essence, a matter that Stump conflates in her list. But this quickly runs into serious conceptual difficulties. If all the divine attributes are identical to each other and identical to the divine essence, then by application of the transitivity of identity, all the divine attributes are identical to the divine essence.[17] But omnipotence is surely distinct from, say, aseity. The two attributes are not identical to one another. Nor are they identical to the divine essence (ascity is not identical to omnipotence, aseity is not identical to the divine nature, and omnipotence is not identical to the divine nature either). To claim otherwise is simply mistaken, even if one does think that natures or essences are attributes or attribute-like (e.g., a rich property). Matters are made worse where God is said to be a substance that instantiates *properties* like other created substances. If he has properties, so this version of the objection goes, then his properties are identical to one another and to the divine essence. But then, by application of the transitivity of identity, God is a property, which is incoherent.[18] For how can a person be a property? How can something concrete be an abstract object (supposing properties are abstract objects)?[19]

---

[16] Notice: *independent* of the pure-act doctrine, but not necessarily *incompatible* with it. Although the version of the doctrine I will develop later in this paper is incompatible with the pure-act account, I am arguing that it might be treated like classical mechanics: useful for certain theological purposes even if it may not be the truth of the matter, in which case it could be that the Thomist doctrine is the truth of the matter, strictly speaking.

[17] According to the transitivity of identity principle, if A is identical to B, and B is identical to C, then A is identical to C.

[18] But what if God is a property cluster, or rich property with no substrate that instantiates the properties in question? I know of no one who seriously adopts this view, for the obvious reason that it would violate the Sovereignty-Aseity Intuition. For how could a bundle of properties collocated in one place be sovereign (in the relevant theological sense) or exist *a se*?

[19] This is the most pointed aspect of Plantinga's critique of the traditional doctrine of divine simplicity in *Does God Have a Nature?*

It has been observed that one reason why this particular problem has arisen since Plantinga's work, though it was not in evidence in the historic discussion of the topic, is that Plantinga (and other analytic philosophers influenced by him) is committed to what Nicholas Wolterstorff calls a *relational* rather than a *constituent ontology*.[20] According to relational ontology, substances are concrete entities that exemplify properties, which are abstract entities. In this way, substances and properties are two very different classes of entity. God is a substance; he is a property bearer. In ascribing certain qualities to God, like omnipotence or omniscience, we are ascribing properties to God. Hence, claiming that one of God's properties is identical to another, or that one or more property is identical to the divine substance that instantiates them, is to confuse two different sorts of ontological entity. It is like mistaking the number 7 for a person. By contrast, the medieval theologians defended a constituent ontology according to which the accidents (i.e., attributes) a substance possesses are parts of that object—its constituents. On this way of thinking, it is much less obviously objectionable to say that a part of a thing is identical to that thing (I have a part that is identical to me; saying that this part is identical to me is therefore true, though of course I also have parts that are not identical to me, like my hand). Nor is it to conflate one sort of entity with another (an abstract one with a concrete one) if we say that God's attributes are part and parcel of God himself rather than being something to which God stands in the relation of exemplification (i.e., God exemplifying or having an instance of the property of omnipotence). Finally, it is worth noting that the medieval constituent ontology allows for some entities to be unlike created substances that exemplify certain accidents. God is (uniquely) an entity of this sort. He does not have distinct properties strictly speaking because he does not stand in the relation of exemplification to something extrinsic to himself. Of course, we speak of his attributes as if they are distinct entities when we speak of his power or knowledge. But this is a sort of *façon de parler*. God does not literally possess distinct properties or attributes as creaturely substances do. The relational ontology typically does not allow for such exceptions. Hence, Plantinga's concern that the doctrine of divine simplicity entails God being a property, which is a kind of category mistake, is really a function of the way he conceives of God and properties. The medieval theologians he criticizes would not have recognized the

---

[20] Nicholas Wolterstorff, "Divine Simplicity," in *Philosophy of Religion, Philosophical Perspectives 5*, ed. James Tomberlin (Atascadero, Calif.: Ridgeview, 1991), 531–52.

objection because it would not have arisen in quite the same way within the ontology with which they were working.

No doubt this distinction between constituent and relational ontology is illuminating. But even if it does offer helpful philosophical context for the discussion of this matter, it does not settle all the points in dispute. For one thing, how would the medieval defender of the maximal version of the doctrine explain God's simplicity without conflating a part (his accidents/properties) with the whole (God)? Claiming that God is unique in having no accidents, including no distinct attributes essentially, appears to be question begging. Moreover, how is God said to be wholly noncomposite—that is, without any parts whatsoever—if he has real distinctions that pertain to the divine persons of the Trinity? Claiming that there may be such distinctions without division in God (a traditional way of attempting to shore up this worry) does no real work here, since any real distinctions are metaphysically impossible in the sort of simple being Stump's version of the traditional doctrine envisages.[21]

Nevertheless, attempts to come to the aid of the medieval account have begun to emerge in the post-Plantinga literature on divine simplicity. Jeffrey Brower has suggested that one way forward is to argue that God is the "truthmaker" for all his attributes. As he puts it, "Divine simplicity just amounts to the claim that God is the truthmaker for each of his true intrinsic predications."[22] In other words, God's having such and such an attribute is true in virtue of something that makes it true. In the case of God, the thing that makes it true that God is such and such is God himself. Or, in Brower's parlance, "God is such-and-such" (where "such-and-such" is a placeholder for a divine attribute) is true in virtue of that fact that God is the truthmaker of this statement.[23] This is a creative way of avoiding Plantinga's "God is a property" objection. For if God is the truthmaker for these attributes—that which grounds them, so to speak—then it does not appear that God is a property or an attribute. However, it is not clear what work this does to show that God is identical to his attributes. Moreover, Brower's argument does not seem to deal with the worry that each of the divine attributes implies

---

[21] Response: the medieval and post-Reformation scholastic theologians did not claim there were real distinctions in the Godhead, only "virtual" or "relative" or "subsistent" ones. But it is notoriously difficult to get a grip on these notions without some sort of conceptual creep toward real relations.

[22] Jeffrey E. Brower, "Simplicity and Aseity," in *The Oxford Handbook of Philosophical Theology*, ed. Thomas P. Flint and Michael C. Rea (Oxford: Oxford University Press, 2009), 112.

[23] Brower, "Simplicity and Aseity," 110–11.

the others. If God is the truthmaker for omnipotence and omnipresence, it is not clear how this claim does any work in making sense of the idea that omnipotence just is omnipresence, and vice versa. Nor does it help explain how God's existence is identical to his essence, as per the Thomist versions of the medieval divine simplicity doctrine.

However, this is not the only way to rehabilitate divine simplicity. Rather than attempting to shore up (an aspect of) the maximal doctrine as Brower does, an alternative way forward involves opting for a weaker account of divine simplicity commensurate with the minimal doctrine—with an eye to its utility for the doctrine of the Trinity. Let us turn to this possibility.

As we have outlined it, the minimal doctrine is commensurate with the maximal doctrine, but it does not imply it. For God could be noncomposite in some manner other than that stipulated by the maximal doctrine. For instance, he could be a metaphysical simple like a soul or a subatomic particle. To be a metaphysical simple is not to be without any parts *whatsoever*, which is what the maximal doctrine requires. It is only to be metaphysically primitive. Entities that are metaphysically primitive in this way are not composed of more fundamental components, as my body is composed of subatomic particles. But being a metaphysical simple like an electron or a soul is consistent with having different properties, such as having a certain mass or spin or conscious state. So metaphysical simples may have parts, if one thinks of properties as parts.[24] They are not *absolutely* mereologically simple. But they are not composite beings in the sense of being composed of more fundamental concrete elements. Suppose God is like this. Such a conception of divine unity is much less stringent than that envisaged in the philosophical doctrine. Because it is a weaker view, it is also more defensible: it is open to fewer of the objections that beset the stronger, maximal doctrine. This is all to the good, as we shall see. But we begin to get ahead of ourselves. Before we can evaluate the merits of this version of the doctrine, it is important to spell out how it might be of theological use.

Let us call the variation on the minimal doctrine that I wish to explore *the parsimonious doctrine*. On this view God is thought of as being metaphysically simple but not absolutely mereologically simple, as per the philosophical doctrine. It has several pertinent theological implications it is worth pausing to note. To begin with, the defender of the parsimonious account regards divine simplicity as a species of apophatic rather than cataphatic

---

[24] Of course, Roman Catholics will think properties are metaphysical parts, and therefore cannot be ascribed to the divine nature. (See Ott, *Fundamentals of Catholic Dogma*, 31.)

theology. The Dominican theologian Brian Davies and the Reformed historical theologian Richard Muller have recently defended this conception of divine simplicity. Davies maintains that an apophatic approach characterized Saint Thomas' account of the doctrine. This is important because, as we have already indicated, Aquinas' position is usually thought to be the apogee of traditional doctrines of divine simplicity. Davies says,

> Aquinas's development of the claim that God is simple amounts to three positions: (1) God is not something changeable; (2) God, in one sense, is not an individual; (3) God is not created or made to exist. This, of course, means that Aquinas's doctrine of divine simplicity is not offered as a *description* of God, or as an attempt to suggest that God has an *attribute* or *property* of simplicity. It is not a description since (in keeping with Aquinas's promise to note ways in which God does *not* exist) it consists entirely of negations, of attempts to say what God *cannot* be. It also is not ascribing simplicity to God as an attribute or property since it explicitly denies that, in a serious sense, God has any attributes or properties. . . . It is not concerned to paint a portrait of God. Its aim is to put up "No Entry" signs in front of certain roads into which we might turn when trying to think about God.[25]

Rather than stipulating how God is simple, the apophatic version of divine simplicity makes the much more modest claim that God is not composite. It seems to me that Saint Thomas makes a number of other remarks that push his views beyond a merely apophatic version of divine simplicity toward the maximal doctrine. Be that as it may, Davies' comments provide the defender of what I am calling the parsimonious doctrine, with an important theological point of departure. Muller takes up a similar theme in his account of the post-Reformation Protestant scholastic theology. He remarks,

> If some of the late patristic and scholastic expositions of the doctrine class as philosophical and perhaps speculative, the basic concept is not: from Irenaeus to the era of Protestant orthodoxy, the fundamental assumption was merely that God, as ultimate spirit is not a compounded or composite being. It is also the case that, from the time of the fathers onward, divine simplicity was understood as a support of the doctrine of the Trinity and as necessarily defined in such a manner as to argue the "manifold" as well as the non-composite character of God.[26]

---

[25] Brian Davies, "Simplicity," in *The Cambridge Companion to Christian Philosophical Theology*, ed. Charles Taliferro and Chad Meister (Cambridge: Cambridge University Press, 2010), 36.
[26] Richard A. Muller, *Post-Reformation Reformed Dogmatics*, vol. 3 (Grand Rapids: Baker Academic, 2003), 276.

We will come to the Trinity presently. For now, it should be clear that the parsimonious doctrine (like the minimal doctrine) is consistent with this apophatic approach to the divine nature, according to which divine simplicity is not so much about stipulating *how* God is noncomposite as affirming *that* God is without composition (though we know not how). The doctrine does not require a full-blown apophaticism, according to which we can predicate nothing substantive about the divine nature. To my mind, such hypertrophied apophaticism is theologically untenable. For it would imply that human creatures can know nothing about the content of the divine nature. But that is plainly false if the incarnation is true (e.g., John 14:8-12).[27] The apophaticism expressed here only calls for caution in attempting to set forth a constructive account of divine simplicity; it is limited in scope; it is, as Davies puts it a "no entry" sign beyond which we dare not stray. We have already noted in passing that this apophatic approach has confessional support among Protestants. So there is good reason to think this a strategy worth pursuing.

The next thing to say about the parsimonious doctrine is that it involves producing a model of the divine nature that approximates to the unity of the divine nature, though it does not capture it. This is very important. It enables the theologian to use the doctrine in a substantive manner, yet without commitment to the particular model of divine simplicity being the truth of the matter all things considered. For it has been conceded at the outset, via apophaticism, that the truth of the matter is not something to which we have epistemic access this side of the grave.

This way of conceiving the doctrine is rather like the model of a subatomic particle that one might find pictured in a physics textbook. The diagram is not what an atom actually looks like. It is an approximation to the truth of something we cannot see with the naked eye—something no one has ever seen. After all, a model is an approximation to a particular thing, and that is just what the model of the subatomic particle is and does. It offers us a picture that helps us conceive (albeit in a partial, incomplete manner) what the particle is like. Given that we cannot examine such a particle with our eyes or even with a powerful microscope, the model is (for the time being) the best we can manage.

I am suggesting that something like this way of thinking about the doctrine of divine simplicity might be a helpful and constructive way forward

---

[27] What is more, this does raise the following worry: Suppose we can know nothing of the divine nature. How can we know that we know nothing of the divine nature?

for theologians wanting to use the doctrine in contemporary constructive theology. Rather than worrying about whether the doctrine is veridical or not, the theologian adopting this approach can be clear from the outset that the divine nature is beyond our ken, so that any notion we have of God will only be an approximation to the truth of the matter. Setting aside the forlorn hope of coming to a veridical account of the doctrine, the theologian may still make headway if he or she adopts a model of divine simplicity that does the work that the more problematic traditional versions of the doctrine do with respect to the doctrine of God without engendering the well-known conceptual problems these thicker doctrines have encountered in the recent literature.

There are other theologians and philosophers who have suggested that the doctrine of divine simplicity should be revised so that the conceptual difficulties of the doctrine are avoided. Thus, Jay Wesley Richards sets out a taxonomy of different accounts of divine simplicity from the most stringent to the most capacious, and opts for a doctrine less strict than what he takes to be the view often thought to be the traditional one, precisely in order to avoid the perceived problems attending the traditional doctrine raised in the recent philosophical literature.[28] Similarly, Richard Swinburne eschews the traditional doctrine, because of its perceived difficulties, in favor of the view that the divine nature is simple in the sense that God (a substance) has only one rich property, which comprises much of what the tradition has taken to be the divine attributes. This property is God's "pure, limitless, intentional power." In this way, God is a much simpler entity than any creature. Yet Swinburne does not have to give up the idea that God is a substance with a property like creatures.[29]

My proposal is not a revisionist approach to the doctrine, as these two recent examples are. I am suggesting that the problem with the doctrine of divine simplicity is that theologians have often been too quick to attempt to trace the shape of the doctrine when they would have been better advised (and perhaps wiser) to have taken a more modest route. This involves generating a model of the doctrine that works alongside a model of the Trinity and even reinforces it. The theological utility of such a maneuver is considerable. Not

---

[28] See Jay Wesley Richards, *The Untamed God: A Philosophical Exploration of Divine Perfection, Simplicity and Immutability* (Downers Grove, Ill.: IVP, 2003), ch. 9.

[29] See Richard Swinburne, *The Christian God* (Oxford: Oxford University Press, 1994), ch. 7. At one point Swinburne writes, "It is because God's essential properties all follow from the very simple property of having pure, limitless, intentional power, that I claim God is an individual of a very simple kind; certainly the simplest kind of person there can be" (154).

only does it avoid some of the most pressing problems that have plagued modern discussion of the divine simplicity, but it also provides a constructive way forward for theologians to use the doctrine in conjunction with the Trinity in order to tackle problems that arise with respect to other theological loci.[30]

A Parsimonious Model of Divine Simplicity

Given the foregoing, we can hazard a version of such a parsimonious doctrine, set out in numbered statements in order to make its form as clear as possible:

(1) God is a concrete entity. That is, he is not an abstract object, like a number or proposition. He is a concrete thing, like a human being.

(2) God is an immaterial person. That is, he is not merely a metaphysical aggregate or artifact (like a chair or table). He is an agent, a living being, but not a material agent.

(3) God is a necessary being. That is, he exists in all possible worlds.[31]

(4) God is metaphysically simple. That is, he is not composed by more fundamental elements, as is the case with material things (e.g., the fundamental subatomic elements that compose objects like tables and chairs at particular times and places).[32]

(5) God is essentially metaphysically simple. That is, it is not the case that he just happens to be metaphysically simple (i.e., accidentally or contingently). He cannot fail to be metaphysically simple; it is part of his nature to be metaphysically simple.

(6) God has distinct attributes that he exemplifies.

---

[30] To be clear: I am not oscillating between saying "the parsimonious doctrine is a useful fiction or model" to "the parsimonious doctrine is a truthful account of divine simplicity." The claim is that the parsimonious model may be better suited to the purposes of constructive ecumenical theology because it only offers a model of the doctrine that aims to be as modest as possible about the claims it makes concerning the manner in which the divine nature is said to be simple. It is a model that approximates the truth of the matter, nothing more.

[31] This is denied by some Christian philosophers, e.g., William Hasker. But it is deeply embedded in the Christian tradition even if it is not always easy to say what it means to claim God is a necessary being. Here I follow the parlance introduced into contemporary philosophy of religion by Alvin Plantinga.

[32] Richards has a conception of divine simplicity weaker than this, according to which "all divine properties are possessed by the same self-identical God" (*Untamed God*, 217). But I do not think this is sufficient for a doctrine of divine simplicity that would pass muster according to the divines whose doctrines are usually thought to be paradigms of the doctrine, such as Saint Anselm or Saint Thomas. It is just too weak. For this reason, I will not discuss this option.

This reasoning proceeds from what I take to be less controversial to more controversial claims. For I suppose that most Christian theologians would agree that God is a concrete object and that he is an immaterial person. That God is a necessary being, though more controversial today, is a constituent of classical theology. The claim that God is essentially metaphysically simple—that is, essentially noncomposite—is a slightly more precise variation on the minimalist doctrine outlined above. Although it is not uncontroversial, I suppose it is much less controversial than the stronger versions of the doctrine of divine simplicity we have discussed, particularly the maximal doctrine. Finally, most Christian theologians when writing about the divine nature proceed *as if* God has distinct divine attributes, even where they are committed to the claim that, strictly speaking, God has no distinct divine attributes, as with Saint Thomas' doctrine of divine simplicity.

Is should also be clear from the foregoing that like any model, the parsimonious doctrine includes claims that are usually thought to be veridical (e.g., that God is a necessary, essentially noncomposite, concrete being that is an immaterial person). The controversial elements are those claims, especially the ones contained in (4)–(6) above, that specify how the divine nature is said to be noncomposite. In this way, the parsimonious doctrine goes beyond the minimal one. It attempts to give a conceptually thin account of the manner in which the divine nature is simple, which concedes the more controversial aspects of the maximal doctrine to its contemporary critics while holding out a hand toward the traditionalists by proposing it as only an approximation to the truth of the matter, which may be beyond our ken. In other words, the doctrine proposes that God is at least this simple, and may be more simple still, though we are not clear at present just how to explain such greater simplicity. This is similar to a Newtonian scientist claiming that physical bodies are composed of numerous simpler entities, namely atoms, that may be comprised of yet simpler entities in turn (i.e., subatomic particles), though early modern science was not capable of explaining what such simpler fundamental entities might be. In this example, like the parsimonious doctrine, the atomic particles that composed physical objects at particular times and places serve to model some more fundamental truth about the fundamental particles of which physical objects are composed. Objects are composed of atoms (that much is true). But it transpires that atoms are not the metaphysically fundamental simples from which objects are composed.

Discussion of the Parsimonious Doctrine

This brings us to some of the major issues and concerns that the parsimonious doctrine raises. First, although it is not made explicit, this doctrine implies that God is a substance, or substance-like entity, because he exemplifies particular attributes. This will be another nail in the coffin of this view from the point of view of defenders of a Thomist doctrine of divine simplicity. And from another direction will come criticism from those who think all talk of substances and their properties (i.e., of "essentialism") is theologically pernicious.

I can sympathize with the Thomists. One way to construe their worry about God as a substance or substance-like thing goes like this: reducing God to one substance among others is a denial of the Sovereignty-Aseity Intuition, which is tantamount to idolatry. God is not a substance that bears properties like creatures. He is a unique entity that is altogether different from any created thing. He does not derive his being from anything else, he is sovereign over all things, and he is not dependent on anything. Moreover, there is no potential in him because he is a perfect being; he cannot grow or diminish. So he is a maximally excellent being, and one that is fully realized, so to speak. For this reason, to claim that God is a substance with attributes is to reduce God to something like an exalted creature, one dependent on things outside himself, one who is not sovereign. This is theologically unacceptable.[33]

However, this is to mistake the nature of what is being proposed here. To repeat: the parsimonious doctrine is *only a model*, a toy example that approximates to the truth of the matter, a proxy. The idea is to provide a model that may be used within theological discourse without running up against the not-inconsiderable conceptual difficulties attending the philosophical doctrine. Consider an analogy with a diplomatic treaty. When several countries engage to produce a jointly signed treaty on a particular issue, this usually involves a protracted period of negotiation leading up to multiple iterations of draft documentation. The language in which the document is cast must be sufficiently precise to do the job the treaty is being drafted to perform (e.g., reduce the CO_2 emissions of signatory states), yet sufficiently porous

[33] Compare Frederick Copleston: "Either we are predicating of God predicates which apply only to creatures, in which case our statements about God are false, or we have emptied predicates of their reference to creatures, in which case they are without content, since they are derived from our experience of creatures and express that experience." Copleston, *A History of Philosophy*, vol. 2, *Medieval Philosophy* (London: Continuum, 2003), 350.

that each member state can affirm what is said according to the cultural differences and political mores that apply in their particular contexts. Often such treaties are the subject of popular derision, as political compromises. However, such documents are usually the result of considerable diplomatic skill and statecraft. My suggestion is that theologians may find such a diplomatic strategy serves the goals of ecumenical theology more effectively than attempting yet another iteration of the maximal doctrine of divine simplicity, given the conceptual problems it presents. This isn't idolatry, because it is offered not as the sober truth of the matter but as something more akin to a political or diplomatic document that attempts a form of words that are acceptable to as many participants in the conversation as possible.

What about those who reject "essentialism" altogether? I have already mentioned the differences between constituent and relational ontologies. Those that reject essentialism must provide some alternative. (Some have been proposed, but without wide acceptance, e.g., the metaphysics of process philosophy.) The fact is that some version of essentialism has been the mainstay of Christian theology in the past two millennia. The prospects for an ontology that offers a better alternative that has explanatory power at least as great as essentialism, and that appeals to as broad a range of Christian thinkers as possible, is unlikely. Given the ecumenical purpose of the parsimonious doctrine, it would seem that the better, more advantageous option is to pursue an account of the divine nature that is essentialist.

Perhaps the most serious concern for the parsimonious view is raised by the Sovereignty-Aseity Intuition. Recall that this is the claim that if God is absolutely sovereign over all he has created, and if he exists independent of all he has created, then he must be a being that does not depend on any other entity for his existence. Yet it appears that according to the parsimonious doctrine, he is dependent on things outside himself—namely, his attributes or properties—in which case his aseity and absolute sovereignty are called into question.

In one respect the parsimonious doctrine does have this implication, but it is not clear to me that this constitutes a fatal objection. What sort of dependency relation is envisaged here? Are all such relations damaging to divine sovereignty and aseity? Perhaps not. Suppose God is a maximally great being. Then (in the parlance introduced into these discussions by Plantinga) he is not merely a being of maximal excellence—that is, excellence in some possible world. He is maximally excellent in all possible worlds, making him maximally great. What is more, he is a necessary being—that is, a being that exists in all possible worlds. To this we may add the presumption, shared with the vast majority of historic Christian theologians, that the attributes he has he has essentially. They are part of his nature. He cannot not be (say) *contingently* omnipotent, omniscient, omnipresent, or necessary in only some worlds. He cannot just happen to have these qualities or be capable of relinquishing them.[34] To switch back to contemporary philosophical-theological parlance, there are no possible worlds in which he exists without these attributes. They are not world-indexed properties but essential properties that he possesses in all the worlds in which he exists, which is all possible worlds.

Suppose, for the sake of argument, that this picture of the divine nature is right. Then it is not possible for there to be a state of affairs in which God exists without these attributes. It is necessarily the case that God is omnipotent, omniscient, and so forth. It may still be true that he "depends" on these attributes in the sense that in order to be the entity he is, he must exemplify omnipotence, omniscience, and the like. But so what? Why is that damaging to the model? If there are no possible worlds in which he fails to exemplify these attributes, then the dependence in question is not one that can damage his greatness, for the reasons just given. Does it damage his aseity? Not obviously. He is independent of his creatures; he is not dependent on anything contingent or accidental. He may be said to "depend" on his nature, and on the attributes he exemplifies. But that seems like a rather Pickwickian sense of "depend." Nothing about the parsimonious view requires a particular account of properties and their exemplification. It is consistent with, say, nominalism (according to which there are no properties, just particulars like the blueness of *this shirt*). But it is also consistent with a theory of universals, according to which particular attributes instantiate universals, like blueness.[35] Granted, rather different metaphysical stories about the divine nature would follow depending on which of these views (if any) one opted for. However, it is no part of the parsimonious doctrine that the attributes God exemplifies

---

[34] There are complications here. The most obvious is the attribute "being the Creator." Is this an essential divine attribute? Must God create? If yes, must he create a world or this world? These are deep waters that we cannot enter into here. Suffice to say that there are options in the tradition. Commitment to the claim that God is indeed essentially a creator do not necessarily compromise divine freedom. For being the creator does not require the existence of any particular created object. For a very helpful recent treatment of issues related to this question, see William L. Rowe, *Can God Be Free?* (Oxford: Oxford University Press, 2006).

[35] There are other theories about properties, predicates, and attributes that I won't go into here. My point is supposed to be illustrative of the sort of worries that may motivate theologians, for many of whom the debate between realists and nominalists will be familiar in its medieval, rather than modern, guise.

are predicates, particulars, tropes, or properties. "Attribute" is metaphysically ambiguous in this respect; it could mean any one of these things.

But suppose that this line of response is inadequate, or mistaken in some way. Why not adopt Brower's claim that God is (uniquely, perhaps) the truthmaker for his attributes instead? Then God's attributes are not true in virtue of something outside of God (e.g., a universal). God makes them true. As far as I can see, this does not necessarily require commitment to the controversial claim that all the divine attributes are identical to one another and to the divine nature, as per the maximal doctrine. It also avoids the worries about aseity, for then God is not dependent on anything outside himself for the attributes he possesses. It also (I think) rebuts the worries about divine sovereignty.

A Further Implication for Constructive Trinitarian Theology

Aside from the conceptual and ecumenical issues surrounding the doctrine of divine simplicity that a model like the parsimonious doctrine may go somewhat toward addressing, there is another consideration in the neighborhood. It is this: the parsimonious model is consistent with a doctrine of differentiation within the divine nature, which appears to be a requirement for the doctrine of the Trinity. There is not the space to offer a complete elucidation of this point here, so perhaps a sketch will suffice. Suppose that the divine persons share a common divine essence, as with classical orthodox Trinitarian thought. What individuates the persons? One traditional response is subsistent relations, such as "being uncreated," "being eternally generated," and "being eternally spirated." But in each case, these are traditionally thought to be subsistent relations within the one divine entity, not distinct properties as such. As we have already noted, much ink has been spilled trying to explain how a relation can be said to be subsistent in this manner. Rather than weigh in on this debate, the parsimonious model of divine simplicity can simply stipulate that, for the sake of argument, God may be said to have certain distinct attributes, including those that historic discussion of the doctrine of God ascribe to one and only one divine person, such as "being the Father," "being the Son," and "being the Spirit."

4

Trinity and Mystery

And the catholic faith is this: That we worship one God in Trinity, and Trinity in Unity; Neither confounding the persons nor dividing the substance. For there is one person of the Father, another of the Son, and another of the Holy Spirit. But the Godhead of the Father, of the Son, and of the Holy Spirit is all one, the glory equal, the majesty coeternal. . . . So the Father is God, the Son is God, and the Holy Spirit is God; And yet they are not three Gods, but one God.

Athanasian Creed c. AD 500

In chapter 2 we considered several conceptual pictures of the divine nature and landed upon what I called *chastened theism* as a way of conceiving the divine nature. In order to provide some concrete indication of how chastened theism might differ from traditional classical theism and from theistic personalism, I offered two examples. These were the doctrine of divine simplicity and the doctrine of the Trinity, respectively. In the previous chapter, I set out a model of divine simplicity that attempts to move beyond the current impasse in the debate about the doctrine, which I called the *parsimonious account of divine simplicity*. We ended that chapter with some hints about how this model may help when it comes to understanding the other fundamental aspect of the Christian doctrine of God—namely, the Trinity.

In this chapter we turn to focus on the Trinity as our second example of a distinctively chastened theistic approach to the doctrine of God. Here, as with the doctrine of divine simplicity, the idea is to provide a model of the doctrine. The result is a conceptually thinner account of the doctrine in question than one often finds in textbooks of Christian theology today, which is (I think) an advantage rather than a liability.

The argument falls into several parts. The first section provides a kind of preamble on the state of the doctrine of the Trinity in systematic and analytic theology. This is important because there are relatively few treatments of the doctrine that take into account both of these literatures, and the constructive account offered in this chapter is an attempt to synthesize these in an analytic systematic theological vein. Having done this, we turn in a second section to clarify some terminology. This includes a brief note on the doctrine of the Trinity followed by some remarks that seek to circumscribe a particular sort of mysterianism about the Trinity. Then in a third section I will set out this mysterian model of the Trinity, which I shall call *chastened trinitarian mysterianism* because it attempts to provide a conceptually thin model of the Trinity along mysterian lines. In a conclusion I draw the threads of the foregoing argument together, along with the threads of the previous two chapters on the doctrine of God, as a segue to the next chapter on the relationship between God and his divine purposes in creation.

Orientation to Discussion of the Trinity

In chapter 2 we noted that Christians confess the following:

(T1) There is exactly one God.
(T2) There are exactly three coeternal divine persons "in" God: the Father, the Son, and the Holy Spirit.
(T3) The Father, the Son, and the Holy Spirit are not identical.
(T4) The Father, the Son, and the Holy Spirit are consubstantial.

This is Trinitarianism. It encapsulates what we may call the dogmatic core of the doctrine of the Trinity, which is one of the central and defining doctrines of Christian theology.[1] There are various ongoing scholarly discussions in this area, on particular models of the Trinity (whether Augustinian/Latin or social, and so on),[2] on the so-called threeness-oneness problem of the Trinity (i.e.,

---

[1] I take it that the Athanasian Creed, though never canonized, adequately represents the catholic faith, as a comparison with, say, the Nicene-Constantinopolitan symbol would quickly demonstrate. This has been challenged in the recent literature by Dale Tuggy. But this represents a minority report. See Dale Tuggy, "Metaphysics and Logic of the Trinity," *Oxford Handbooks Online* (Dec 2016), https://doi.org/10.1093/oxfordhb/9780199935314.013.27. (Interestingly, it is included in article 8 of the 1662 edition of the Anglican Articles of Religion as one of three creeds to which assent should be given.)

[2] See, e.g., the essays in these recent symposia: Oliver D. Crisp and Fred Sanders, eds., *Advancing the Trinity: Explorations in Constructive Dogmatics* (Grand Rapids: Zondervan Academic, 2014); Gilles Emery and Matthew Levering, eds., *The Oxford Handbook of the*

how God can be both one and three at one and the same time), and on issues pertaining to God's life *ad intra*, such as the eternal generation of the Son or the right way in which the process of the Spirit should be understood—what is sometimes called "Third Article theology" (because it refers to the third article of the Nicene Creed regarding the person of the Spirit).[3] There have also been several important studies on the doctrine as a whole in recent years.[4]

In addition to these areas of debate, there has also been constructive philosophical-theological work done toward new models of the Trinity. This has been underreported in recent systematic theology, but analytic theological work has generated a range of such models.[5] Perhaps the best known of

---

Trinity (Oxford: Oxford University Press, 2011); Peter C. Phan, ed., *The Cambridge Companion to the Trinity* (Cambridge: Cambridge University Press, 2011); Jason Sexton, ed., *Two Views on the Trinity,* Counterpoints Series (Grand Rapids: Zondervan Academic, 2014); and Thomas H. McCall and Michael C. Rea, eds., *Philosophical and Theological Essays on the Trinity* (Oxford: Oxford University Press, 2009). There is some debate about the nomenclature. Should we speak of "Augustinian" models of the Trinity, or of "Latin" models? I have opted for the term "Latin" models, though they are not necessarily restricted to Latin, or Western, theologians, because there are ways in which this family of views develops over time from the work of Augustine of Hippo in *De Trinitate*, to, say, the work of Thomas Aquinas in his treatise on the Trinity in *Summa theologiae*. In what follows I shall be concerned more with the Thomist iteration than with the Augustinian iteration of this model (or models).

   [3] See, e.g., Kevin Giles, *The Eternal Generation of the Son: Maintaining Orthodoxy in Trinitarian Theology* (Downers Grove, Ill.: IVP Academic, 2012); and the essays collected together in Myk Habets, ed., *Third Article Theology: A Pneumatological Dogmatics* (Minneapolis: Fortress, 2015).

   [4] Examples from systematic and philosophical theologians include Fred Sanders, *The Triune God,* New Studies in Dogmatics (Grand Rapids: Zondervan Academic, 2016); Sarah Coakley, *God, Sexuality, and the Self: An Essay 'On the Trinity'* (Cambridge: Cambridge University Press, 2013); William Hasker, *Metaphysics and the Tripersonal God,* Oxford Studies in Analytic Theology (Oxford: Oxford University Press, 2014); Veli-Matti Kärkkäinen, *Trinity and Revelation*, vol. 2 of *Constructive Christian Theology for the Pluralistic World* (Grand Rapids: Eerdmans, 2014); and Thomas H. McCall, *Which Trinity? Whose Monotheism? Philosophical and Systematic Theologians on the Metaphysics of Trinitarian Theology* (Grand Rapids: Eerdmans, 2010). The recent historical-theological work on the Trinity has been very important here as well. See, for example, Khaled Anatolios, *Retrieving Nicaea: The Development and Meaning of Trinitarian Doctrine* (Grand Rapids: Baker Academic, 2011); Lewis Ayres, *Nicaea and Its Legacy: An Approach to Fourth-Century Trinitarian Theology* (Oxford: Oxford University Press, 2004); and Stephen R. Holmes, *The Quest for the Trinity: The Doctrine of God in Scripture, History and Modernity* (Downers Grove, Ill.: IVP Academic, 2012).

   [5] For a very illuminating discussion of recent analytic-theological models of the Trinity, see Daniel Howard-Snyder, "Trinity," *Routledge Encyclopedia of Philosophy Online* (2015), https://www.rep.routledge.com/articles/thematic/trinity/v-2; and Tuggy, "Metaphysics and Logic of the Trinity." In addition to the constitution view that is discussed in this chapter, there are also versions of social Trinitarianism, including Richard Swinburne's approach, and the Trinity monotheism of William Lane Craig. There are also versions of a Latin account,

these is the constitution account of the Trinity. This turns on the notion of numerical sameness without identity. Very roughly, we might put it like this: for any two (or more) things that are both God and both a divine person, the first entity may be the same deity as the second (i.e., numerically the same thing) but not the same divine person as the second (i.e., not the same member of the Trinity). So, to use the example often cited in this literature, a block of marble fashioned into a statue that is also a pillar in a large public building is so constituted that the block of marble is numerically the same as the statue and the pillar. Yet the three things are distinct from one another, relative to the sortals "block," "pillar," and "statue." In fact, it might be thought that there are three distinct entities that occupy the same space and that are composed of the same matter—namely, the block, the statue, and the pillar. They are distinct entities at least in part because they have different persistence conditions. For instance, the statue could be effaced and yet the marble block and pillar still exist. Yet one block of marble composes all three entities. In a similar manner, so defenders of the constitution view of the Trinity aver, the persons of the Trinity may be distinct from one another relative to the sortal terms "Father," "Son," and "Spirit," and yet all "composed" by the one divine essence.[6]

The constitution account is not clearly either a Latin model of the Trinity or a social account of the Trinity. I take it that Latin accounts of the Trinity suppose that the Trinitarian Law is true, according to which *in God all is one except for the opposition of relations*.[7] In the Thomist version of this model, which is arguably the most sophisticated historic version of the model, there is one God, two processions within the Godhead (the Son's eternal generation and the Spirit's eternal spiration), three divine persons, and four relations (paternity, filiation, common spiration, and procession). This is said

---

including Brian Leftow's model of the Trinity in terms of three streams of one life. What is interesting about the constitution view, as I shall argue in due course, is that it is a new (analytic) model of the Trinity that does not clearly fall into one or the other of these two traditional families of views on the Trinity (viz., either Latin or social views).

[6] For an accessible treatment of the constitution view, see Michael C. Rea, "The Trinity," in *The Oxford Handbook of Philosophical Theology*, ed. Thomas P. Flint and Michael C. Rea (Oxford: Oxford University Press, 2009), 403–29. See also the essays in part 3 of McCall and Rea, *Philosophical and Theological Essays on the Trinity*.

[7] Ludwig Ott, *Fundamentals of Catholic Dogma*, 4th ed. (Rockford, Ill.: TAN Books, 1960), 70. As Ott notes, this doctrine is *de fide* for Roman Catholic Christians (i.e., part of the core of the faith that should be believed by the faithful). It was first formulated by Anselm of Canterbury in his *De processione Spiritus* §2, and affirmed by the Council of Florence (AD 1441). Ott comments, "According to this assertion, the real distinctions of the Persons rests exclusively on the opposition of the relations."

to be consistent with the traditional, catholic theological claim that God is metaphysically simple and yet triune.

In the Thomist version of the model, this means that the divine persons are distinguished by their relations of origin only. They are, to use a rather sibylline Thomistic phrase, *subsistent relations* within the Godhead—a very thin account of the divine persons indeed.[8] This is not a Thomist idiosyncrasy, however. As Richard Cross puts it, "The *vast consensus in the west* [is that] the only distinguishing features among the [divine] persons are their relations—that, in the standard terminology, they are subsistent relations."[9] These subsistent relations are expressed in terms of the relations of origin that the divine persons bear to one another in the divine life. So the Father is said to be the fount or source (*arche*) of the Trinity. He is innascible—that is, "originates from no one" (*innascibilitas*). The Son is eternally begotten of the Father; and the Holy Spirit is spirated by the Father (as well as by the Son, according to Western Christians). Yet these are said to be the only real distinctions in God according to defenders of Latin models of the Trinity. All other distinctions in God are said to be "virtual," or "formal." Consequently, on the Latin model, will and understanding in God belong to the divine essence, not to the persons. There is only one will and one understanding shared by the divine persons.

Social Trinitarians claim that Latin models are problematic at precisely this juncture. God is, they maintain, three distinct divine persons, each of which has a will and center of action. There are differences among social Trinitarians about how to parse the central claims of the model, which may be most helpfully expressed by saying that there is a family of different social models of the Trinity, just as there are variations on the Latin model. Nevertheless, they share in common the following assumptions: First, that the Father, Son, and Spirit are not numerically the same substance. Second, that the divine persons are consubstantial in the sense that they each share in a common divine nature (on analogy with the way in which three human persons may be said to each share in a common human nature). Third, social Trinitarians tend to think that monotheism implies only that all divine

---

[8] "Distinction in God arises only through the relations of origin . . . but a relation in God is not like an accident inherent in a subject, but is the divine essence itself. So it is subsistent just as the divine essence is subsistent. Just as, therefore, the Godhead is God, so the divine paternity is the Father, who is a divine person. Therefore, 'divine person' signifies a relation as subsistent." Thomas Aquinas, *Summa theologiae* 1.29a.4c.

[9] Richard Cross, "Two Models of the Trinity?" *Heythrop Journal* 43 (2002): 287 (emphasis added).

substances stand in a particularly intimate relation to one another that is not the same relation as being numerically the same divine substance. (Often this involves invoking the notion of perichoresis as a kind of relation that binds the divine persons together in some sense.[10]) The persons of the Trinity stand in this intimate relation to one another; hence, social Trinitarianism is monotheistic.[11]

The constitution model of the Trinity is not equivalent to either of these models. It is not clearly a Latin view, and it is not clearly a social view; it bucks the usual typology of these matters given in textbooks of Christian theology. In the natural sciences, the generation of new ways of looking at data, including new models that reframe old questions, is usually thought to be the sign of a flourishing research program. If analytic theology is a kind of theological research program, then on this way of thinking it has already begun to show it can generate new models of data on the most central and defining Christian dogma, of which the constitution model is perhaps the most intriguing. That is no mean feat.

The task of this chapter is not to provide another version of a Latin, social, or constitution model of the Trinity, however. The reason is that I think all these existing ways of conceiving the Trinity fail for a similar reason—namely, *they attempt to say too much about the triunity of God*. The Latin Trinitarians think that they can give an account of the divine persons as subsistent relations. But it is not at all clear how a relation can be said to subsist—that is, to exist independently like a substance. So how can such relations be divine persons? And, in any case, how can a *relation* be a *person*—even in some sort of attenuated or analogical sense of the word "person"? Despite strenuous attempts to explicate this among Latin Trinitarians, it is still very difficult to see what sense can be made of such a claim.

The major concern with social Trinitarians is that their accounts of the triunity of God seem to collapse into tritheism, where the divine persons, like Zeus, Poseidon, and Hades, share in, or instantiate, or exemplify a common property, "divinity." This social Trinitarian commitment to a strong sense of

---

[10] See my discussion of this in Crisp, *Divinity and Humanity: The Incarnation Reconsidered* (Cambridge: Cambridge University Press, 2007), ch.1.

[11] Jürgen Moltmann is a social Trinitarian who denies that Christianity is monotheistic. For a critical discussion of this, see Randall Otto, "Moltmann and the Anti-monotheism Movement," *International Journal of Systematic Theology* 3, no. 3 (2001): 293–308.

distinctions within the Godhead appears to jeopardize the monotheism of Christianity and a commitment to divine simplicity.[12]

As I have already indicated, the constitution view depends upon the controversial Aristotelian thesis that one can have numerical sameness without identity.[13] The Trinity, then, is a kind of hylomorphic compound (that is, a compound of form and matter). The analog to "matter" in the Trinity is the divine essence, while the divine persons of the Trinity play the role of "forms." In Aristotelian philosophy matter is organized by its form. Together the matter-plus-form constitute one hylomorphic compound. Thus, the human soul is the form of the body. The body is the matter that the soul organizes. Together they constitute a hylomorphic compound of body-plus-soul. God, on this way of thinking, is like this. The divine nature is the "matter" that is organized by the three divine persons, who are the "forms" of the Godhead. There is still numerically one God on this view. But God is organized according to three "forms." An example often used in connection with the constitution model of the Trinity is that mentioned above, of the material constitution of a statue that is also a pillar and that is composed of a marble slab. (Think of a monumental statue in a public building that also acts as a pillar, propping up the ceiling of the building.) In this case, the marble is the matter which composes the three objects. The statue, the pillar, and the marble slab are the "forms" that organize the marble. This appears to be a good example of numerical sameness without identity that is analogous to the constitution account of the Trinity.

Now, obviously, this model is a controversial way of construing the Trinity. Yet it is also a novel way of doing so that does not obviously fall into either of the traditional genera of Trinity doctrines and that has certain advantages over these traditional alternatives. For it makes a lot of sense to say that the divine persons of the Trinity all share in a common deity, while treating the distinctions pertaining to the divine persons as sortal-relative. For those willing to bear the conceptual cost of endorsing

---

[12] Perhaps the most comprehensive critique of versions of social Trinitarianism can be found in Brian Leftow, "Anti-social Trinitarianism," reprinted in McCall and Rea, *Philosophical and Theological Essays on the Trinity*, 52–88.

[13] Alongside the constitution account of the Trinity there is also the closely related relative-identity account. But, as Michael Rea has pointed out, one can be a constitution-Trinity defender and yet resist the core claim of the relative-identity account that relative identity claims are more fundamental than classical identity claims. See Michael C. Rea, "Relative Identity and the Doctrine of the Trinity," in McCall and Rea, eds., *Philosophical and Theological Essays on the Trinity*, 249–62. See also the useful overview of recent analytic discussion in Howard-Snyder, "Trinity."

the numerical-sameness-without-identity claim at the heart of this view, it is a viable alternative to traditional ways of thinking about the dogma of the Trinity that has considerable appeal, without the costs associated with other, historical accounts of the Trinity.

Although there are conceptual costs to each of the extant families of models on the Trinity, their defenders have things to say by way of response. An adequate treatment of each of these families of Trinitarian models would require us to take account of such counterarguments. However, that is not our task here. Rather than wade into such deep waters, I shall set out another way of thinking about the divine nature, one which belongs in a family of views that has come to be known in the analytic literature as *Trinitarian mysterianism*. In an attempt to bridge some of the discussion between historians and systematicians, I want to focus on this way of thinking about the dogma of the Trinity, offering an argument in favor of the notion that the Trinity is a mystery that we cannot penetrate. Although I am sympathetic to the intuition that motivates some apophatically minded systematic theologians to be leery of any but the thinnest conceptual content to the doctrine of the Trinity, I am also skeptical of the claim that we can know nothing, or next to nothing, about the divine nature, for reasons that will become clear presently. But nor am I as optimistic as some analytics and social Trinitarians seem to be about what we can say regarding the divine nature. What I am after is something between these two sorts of views. We might say it is a kind of conceptually restricted model of the Trinity that is a version of Trinitarian mysterianism. One important advantage of this view over others we have discussed thus far is precisely that it says very little about the divine nature, and about what divine persons are or how they are related to one another in the divine life.

Circumscribing Mysterianism

A note on the formation of the doctrine of the Trinity

With this preamble in place, we can turn to the task of circumscribing the sort of mysterianism in view. We begin with a brief sketch of the dogma of the Trinity itself. In the previous chapter we noted that a doctrine is a second-order human reflection upon the first-order language of Holy Writ— the divine revelation against which all doctrine must be measured. A doctrine also has an ecclesial location. It is (minimally) a comprehensive account of a particular teaching about a given theological topic held by some community of Christians or some particular denomination.

We also saw in the previous chapter that a particular dogma is a theological doctrine with a canonical shape and that it is part of the conceptual core of the faith. The Trinity is surely a paradigm of such a doctrine, along with the incarnation. For it is clearly set forth in the ecumenical creeds, in the Nicene-Constantinopolitan symbol of AD 381. Yet, as is well known, it is not until the Nicene-Constantinopolitan Creed was promulgated by the Catholic Church that there was an official canonical form to the doctrine. Earlier creedal statements, including the Creed of Nicea of AD 325, do not provide a complete doctrine of the Trinity. Of course, the fathers of the church who compiled the Nicene-Constantinopolitan Creed did not think they were creating new doctrine out of whole cloth. They believed they were engaged in preserving and articulating the apostolic faith.[14] I think that they were right in their judgment, and the overwhelming majority of Christians since then have concurred. Nevertheless, a clear, unambiguous doctrine of the Trinity is not to be found in the pages of the New Testament. It is a dogma that, at best, is a kind of theological inference to the best explanation given the data of Scripture and the testimony of the earliest witnesses to the apostolic message.

One could give a plausible account of the divine nature rooted in the New Testament texts that was, say, Arian in nature. However, the leaders of the early church saw that such an Arian picture of God was not wholly adequate. It failed in important respects to take the deity of Christ with sufficient seriousness. It failed to provide an account of the divine nature that included Christ within the divine identity. Similar problems were apparent in inadequate accounts of the divinity of the Third Person of the Trinity as well. This is why it is only with the Nicene-Constantinopolitan Creed that we have a dogmatically adequate account of the divine nature. Through reflecting on the apostolic message and the New Testament witness, and through engagement and disagreement with alternative ways of understanding the same deposit of material (particularly with reference to Arianism), the fathers of the early church came to a clearer understanding of the implications of this material, concluding that God is, in fact, triune.

So it seems to me that the Trinity is a very good case of a doctrine formed by the early church on the basis of their reception of the apostolic faith,

---

[14] This can be seen in the implicitly Trinitarian baptismal formula of Matt 28:19 and in the way in which both the Father and Holy Spirit are identified with Christ's ministry in his baptism (Matt 3:16-17)—something that is echoed later in the New Testament in passages like Eph 4:4-6. Other New Testament passages are more obviously binitarian, including Christ in the divine identity, e.g., John 10:30-36, John 14:9-11, Phil 2:5-8, Col 1:15-17.

including the texts of the New Testament. It is a plausible interpretation of those texts and the apostolic tradition. And moreover, as far as Christians are concerned, it is also a warranted and true understanding of those texts and that apostolic tradition. Nevertheless, it is with the creedal tradition that we have the beginnings of a dogmatic understanding of the Trinity. It is not a doctrine that is clearly and unambiguously set forth in the New Testament documents, though there are hints and indications that this is the right view for those who have eyes to see (e.g., Matt 28:19). It is this ecclesiastical dogmatic deposit with respect to the Trinity that informs the argument of what follows.[15] We can summarize it thus:

TRINITY: The conjunction of dogmatic propositions concerning the divine nature, expressing the claim that God is one in essence and subsists in three persons, that are found in the dogmatic deposit of the ecumenical creeds, especially the Nicene-Constantinopolitan Symbol, and that reflect (a particular way of understanding) the teaching of Scripture and the apostolic faith. The dogmatic core of this conjunction of claims is as follows:

(T1) there is exactly one God;
(T2) there are exactly three coeternal divine persons "in" God: the Father, the Son, and the Holy Spirit;
(T3) the Father, the Son, and the Holy Spirit are not identical;
(T4) the Father, the Son, and the Holy Spirit are consubstantial.

Models and the Trinity

We have already encountered the notion of a conceptual model in the previous chapter. Nevertheless, given the importance of doctrinal models in this work, it is worth pausing to recap. By a model I mean something like the following: *a simplified conceptual framework or description by means of which complex data sets, systems, and processes may be organized and understood.* Models are usually *simplifications* or pared down descriptions of particular data sets, systems, and processes. They are incomplete and strictly inaccurate, but informative and imaginative, attempts to get at something that is usually too complex to be grasped as a whole. This applies to models used in scientific and mathematical theorizing, of course. It could also be applied to more

---

[15] For a somewhat similar recent short treatment of these matters, see Kathryn Tanner, "The Trinity as Christian Teaching," in Emery and Levering, *Oxford Handbook of the Trinity*, 349–58.

mundane things. For instance, a toy model of an airplane need not have scaled-down working engine parts; it may have no replica engine parts at all! Nor do the wings have to be properly aerodynamic so that they would give the model lift. The propellers in relation to the fuselage may be out of scale, the rudder and tail plane may not work at all (they may be made of one whole piece of wood or plastic or whatever). The dimensions of the model may be such that, even if all the other matters were attended to, it could never fly. (It might be too heavy relative to its size, its wings may be too short, its body oddly shaped or weighted, and so on.) We would not necessarily think such a replica a poor model of an airplane. It may be a very good model, depending on the use to which it is put.

Such a conception of a model may also have theological utility. However, here we must exercise caution lest this be misunderstood. I have said that a model is, strictly speaking, incomplete and inaccurate. That is true. A model airplane with no working engine is certainly an incomplete airplane that is in one important sense an inaccurate representation because it lacks something all working airplanes must possess. But it is in the nature of a model to be like this. Note that one can use models for various tasks without any commitment to whether the model represents something that is actual, or concrete, or *real*. Suppose I have a model of the *Millennium Falcon*. There is nothing that corresponds to the model in the real world, so to speak. It is a fictional entity, depicted on celluloid in the *Star Wars* saga. However, my model can be a better approximation to the *Falcon* depicted on the silver screen than another one, provided it has more of the properties that the film version appears to have as well (e.g., size, shape, mass, hyperdrive, and so on).

A model of the Trinity is a simplified description of something too complex to grasp altogether: the nature of God.[16] But I suppose that what the model describes is ontologically real. There is a Trinity. If one were of the view that there is no actual existent that corresponds to a model of the Trinity (because, say, God is a fictional object, or a projection of our imaginations, or

---

[16] It might be objected that if God is simple, it is odd to say that we cannot comprehend God altogether because he is too complex. Surely if God is simple, then it is a simple matter to understand what he is. This mistake, recently popularized by Richard Dawkins, falls under the fallacy of equivocation. The claim that God is a simple being (that is, essentially noncomposite) is semantically distinct from the claim that a concept is simple (i.e., that it is easily grasped). Hence, it is perfectly feasible to have an entity that is simple in the sense of being essentially noncomposite and yet to discover that making sense of that entity is so complex a matter that a model is needed to assist the limited human reason in contemplating it. Something similar may be said, mutatis mutandis, about simples in physics, such as subatomic particles, as we saw in the previous chapter.

whatever), then one might still find this model an interesting way in which religiously benighted individuals might give account of their apparently counterintuitive views about the divine. In the middle ground, there will be those who think there is a deity of some sort but that we have no reliable access to him/her/it, or that we cannot grasp anything substantive about his/her/its nature, if he/she/it even has a nature. Such strong theological apophaticism is an important constituent of much Christian theology and has been defended by several notable contemporary philosophers, such as Jean Luc Marion and John Caputo. Important though this is, I shall not attempt to offer a model that deals with the challenges presented by an apophatic account of God that prescinds from ascribing any conceptual content to the divine beyond some bare definite description or proper name.

Here we should raise a well-known objection to the use of conceptual models in theology. We can call it *the idolatry objection*. The worry is that it is a kind of idolatry to construct a model of some aspect of the divine nature—for aren't all such models, strictly speaking, false and inaccurate pictures of what they seek to represent? And isn't an account of the divine nature that is false and inaccurate something other than God—a simulacrum of our own imaginations?[17]

In response to this worry, several things can be said. First, as I have labored to explain, models are indeed, strictly speaking, false reports because they simplify complex data into a picture or account that can be grasped. Think once more of the model airplane. Not all the actual airplane parts are represented by the model. It does not fly, unlike the actual plane. Yet it represents something of the entity that it approximates. That, I suggest, is how we should think of the model of divine simplicity offered in the previous chapter, and the model of the Trinity that will be set forth in this chapter. Second, rather than being an exercise in hubris and idolatry, the opposite is the case. The sort of theological models in view here and in the previous chapter are ways of *preserving* the divine mystery and indicating the limitations of human comprehension of the divine. God is beyond human ken. He is concealed by a brilliant darkness (as Pseudo-Dionysus memorably put it[18]). What he does reveal of himself is piecemeal and limited. Yet we can provide some conceptual account of these things, albeit in models that are limited, fallible, and subject to revision because they are constructed by fallen human beings who see these things "through a glass darkly."

---

[17] This is a point made by William Wood in "Modeling Mystery," *Scientia et Fides* 4, no. 1 (2016): 40. His account is very helpful.

[18] Pseudo-Dionysius, *The Mystical Theology*, in *Pseudo-Dionysius: The Complete Works*, trans. Colm Lubheid (Mahwah: Paulist Press, 1985), 135.

In other words, a few moments of reflection should enable us to see that no serious theologian mistakes the role played by models in thinking about Christian doctrine with the object of Christian doctrine—namely, God. Similarly, no physicist of repute mistakes the model of an atom with an atom. Models should not be mistaken for the thing that they represent.

It is difficult to adjudicate between competing models of the Trinity beyond what we might think of as intuitive criteria such as coherence, consistency with the biblical and apostolic traditions as well as other areas of knowledge, and, perhaps, parsimony. I shall also presume that a model of the Trinity is better or more satisfactory if it provides an account that requires less revision to the traditional understanding of the doctrine of God stemming from the Nicene settlement of the fourth and fifth centuries. This is a stipulation that is not uncontroversial. Those who regard the task of contemporary Trinitarian theorizing as part of a larger theologically revisionist program, overturning or significantly altering aspects of the classical Trinitarian settlement that they regard as mistaken in important respects, may resist or even reject this stipulation. It is, however, a provision that I think is theologically respectable and important. Not only has it been historically significant, but it is also arguably the default option in the Christian tradition. However, I shall not defend it here.[19] For present purposes, we can simply summarize the notion of model we will deploy later in the constructive section of the chapter in this way:

MODEL: A simplified conceptual framework or description by means of which complex sets of data, systems, and processes may be organized and understood.

Mystery and the Trinity

We turn now to the relationship between the notion of mystery and that of the Trinity. According to Dale Tuggy, there are five ways of understanding the word "mystery":

[1] a truth formerly unknown, and perhaps undiscoverable by unaided human reason, but which has now been revealed by God and is known to

---

[19] I have offered a partial defense of the place of tradition in Christian theology in Crisp, *God Incarnate: Explorations in Christology* (London: T&T Clark, 2009), ch. 1. A much richer defense of the role of tradition in Christian theology can be found in William J. Abraham, *Canon and Criterion in Christian Theology: From the Fathers to Feminism* (Oxford: Oxford University Press, 1998); and William J. Abraham, Jason E Vickers, and Natalie B. Van Kirk, eds., *Canonical Theism: A Proposal for Theology and the Church* (Grand Rapids: Eerdmans, 2008).

some; . . . [2] something we don't completely understand; . . . [3] some fact we can't explain, or can't fully or adequately explain; . . . [4] an unintelligible doctrine, the meaning of which can't be grasped; . . . [5] a truth which one should believe even though it seems, even after careful reflection, to be impossible and/or contradictory and thus false.[20]

Of these, Tuggy suggests that (4) and (5) are the meanings used by "sophisticated mysterians about the Trinity."[21] However, without some qualifications, this seems mistaken. For one thing, if the doctrine is *literally* unintelligible (as per [4] above), then there is nothing to be said about it. It cannot be articulated in a sensible way, let alone believed by a rational person, for the very good reason that it is impossible to understand. That is just what it is for a thing to be unintelligible. However, this should not be confused with the claim that *x is a doctrine the complete understanding of which is beyond our ken*. I take it that just such a position is proposed by those who are mysterians about the mind-body problem. In that discussion the idea is that, at our current stage of evolutionary development, human beings are incapable of resolving the mind-body problem because we do not have sufficiently developed hardware. It is a problem of cognitive limitation. Similarly, it could be that the Trinity is a perfectly intelligible doctrine for someone that has an infinite intelligence, or even a very great finite intelligence, but not intelligible to creatures of limited intelligence, such as human beings. It seems to me that this thesis about the cognitive limitation of human beings is what lies behind much Trinitarian mysterianism—or at least, it is what lies behind the sort of Trinitarian mysterianism that I am interested in pursuing.

Let us turn to (5), which was the notion that a mystery is "a truth which one should believe even though it seems, even after careful reflection, to be impossible and/or contradictory and thus false." It is difficult to know what to say about this. If a doctrine is impossible, which I take to be a modally robust claim equivalent to its being in some sense *not possibly true* or even *necessarily false*, then it is difficult to see how anyone can believe it. This would be equivalent to heeding the counsel of the White Queen, who enjoins Alice in *Through the Looking Glass* to practice "believing six impossible things before breakfast."[22]

---

[20] Dale Tuggy, "The Unfinished Business of Trinitarian Theorizing" *Religious Studies* 39, no. 2 (2003): 175–76.

[21] Dale Tuggy, "Trinity," *Stanford Encyclopedia of Philosophy* (March 2016), http://plato .stanford.edu/entries/trinity/, accessed September 13, 2016.

[22] If a doctrine is contradictory, then I take it that it is false on other grounds, and necessarily so. I shall not venture into nonstandard logics where the principle of bivalence

I reject (5) as an adequate account of mystery. Tuggy equates this with what he calls *positive mysterianism*. This is the view that "the trinitarian doctrine can't be understood because of an abundance of content. That is, the doctrine seems to contain explicit or implicit contradictions."[23] It is not clear to me that an abundance of content is the problem according to (5). The more modest doctrine of mystery expressed in (4) might also be a candidate for having too much content for the cognitively limited human to grasp (though Tuggy appears to think otherwise). The real issue for those who advocate something like (5) is that it requires assent to an understanding of mystery that contains implicit or explicit contradictions. But then, on the widely held assumption that there are no true contradictions, it would seem that no defender of (5) could command assent to a mystery like the Trinity. That does not appear to be a very appealing doctrine of mystery.

In contrast to positive mysterianism, Tuggy posits a weaker *negative mysterianism* (while granting that in many theological presentations of mysterianism, these two are not clearly distinguished and may be conflated). According to this view, "The true doctrine of the Trinity is not understandable because it is too poor in intelligible content for it to positively seem either consistent or inconsistent to us."[24] He cites Saint Gregory Nazianzus as an example of this sort of mysterianism. At the end of his *Fifth Theological Oration: On the Holy Spirit*, and despairing of finding any image of the Trinity in things that are created adequate to the purpose, he writes,

> Finally, then, it seems best to me to let the images and the shadows [i.e., various attempts to image the Trinity] go, as being deceitful and very far short of the truth; and clinging myself to the more reverent conception, and resting upon few words, using the guidance of the Holy Ghost, keeping to the end as my genuine comrade and companion the enlightenment which I have received from Him, and passing through this world to persuade all others also to the best of my power to worship Father, Son, and Holy Ghost, the One Godhead and Power. To Him belongs all glory and honour and might for ever and ever. Amen.[25]

---

is suspended or done away with. Whatever is made of such logics, it seems intuitive that the doctrine of the Trinity is not a good candidate for a "true contradiction."

[23] Tuggy, "Trinity." Tuggy takes up the issue of positive mysterianism in greater detail in "On Positive Mysterianism," *International Journal for Philosophy of Religion* 69, no. 3 (2011): 205–26.

[24] Tuggy, "Trinity."

[25] Nazianzus, *The Fifth Theological Oration: On the Holy Spirit* (*Oration 31*) 33, in *Cyril of Jerusalem, Gregory Nazianzen*, vol. 7 of NPNF Second Series, ed. Philip Schaff and Henry Wace (Edinburgh: T&T Clark, 1893), 328.

The "practical upshot of this," says Tuggy, "is being content to merely repeat the approved trinitarian sentences."[26] This also has little to commend it, even if so eminent a divine as Saint Gregory Nazianzus approves it. Suppose someone informs me that scientists have found a new object that only exists in the reaches of deep space. They have labeled it the Deep-Space Unidentified Object, or DSUO. Upon asking what this object is, I am told that the scientists studying it have absolutely no idea. That is why it is called DSUO. I inquire about its general properties and am told these remain mysterious and no particular property has yet been isolated and identified. Suppose this discussion continued and it transpired that the scientific team that has made this discovery has no direct empirical data on DSUO at all. They have postulated its existence indirectly or abductively, on the basis of other phenomena. (Perhaps it generates a gravitational disturbance, or is picked up on the basis of an unexplained radiation signature in the surrounding region, or something like that.) There is sufficient data to make the scientists think something is there, though they have insufficient data to know what is there. Perhaps I might believe that there is such a thing as DSUO, upon consulting the data myself, though I might also remain skeptical without more information. But even if DSUO does exist, I can know almost nothing about it and can reasonably be expected to adopt no particular attitude toward it. Transpose this reasoning onto negative mysterianism. According to this way of thinking about the Trinity, I appear to know next to nothing substantive about the divine nature. I know nothing about particular divine attributes, even if God has particular divine attributes—apart from the fact that he is in one fundamental respect one, and in another fundamental respect three. When pressed, I say I can affirm nothing more or less about the divine nature because I have no other information. This is as much of the mystery as has been revealed by divine revelation.

Tuggy correlates negative mysterianism with (4). But we have already seen that (4) presents the Trinitarian theologian with apparently insurmountable problems: we cannot be expected to believe things that are literally unintelligible. However, as he characterizes negative mysterianism, there is no need to hold (4). The negative mysterian is only committed to the weaker claim that we cannot understand the doctrine of the Trinity because there is not enough intelligible conceptual content to the doctrine for us to judge whether it is coherent or incoherent. But, as I have already indicated, this is not the same as saying the doctrine of the Trinity is literally unintelligible.

---

[26] Tuggy, "Trinity."

Jones may not understand a particular interpretation of quantum mechanics. (As the adage goes, "If you say you understand quantum mechanics, then you only show that you don't understand quantum mechanics."[27]) This may simply be because Jones is not capable of understanding the work, or does not have the "hardware" with which to make sense of it. Clearly, this does not mean sense cannot be made of it. There are other more intelligent beings than Jones who are able to make sense of it and use it to good scientific effect. If the negative mysterian is in this position with respect to the dogma of the Trinity, then Jones is not clearly in a position equivalent to (4). What is more, there seems little that is objectionable in the cognitive-limitation view just outlined. Just as there is nothing surprising in the claim that Jones, like most moderately intelligent human beings, cannot understand a particular interpretation of quantum mechanics, so there is nothing particularly surprising in the claim that something as profound as the Trinity might be beyond Jones' ken. But note, the reason why Jones cannot penetrate the mysteries of quantum mechanics has nothing to do with contradictions, though it may have to do with apparent paradoxes. It is just that Jones is not in an epistemically advantageous position with respect to the conceptual content of quantum mechanics. And the same may be true for all we know, mutatis mutandis, with respect to Jones' understanding of the Trinity.

In place of Tuggy's characterization of mystery, I offer the following:

MYSTERY: A truth that is intelligible in principle but that may not be entirely intelligible to human beings in their current state of cognitive development.

Note that on this way of thinking about mystery, it is not necessarily entirely unintelligible even for the person who does not completely grasp its meaning. Moreover, it is possible, on this construal, that most if not all humans can only have a partial, incomplete grasp of the doctrine. This is similar in some respects to James Anderson's notion of a *merely apparent contradiction resulting from unarticulated equivocations*, or MACRUE for short.[28] Christian doctrine may contain such MACRUES, articulations of the Trinity included. But this is a far cry from the claim that the Trinity is a true contradiction or that it is unintelligible *simpliciter*.

---

[27] A saying often attributed to Richard Feynman.

[28] See James Anderson, *Paradox in Christian Theology: An Analysis of Its Presence, Character, and Epistemic Status* (Milton Keynes: Paternoster, 2007).

Divine transcendence

Alongside notions of the Trinity and mystery go discussions of the transcendence of the divine nature. It seems that transcendence is something that surpasses ordinary experience or existence. In the case of God, he surpasses creaturely experience and existence. (He surpasses creaturely experience because he is omniscient, omnipresent, and omnipotent as well as eternal; and God surpasses creaturely existence because he is a necessary being.) But more than that, he is transcendent over all creatures because he is the creator of all things.[29] For many theologians, however, transcendence is closely related to a much stronger account of the difference between divine and human existence. Thus, for example, Elizabeth Johnson writes,

> The holiness and utter transcendence of God over all of creation has always been an absolutely central affirmation of the Judeo-Christian tradition. God as God—source, redeemer, and goal of all—is illimitable mystery who, while immanently present, cannot be measured or controlled. The doctrine of divine incomprehensibility is a corollary of this divine transcendence. In essence, God's unlikeness to the corporal and spiritual finite world is total; hence we simply cannot understand God. No human concept, word, or image, all of which originate in experience of created reality, can circumscribe the divine reality, nor can any human construct express with any measure of adequacy the mystery of God, who is ineffable.[30]

There are very good historical-theological reasons for thinking of transcendence in this way, and some recent analytic theological work has taken up the task of trying to give an account of the divine nature that begins with the claim that God is ineffable (literally, beyond our capacity to express in words) and incomprehensible (beyond human comprehension).[31] But there are significant conceptual obstacles for any such project, as we have already

---

[29] This is the conclusion to which Jonathan L. Kvanvig comes in his article, "Divine Transcendence," *Religious Studies* 20, no. 3 (1984): 377–87.

[30] Elizabeth Johnson, "The Incomprehensibility of God and the Image of God as Male and Female," *Theological Studies* 45, no. 3 (1984): 441.

[31] Jonathan D. Jacobs, "The Ineffable, Inconceivable, and Incomprehensible God: Fundamentality and Apophatic Theology," in *Oxford Studies in Philosophy of Religion*, vol. 6, ed. Jonathan L. Kvanvig (Oxford: Oxford University Press, 2015), 158–76; Sameer Yadav, "Mystical Experience and the Apophatic Attitude," *Journal of Analytic Theology* 4 (2016): 18–43; and Sebastian Gäb, "The Paradox of Ineffability," *International Journal of Philosophy and Theology* 78, no. 3 (2017): 289–300. See also Michael C. Rea, "Hiddenness and Transcendence," in *Hidden Divinity and Religious Belief: New Perspectives*, ed. Adam Green and Eleonore Stump (Cambridge University Press, 2015), 210–25.

had cause to note in passing in chapter 2. For our purposes, it is enough to hold that God is transcendent *in at least this way*: he is the creator of all things. This is a much weaker sense of transcendence than that articulated by Johnson. But it is sufficient for the purposes of our model.

Now, it may seem that analyzing transcendence in terms of being the creator of all things implies that transcendence is a relational property. However, it is not necessarily a relational property because, as Jonathan Kvanvig points out, there is no contingent thing that must exist in order for God to have this property.[32] There is a possible world that contains only God and nothing else.[33] Yet in that world God is still the creator of all things—it is just that the referent of "all things" in that world is not mind independent. "All things" in that world comprises some set of divine ideas God has not brought about. Of course, some stronger version of divine transcendence may be true, all things considered—one that includes the notions of ineffability and incomprehensibility. But these two notions are not entailed by the concept of transcendence understood in terms of Kvanvig's analysis as a claim about God as creator of all things. To sum up:

TRANSCENDENCE: God is transcendent in virtue of being the creator of all things.

Chastened Trinitarian Mysterianism

With this understanding of mystery in place, we may proceed to set out the chastened Trinitarian mysterian model of the Trinity. Recall that we are after a doctrinal account of the divine nature that conforms to TRINITY and MODEL and that reflects MYSTERY and TRANSCENDENCE. Moreover, it is not enough simply to confess the words of the Nicene-Constantinopolitan Creed, or the Athanasian Creed, or any other confession as per negative mysterianism. Some conceptual content must be supplied in order for this to be a meaningful dogmatic framework, even if the result is a rather thin positive mysterianism. In a similar fashion, merely reiterating the words of the Declaration of Independence does no work in *explaining* what we take the scope of this document to be, or its political relevance. A conceptual framework must be supplied in order that we may have some idea of what it is that the document conveys to us about its scope and political relevance for today.

---

[32] Kvanvig, "Divine Transcendence," 386.

[33] Or, at least, so it seems to me. Of course Platonists will deny this. But I am not a Platonist.

In order to get clearer the sort of view I have in mind here, let us briefly consider Edwin Abbott's nineteenth-century mathematical novel, *Flatland*.[34] Abbott conceives of a two-dimensional world populated by sentient plane figures that have no notion of a third dimension. How are such beings to understand the existence of a three-dimensional world beyond their own? It is literally outside their experience. Perhaps the denizens of Flatland can begin to apprehend something of three-dimensional existence by means of careful modeling in two dimensions. Think of the way in which we can draw a two-dimensional representation of a sphere on a page (see fig. 1).

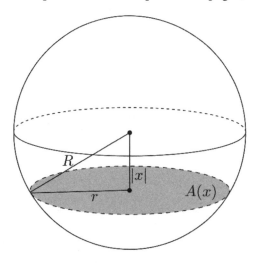

Figure 1. Sphere with cross section. Source: Wikicommons, *2009.*

Even though such a picture is an illusion, strictly speaking, it does offer an approximation of what an actual sphere looks like that is consistent with MODEL. Yet without a concept of "depth" (or some other term that entails three-dimensions in space like "height," "width," or "breadth"), it is difficult to know what Flatlanders would make of a two-dimensional model of a sphere. We humans know what life in three-dimensions is like. Those dwelling in Flatland do not. Perhaps they are incapable of understanding this without some further cognitive development, along the lines of MYSTERY.

This problem is one of the central preoccupations of Abbott's mathematical novel. In one chapter, a plane-figure Flatlander encounters a sphere from

---

[34] See Edwin A. Abbott, *Flatland: A Romance in Many Dimensions* (London: Seeley, 1884).

Spaceland. As he tries to explain to the Flatlander what it is like to live in three-dimensions, the sphere says this:

> You are living on a Plane. What you style Flatland is the vast level surface of what I may call a fluid, on, or in, the top of which you and your countrymen move about, without rising above it or falling below it. I am not a plane Figure, but a Solid. You call me a Circle, but in reality I am not a Circle, but an infinite number of Circles, of size varying from a Point to a Circle of thirteen inches in diameter, one placed on top of the other. When I cut through your plane as I am now doing, I make your plane a section which you, very rightly, call a Circle. For even a Sphere—which is my proper name in my own country—if he manifests himself at all to an inhabitant of Flatland, must needs call himself a Circle.[35]

It is not hard to see how a sphere from Spaceland would appear as a circle to a Flatlander. And it is not hard to understand how a geometric plane figure would find it difficult to conceive of the concept of "space" and of the notion of a three-dimensional entity composed of an infinite number of circles and of varying diameters.

This illustration provides us with an intuition pump. It delivers some independent reason for thinking that a truth about three-dimensional space might be mysterious to an entity more epistemically limited than we occupants of Spaceland. It is not that the notion of space or of three dimensions is contradictory or nonsensical, though it may appear to be so to the Flatlanders. Rather, the concept of space is a notion the complete understanding of which is beyond the ken of the Flatlander. Even when the sphere reveals himself to the Flatlander, it is in terms that the Flatlander can understand, as a circle. We might say that the sphere accommodates himself to the cognitive limitation of the Flatlander in order to convey certain truths about things beyond the ken of the Flatlander. What appears to the Flatlander to be a circle is in fact the plane section of the sphere. But without a concept of space, and without an experience of three dimensionality, the Flatlander is incapable of making the cognitive leap necessary to comprehend this. In other words, the partial or piecemeal understanding of the plane figure requires conceptual supplementation by means of revelation—that is, further information, including further conceptual content, to which the plane figure has no independent cognitive access. Such revelation includes the sphere accommodating himself to the concepts and terms understood by two-dimensional plane figures—such as the notion that the sphere is composed of an infinite

[35] Abbott, *Flatland*, 106.

number of circles of varying diameters from a point to thirteen inches, or the notion that the sphere appears as a circle to the Flatlander because the intersection of a solid with a plane generates a two dimensional cross-section.

The relevant changes having been made, we can apply the reasoning of this intuition pump to the doctrine of the Trinity. A traditional theological claim is that the Trinity is a revealed doctrine. Suppose that is right. And suppose with much classical, orthodox Christian theology that God's transcendence means there are important ways in which God is beyond our ken in a very strong sense—rather like the way in which the sphere, as a three-dimensional entity, is beyond the ken of the Flatlander. Suppose further that in order for God to give us some inkling of what he is like, he must accommodate himself to our limitations and convey to us something of himself that is, at best, a partial account of his divine nature. This, too, is like the explanation the sphere gives to the Flatlander, and the appearance of the sphere to the Flatlander (as a circle). Finally, suppose that God does not provide us with a complete explanation of the MACRUES that result from what he does reveal of himself to us. In particular, he does not give us a complete explanation of how he can be both one and three at one and the same time. In a similar fashion, the sphere is unable to give the Flatlander a complete explanation of himself because, in order to do that, he would need to supply other conceptual information that would make little sense to the Flatlander—including, most fundamentally, the concept of three-dimensional space.

Now, this little just-so story about the Trinity seems consistent with what Christians have traditionally professed concerning the divine nature. God is triune; this is a revealed doctrine; what God reveals of himself in Scripture and in the Christian tradition is incomplete in important respects, and this is at least in part because of our limited cognitive capacities. Note also that, by bringing in the example from Flatland, we have an intuition pump that provides us with some explanation of why there is so much misunderstanding about the threeness-oneness problem of the Trinity. In the case of the Flatland example, this is because the idea that an entity may present itself as a circle and yet also be composed of an infinite number of circles of varying diameters from a point to thirteen inches seems incredible—perhaps even paradoxical or contradictory—to a two-dimensional plane figure. (It may seem contradictory because the sphere claims to be both a circle, like some other Flatland figures, and yet also an infinite number of circles of varying diameters at one and the same time.) In the case of the Trinity, this is because the idea that an entity may present itself as one in essence and yet subsisting in three persons seems incredible, paradoxical, and, to many, contradictory.

But this makes sense if, like the sphere, God is transcendent. That is, God is beyond our mere human experience in a way similar to the manner in which the sphere is above and beyond the experience of the Flatlander. Perhaps, like the sphere, God is in some important sense incomprehensible to human beings in their present state of development. It may even be that certain qualities of God's nature are, like the sphere, incommunicable to human beings. But, for present purposes, all we need is the notion that God is transcendent—for what we are after is a model of the Trinity.

We are now in a position to sum up the chastened mysterian account of the Trinity. We begin with the stipulations previously stated:

MODEL: A simplified conceptual framework or description by means of which complex sets of data, systems, and processes may be organized and understood.

MYSTERY: A truth that is intelligible in principle but that may not be entirely intelligible to human beings in their current state of cognitive development.

TRINITY: The conjunction of dogmatic propositions concerning the divine nature, expressing the claim that God is one in essence and subsists in three persons, that are found in the dogmatic deposit of the ecumenical creeds, especially the Nicene-Constantinopolitan Symbol, and that reflect (a particular way of understanding) the teaching of Scripture and the apostolic faith. The dogmatic core of this conjunction of claims is as follows:

(T1) there is exactly one God;
(T2) there are exactly three coeternal divine persons "in" God: the Father, the Son, and the Holy Spirit;
(T3) the Father, the Son, and the Holy Spirit are not identical;
(T4) the Father, the Son, and the Holy Spirit are consubstantial.

TRANSCENDENCE: God is transcendent in virtue of being the creator of all things.

What we want is an account that is consistent with the conjunction of MODEL, MYSTERY, TRINITY, and TRANSCENDENCE—something like this:

(1) The triunity of the divine nature is an instance of MYSTERY because God is transcendent (as per TRANSCENDENCE).
(2) Human beings cannot apprehend the triunity of God absent divine revelation.
(3) In revealing himself to us, God accommodates himself to the epistemic limitations of human beings. (Presumably, this includes allowing for the noetic effects of sin.)
(4) TRINITY is a revealed dogma (that is, a doctrine that has a particular canonical form).

(5) TRINITY provides a dogmatic framework for understanding the divine nature that is theologically minimal.[36]

(6) TRINITY does not *explain* how God is triune; it does not in and of itself offer a particular MODEL of the Godhead; it is metaphysically underdetermined. (For this reason it is consistent with more than one dogmatic extrapolation, including a range of Trinitarian doctrines and MODELS.)

(7) The terms "person" and "essence," and their cognates that demarcate the way in which God is three and the way in which God is one in TRINITY, are referring terms that are placeholders; we do not have a clear conceptual grip on their semantic content. (This is consistent with the claim that we may have a partial, piecemeal, or analogous sense of these terms.)

(8) TRINITY is consistent with MYSTERY.

With this we complete the constructive section of the argument. (1)–(8) constitute the chastened mysterian MODEL.

Conclusion

In this chapter we have set out an account of a chastened Trinitarian mysterianism. When this is set beside the parsimonious model of the doctrine of divine simplicity set forth in the previous chapter, a particular picture of God emerges. This picture is consistent with the chastened theism offered in chapter 2. In keeping with much analytic theology, the accounts of divine simplicity and the Trinity offered here have been given as doctrinal models. They do not capture all that there is to say about the divine nature; they are simplified descriptions of something much more complex. This more complex thing has to do with the two "poles" within the Christian doctrine of God that need to be addressed by any adequate systematic theology: God's unity and triunity. A more complete account of the Christian doctrine of God would fill this picture out with other components, such as an account of the divine attributes. While I do not propose to do that here, the next chapter does segue from the doctrine of God to the doctrine of creation. In so doing, it gives some account of the notion of divine eternity and election in relation to God's purposes in creation. This will lead, in chapter 6, to a discussion of the reasons for the incarnation—a matter at the heart of God's purpose for the created order.

---

[36] Objection: How is TRINITY theologically minimal? Reply: It is theologically minimal in the sense that the tenets of TRINITY are consistent with more than one model of the Trinity.

5

God's Eternal Purpose

The doctrine of election is the sum of the gospel, because of all the words that can be said or heard it is the best: that God elects man; that God is for man too the One who loves in freedom. . . . Its function is to bear basic testimony to eternal, free and unchanging grace as the beginning of all the ways and works of God.

Karl Barth[1]

In this chapter we move from discussion of Theology Proper—that is, the doctrine of God—to discussion concerned with the purposes of God in creation, eventually focusing upon God's work in the incarnation. This chapter segues from the doctrine of God to the doctrine of creation and God's purposes in election in light of the end for which God created the world. Then we will be in a position to consider whether the incarnation was only a response to the appearance of fallen creatures or whether God had other, more general reasons for bringing about the incarnation—reasons to do with uniting human beings to Godself. This is the topic of the next chapter.

The argument of this chapter falls into three parts. In the first I shall give a dogmatic sketch of the doctrine of divine eternity, the main contours of which are well known.[2] Following an outline of this aspect of the classical theistic picture of the divine nature, we shall turn in a second section to consider three theological theses about God's life in relation to his purposes

---

[1] Karl Barth, *Church Dogmatics* II/2, ed. T. F. Torrance and Geoffrey W. Bromiley (London: T&T Clark, 1957), 3.

[2] At least, this is the case on the classical Boethian account, about which, more below. The modern notion that divine eternity can include a concept of duration is discussed by Brian Leftow in *Time and Eternity* (Ithaca, N.Y.: Cornell University Press, 1991), and was introduced into the modern discussion by Eleonore Stump and Norman Kretzmann, "Eternity," *Journal of Philosophy* 78, no. 8 (1981): 429–58.

in election and creation. Each of them in different ways undermine the claim that God is eternal or atemporal, preferring instead the notion that God is in time or everlasting. Then, in a third section, I shall offer some reflections on the findings of this analysis as a prelude to the constructive argument for a supralapsarian Christology to be taken up in the next chapter.

Divine Eternity and the Classical Picture of the Divine Nature

According to the classical theistic picture, God is not a temporal being like us. He is an atemporal being. He exists without time. That is, no temporal relations bear upon the divine life. He has no beginning, middle, and end. He has no past and no future.[3] As the great Roman theologian Boethius put it,

> Eternity, then, is the complete, simultaneous and perfect possession all at once of illimitable life. . . . Therefore, whatever includes and possesses the whole fullness of illimitable life at once and is such that nothing future is absent from it and nothing past has flowed away, this is rightly judged to be eternal, and of this it is necessary both that being in full possession of itself it be always present to itself and that it have the infinity of mobile time present to it.[4]

This view is not merely one among several that are each of equal dogmatic worth. It is the default position in historic Christianity.[5] It is also *de fide* for Roman Catholics (for God is said to be eternal according to Lateran IV and

[3]   Recent defenses of the timelessness view include Paul Helm in *Eternal God: A Study of God without Time,* 2nd ed. (1988; repr., Oxford: Oxford University Press, 2010); Leftow, *Time and Eternity*; Katherin A. Rogers, *Perfect Being Theology* (Edinburgh: Edinburgh University Press, 2000); and *idem, Anselm on Freedom* (Oxford: Oxford University Press, 2008). For recent defenses of versions of the everlastingness view, see Garrett J. DeWeese, *God and the Nature of Time* (Aldershot: Ashgate, 2004); William Hasker, *God, Time, and Knowledge* (Ithaca, N.Y.: Cornell University Press, 1989); and, most recently, R. T. Mullins, *In Search of the Timeless God*, Oxford Studies in Analytic Theology (Oxford: Oxford University Press, 2016). Nelson Pike's *God and Timelessness* (London: Routledge and Kegan Paul, 1970), is also still worth reading. A useful comparison of the different views on this matter can be found in Gregory Ganssle, ed., *God and Time: Four Views* (Downers Grove, Ill.: IVP, 2001).

[4]   Anicius Manlius Severinus Boethius, *The Consolation of Philosophy*, in *Theological Tractates*, trans. H. F. Stewart, Loeb Classical Library (1918; repr., Cambridge, Mass.: Harvard University Press, 1973), bk. 5, §6.

[5]   Or, perhaps more precisely, divine eternity understood in terms of divine timelessness is a family of views about God's relation to time within which there are several different options. See Leftow, *Time and Eternity,* for discussion of this.

Vatican I),[6] and appears to be enshrined in a number of Protestant symbols as well. For example, article 1 of the Belgic Confession states, "We all believe with the heart and confess with the mouth, that there is only one simple and spiritual Being, which we call God; and that he is eternal, incomprehensible, invisible, immutable, infinite, almighty; perfectly wise, just, good, and the overflowing fountain of all good."[7] Similarly, the first article of the Augsburg Confession reads, "There is one divine essence, which is called and which is God: eternal, incorporeal, indivisible,"[8] and the first chapter of the Scots Confession says something similar: God "is eternal, infinite, unmeasurable, incomprehensible, omnipotent, invisible."[9] These symbols speak of God in terms reminiscent of the influential Boethian characterization, as *eternal*. The alternative idea, that God is somehow temporal, or everlasting, is without significant dogmatic support in the tradition. Even defenders of the everlastingness view concede as much. Thus, William Hasker admits that the everlastingness view "has . . . been a minority view in the history of theology, with preference rather for the claim that God is timeless, outside of time altogether."[10]

For defenders of this classical Christian theistic view that we find in the historic creeds and confessions of Protestantism and Roman Catholicism, the idea that "God has a future" makes no sense, when interpreted literally. He has no future because he is not in time. Nevertheless, God creates the world *with* time. He brings about the cosmos and everything in it, but not at a particular moment "prior" to which he was doing something else. For (to repeat) it is an entailment of this view that there is nothing chronologically prior in the divine life because temporal relations have no purchase upon God. Naturally, as creatures of time, we cannot fathom what such a life is like; it is

[6] See Ludwig Ott, *Fundamentals of Catholic Dogma*, 4th ed. (Rockford, Ill.: TAN Books, 1960), 36–37.

[7] Translation in Philip Schaff, ed., *The Creeds of Christendom: With a History and Critical Notes*, vol. 3, *The Evangelical Protestant Creeds*, rev. David Schaff, 6th ed. (1931; repr., Grand Rapids: Baker Books, 1983), 383–84.

[8] This translation of the Latin edition of the Augsburg Confession, along with a parallel translation of the text of the German version of the confession, can be found in Theodore G. Tappert, trans. and ed., *The Book of Concord: The Confessions of the Evangelical Lutheran Church* (Philadelphia: Fortress, 1959), 27.

[9] The text of the Scots Confession can be found in Schaff, *Creeds of Christendom*, 439. Similar ideas can be found in the first article of the Anglican Articles of Religion and in the Westminster Confession.

[10] William Hasker, "Eternity and Providence," in *The Cambridge Companion to Philosophical Theology*, ed. Charles Taliaferro and Chad Meister (Cambridge: Cambridge University Press, 2010), 81.

even difficult to give an account of such a life, let alone an adequate account. The conceptual apparatus needed for such an account is, if not beyond us, at least at the very conceptual limits of what we are able to conceive and express in natural human terms (as we have already had cause to note with respect to the doctrine of God in earlier chapters).

That said, the fact that we cannot give a complete account of a particular thing should not lead us to presume that such a thing is therefore incoherent, as if the only things that can exist are the things we can conceptually grasp, or at least, are things humans should, in principle, be capable of grasping. There are many things in the world independent of theology that we cannot grasp, even things that we may be incapable of grasping in our current state of evolutionary development. We have already mentioned one example of this in the previous chapter: Colin McGinn and those who follow his "mysterianism" about the philosophy of mind claim that we may be incapable of figuring out the mind-body problem because we are not sufficiently evolved. It is not that the problem cannot be resolved, only that, given our current stage of evolutionary development, we don't have the hardware with which to successfully resolve the matter. In theological circles the idea that there may be things beyond our ken is hardly novel. Demarcating the difference between what we are in principle capable of knowing as creatures and what is beyond the ken of any human creature is not always easily done. However, that does not mean there is no line to be drawn, any more than the fact that a myopic man cannot see a line in the sand means that there is no line in the sand to be seen.

But perhaps there is a proper theological curiosity about the divine life, one that historic defenders of divine timelessness like Boethius might approve. Suppose we approach the doctrine of God with a healthy dose of apophaticism, as I have been recommending up to this point in earlier chapters. That is, suppose we begin our thinking about God by saying to ourselves, "There will be aspects of the divine life that are beyond my ken. But there will be other things about the divine life that I can have some apprehension of, because God has revealed these things to us in Scripture and via the witness of the Christian tradition." That seems to reflect the sort of healthy apophaticism I have in mind. Not that everything about the divine nature is forever beyond our ken—for then we could know nothing about God. But rather, there are certain limited things we can know about God and certain things that we cannot. In the latter cases we must leave the veil of mystery in place.

Some will think that such a modest apophaticism with regard to the doctrine of God is not strong enough. For, say such critics, we can know *nothing* about the divine life if by "the divine life" we mean the divine essence. We cannot know God as he is in himself. We can only know the emanations of God, or the energies of God, or some communication of the divine that is not identical to the divine essence. Perhaps, like the distinction in contemporary metaphysics between fundamental and derived properties, we can know certain things that are derived attributes of God but not things that are fundamental to the divine essence.[11] In a similar manner, perhaps we can know the derived properties of the table: that it appears hard to the touch; that it resists my pressure upon it; that it is solid, wooden, of certain height, width, and depth in three-dimensional space, and so on. Yet we cannot immediately apprehend certain fundamental properties of the table such as the fact that it is composed mainly of a huge number of tiny subatomic particles arranged table-wise. Applied to God the claim is that there are certain things about the divine nature that we can apprehend, things that God has communicated to his creatures in Holy Writ, or perhaps in the created order. But such things are not fundamental to who he is, to his divine life. Instead, they are derivative, like the superficial attributes of the table with which we come into contact on a daily basis.

This is an attractive picture of the divine life, and it (or something very like it) has had a grip on many historic orthodox Christian theologians. According to these thinkers, the divine nature is literally incomprehensible (that is, is such that we cannot *comprehend* anything about the divine nature) as well as ineffable (that is, is such that we cannot *express* anything about the divine nature accurately).[12] Yet to my way of thinking, this is a beguiling picture. Here is why: if Jesus of Nazareth is God Incarnate, then when Jesus speaks, God speaks. Or, more precisely, when Jesus speaks, God Incarnate speaks. That is, God the Son speaks by means of his human nature, in which case when Jesus says something about God, it is God speaking about himself. Or, more precisely, when Jesus says something about God, it is God the Son speaking by means of his human nature about his own divine nature. That

---

[11] As we saw in the previous chapter, this has been recently suggested by Jonathan D. Jacobs, "The Ineffable, Inconceivable, and Incomprehensible God: Fundamentality and Apophatic Theology," in *Oxford Studies in Philosophy of Religion*, vol. 6, ed. Jonathan L. Kvanvig (Oxford: Oxford University Press, 2015), 158–76.

[12] Compare Lewis Ayres: "Pro-Nicenes universally assert that God's nature or essence is incomprehensible" (*Nicaea and Its Legacy: An Approach to Fourth-Century Trinitarian Theology* [Oxford: Oxford University Press, 2004], 282). The apogee of this sort of strong apophaticism can be found in the work of Pseudo-Dionysius. See *Pseudo-Dionysius: The Complete Works*, trans. Colm Lubheid (Mahwah, N.J.: Paulist, 1987).

seems to be an obvious correlate to the doctrine of the incarnation as it has been classically understood.

I take it that Jesus of Nazareth is God Incarnate. He is a divine person personally united to a human nature, which he assumes at the first moment of incarnation and retains forevermore thereafter. So when Jesus says things like "I and the Father are one" (John 10:30), or agrees with Pilate's accusation that he is the Son of God (Luke 22:70), or identifies himself with the divine name revealed in Exodus 3 by saying, "Before Abraham was, I am" in John 8, he is making claims about himself and his relation to God. Or consider the saying of Jesus reported in Matthew's Gospel: "All things have been delivered to me by my Father, and no one knows the Son except the Father. Nor does anyone know the Father except the Son, and the one to whom the Son wills to reveal Him" (11:27). This tells us something about the divine nature that is surely fundamental (in the sense of "fundamental" at issue)—namely, that the Father is only known by the Son, and those to whom the Son chooses to reveal him. I take it that the referent of "Son" in this passage is the divine person speaking by means of his human nature.[13]

So we have two sorts of material here. The first includes sayings of Jesus that imply that he is divine or otherwise included in the divine life. The second includes sayings that report things about the divine nature by the Son who, we are told, has privileged access to the divine life. Given that Scripture is the word of God, and that Jesus is God Incarnate, I take it that we have good prima facie theological reasons for thinking that we can know things about God and about the divine life that count as being fundamental rather than derivative—in which case the claim of the strong apophaticists that we can know nothing about the divine nature whatsoever must be mistaken.[14]

---

[13] Now, I realize some will worry that it is hermeneutically naive to think that when we read the words of Christ reported in the canonical Gospels we are reading what Christ actually said. However, whether one thinks that the historical Jesus said such things, and whether one thinks that the historical Jesus was making claims to divinity, I take it that these sayings contained in the canonical Gospels are supposed to be understood as claims about the nature of God. And I am sure one could find many other such sayings put into the mouth of Jesus of Nazareth—sayings that tell us something about who God is—that is, about the divine nature.

[14] Similarly, in John 17:3 we read, "And this is eternal life, that they may know you, the only true God, and Jesus Christ whom you have sent." In a similar fashion, Paul says to Timothy that he should "take hold of eternal life" (1 Tim 6:12, 19). But it is difficult to know how a person might take hold of eternal life if the source of that life is not capable of being *truly* known. Thanks to Jesse Gentile for pointing me to these passages.

There are other reasons for thinking this is right independent of specifically biblical arguments, of course. For one thing, as we noted in previous chapters, if God is literally incomprehensible to us, then we can know precisely nothing about God. But that is plainly false, because (ex hypothesi) we know at least one thing about God—namely, that we can know nothing about God. Similarly, if divine ineffability is true, then we can express nothing about the divine nature. But plainly that is false because (ex hypothesi) we can express at least one thing about the divine nature—namely, that we are incapable of expressing anything about the divine nature. But neither of these objections pertain to the modest version of apophaticism, which doesn't imply these strong notions of divine incomprehensibility or ineffability. Moreover, the modest version of apophaticism has the virtue of preserving the mystery of the divine nature while, at the same time, giving reasons for thinking that we can know something about the divine nature, something that can be expressed (given the incarnation, revelation in Scripture, and so on).

Suppose this modest apophaticism is on the right track. In and of itself, the claim that some of the canonical sayings of Christ reveal to us things about the divine nature does nothing to show that God's life is atemporal. This is not surprising: Scripture is metaphysically underdetermined on a number of important matters, and this includes the question of whether God's life is temporal or atemporal.[15] Does anything Christ is reported to have said *suggest* that God is atemporal? Perhaps. When Jesus is reported as saying in John 8:58, "Before Abraham was, I am," this is clearly a claim to divinity. It might also suggest something about what the divine life is like. For Jesus is not reported as saying, "Before Abraham was, I was," or even, "Before Abraham was, I will be what I will be." He is reported as saying, ἀμὴν ἀμὴν λέγω ὑμῖν, πρὶν Ἀβραὰμ γενέσθαι ἐγὼ εἰμί. That is, before Abraham was, *I am*.[16] As for what he claims here, it is not only startling; it suggests (I put it no stronger than that) that the sort of divine life in which Jesus includes himself is one that is not temporal in any conventional sense.

---

[15] I owe this insight to Paul Helm. See his contribution to Ganssle, *God and Time.*

[16] The fact that this saying comes in a passage often thought to be an addition to the Fourth Gospel, or an interpolation, doesn't really affect the point being made here. For suppose it is an interpolation or later scribal gloss, the work of some editor that postdates the work of the original Johannine community. It is still the case that the canonical form of the text as received by the church includes this passage, and that Christians down through the ages have believed that it reflects something important about Christ's claims regarding himself, on the basis of this canonical form of the text.

More would need to be said about this matter if our primary concern was to expound the account of the divine life given by Christ in the canonical Gospels. But that is not our task. Nevertheless, there is at least some evidence that suggests Jesus' sayings are *consistent* with the claim that God is atemporal, and that may even suggest that God *is* atemporal. But my broader claim is a modest one—namely, that Scripture is underdetermined on this question (though it is consistent with the notion that God is atemporal—a view that can claim to be the default option in historic Christianity, even if it is currently out of favor). If God is atemporal, as Boethius claims, then our conception of the doctrine of election must be framed accordingly. For then God ordains all that comes to pass in an eternal moment, as it were. He does not ordain what he does successively, or chronologically, for that presumes that some temporal relation pertains to the divine life. This is a point to which we shall return at the end of the chapter.

Three Modern Claims about the Divine Life

With this in mind, we turn to consideration of the three modern theological theses about God's purposes in election and creation, all of which in some way deny that God is eternal in the sense of being timeless.

The Hellenization Thesis

The first of these theses is the *Hellenization Thesis*. The eternalist picture of God has been the subject of sustained criticism in modern theology (and philosophy). Colin Gunton speaks for many when he writes, "It is one of the tragedies—one could almost say crimes—of Christian theological history that the Old Testament was effectively displaced by Greek philosophy as the theological basis of the doctrine of God, certainly so far as the divine attributes are concerned."[17] This view has been trumpeted in recent systematic theology by Gunton's teacher and mentor, Robert Jenson. He is well known for his assertion that philosophy is just a secularized theology, the theology of the ancient world, or what he refers to as *Olympian-Parmenidean religion*—an assertion we encountered in chapter 1.[18]

---

[17] Colin E. Gunton, *Act and Being: Towards a Theology of the Divine Attributes* (Grand Rapids: Eerdmans, 2002), 3.

[18] He writes, "The secular mood by which some forms of 'philosophy' contrast with Christian theology and that tempts us to take them for a different kind of thinking is simply a character of Olympian religion itself, which pursued a divinity purged of mystery. Insofar as Western philosophy is now reduced to the pure study of logic, it is still in fact theology,

A number of other recent theologians and philosophers echo the sentiment expressed by Gunton and Jenson—notably Jürgen Moltmann and Wolfhart Pannenberg among German-speaking theologians, and Nicholas Wolterstorff among Anglo-American philosophers.[19] But its most famous defender is the liberal historian of dogma Adolf von Harnack, who declared, "The development of the Christian faith into an all-embracing theosophy, and the identification of faith with theological knowledge, are proofs that the Christian religion on Greek soil entered the prescribed circle of the native religious philosophy and has remained there."[20]

Divine eternity is a test case for the Hellenization Thesis, because (so it is claimed) it is the Greek fixation with finding some perfect, immutable, and nontemporal truth not subject to the ravages of time and change that led early Christian thinkers to posit timelessness as the only adequate conception of the divine nature. But, as we have already seen in sketching out the eternity view, this characterization of divine atemporality is contentious. It trades upon the assumption (for assumption it is) that the biblical God must be in time because various relations and predicates are ascribed to him that imply he is temporal. He changes his mind (Isa 38), he repents (Gen 6:6), he deliberates (Gen 18, 1 Sam 23), he acts in different ways at different times (Num 14), and so on.

Two things can be said about such claims. The first, and most fundamental, is that this way of reading the biblical material is not metaphysics-free. It presumes that a certain view of the material—namely, that the view according to which God is everlasting, not timeless—is the right way to read the texts because it is the most straightforward, commonsense, or obvious way to read the texts. But this is by no means incontestable if it transpires that there are good reasons for reading the texts differently. By analogy, it might

---

Christian or Olympian-Parmenidean. Theologians of Western Christianity must indeed converse with the philosophers, but only because and insofar as both are engaged in the *same* sort of enterprise." See Robert Jenson, *Systematic Theology,* vol. 1, *The Triune God* (New York: Oxford University Press, 1997), 10 (emphasis in original).

[19] See, e.g., Jürgen Moltmann, *The Trinity and the Kingdom: The Doctrine of God,* trans. Olive Wyon (1980; repr., London: SCM, 1981), ch. 1; Wolfhart Pannenberg, *Systematic Theology,* 3 vols., trans. Geoffrey Bromiley (Grand Rapids: Eerdmans, 1991–1998); and Nicholas Wolterstorff, "God Everlasting," in *God and the Good: Essays in Honor of Henry Stob,* ed. Clifton Orlebeke and Lewis Smedes (Grand Rapids: Eerdmans, 1975), 181–203.

[20] Adolf von Harnack, *What Is Christianity?* trans. Thomas Bailey Saunders, 2nd ed. (New York: G. P. Putnam's Sons, 1901), lecture 13, p. 245. I do not presume that the Hellenization Thesis is mistaken *just because* it was made famous by von Harnack. But I do think it strange that many modern theologians are ready to follow him with such enthusiasm.

be commonsense to think that the sun revolves around the earth, for it rises in the east each day and sets in the west. We do not move; it moves across the heavens. Yet we now know that this initially plausible view is in fact mistaken: heliocentrism, not geocentrism, is the truth of the matter.

The second thing to be said about such an approach to Scripture is that it makes certain tacit hermeneutical assumptions about how to treat texts that tell us that God repents, deliberates, and otherwise (apparently) changes over time. These assumptions include presuming that such material should be treated straightforwardly as predicating these actions of God. But this is not at all obvious, and was not obvious to precritical readers of Scripture. Certainly God is said to repent, deliberate, and so on. That is undeniable. But whether we should ascribe such predicates unequivocally to God is another matter. We don't commonly think God has an arm (Isa 59:1) or an eye (2 Chron 16:9), or is spatially located (Ps 47:8, Isa 6:1). Yet Scripture says all these things about God. Why do we think this latter class of ascriptions are anthropomorphic in nature, whereas the former class are not? Where do we draw the line between passages that ascribe predicates to God that should be understood in terms of anthropomorphism and those that should not? At the very least, it is not obvious from a plain reading of the texts of Scripture which are which, or where the line should be drawn. These are decisions we make as readers of the texts, but they are hermeneutical decisions nonetheless. As Paul Helm observes, "If there is no evidence of either the acceptance or rejection of the abstract idea of timelessness then what this allows one to infer is not that the biblical writers rejected the idea of timeless eternity but that they neither rejected it nor accepted it and that the idea of timeless eternity may be consistent with what they did accept."[21] Like Helm, it seems to me that the biblical case for the Hellenization Thesis is, as Scots criminal law says, "not proven."

The Hegelian Thesis

Alongside this Hellenization Thesis is a second modern theological concern that runs counter to the traditional doctrine of God and, therefore, to the notion of divine eternity. This is *the Hegelian Thesis*. The central notion of this thesis is that, in some manner, God's life unfolds in history. The particular way in which this thesis is stated differs from one theologian to another. But they share in common the idea that because God is in time, his life unfolds in history. Let us consider the contributions of two recent American

---

[21] Helm in *Eternal God*, 4. Helm's study repays careful attention on this matter.

theologians to this discussion: Robert Jenson and Bruce McCormack. We shall see that both, in important respects, work from Karl Barth's mature theology of election encapsulated in *Church Dogmatics* II/2, using his contribution as the point of departure for their own constructive projects.

Jenson holds that God's life is embedded within the history of Israel. In the first volume of his *Systematic Theology,* he says that the Son is "his own presupposition in God's eternity"; he appears in the Old Testament not as unincarnate but as the "narrative pattern of Israel's created human story" before he may appear as a particular Israelite in that story. He goes on: "What in eternity precedes the Son's birth to Mary is not an unincarnate state of the Son, but a pattern of movement within the event of the incarnation, the movement to incarnation, as itself a pattern of God's triune life."[22]

More recently, while conceding that his earlier claim about Christ's preexistence as a pattern of movement in the life of Israel was "hopelessly vague," he offers the following clarification of his position:

> What in the triune life has ontological *pre*-cedence to the Son as subsistent relation, is the "monarchy" of the Father: his relation to Jesus is the condition of the possibility of Jesus' relation to him. Yet the Father himself does not subsist otherwise than as a relation to the Son—the circle is the very point. Therefore, since there is no way in which anything could be precedent to the Father, there is nothing precedent to the Son as subsistent relation.[23]

That is, there can be no sense to talking about Christ's preexistence if the Second Person of the Trinity just is the subsistent relation within the Godhead that is identical to the history that we see in Christ. Or, to attempt to put it less gnomically, if Christ is identical to the Second Person of the Trinity, then, says Jenson, there is no life of the divine Second Person independent of Christ, no residue or overflow that is not accounted for when we refer to Christ. In one respect this is a bold, courageous move that in one fell swoop attempts to shore up the identification of Christ with God while denying any room for speculation about the life of the Second Person of the Trinity "before" his incarnate state. But, like all substantive theological claims, this way of construing the Hegelian Thesis comes at a price. First, it requires us to swallow the claim that Christ is identical to God the Son, which has significant modal implications. (For instance, it means that a divine person

---

[22] Jenson, *Systematic Theology*, 1:141.
[23] Jenson, "Once More, the *Logos asarkos*," *International Journal of Systematic Theology* 13, no. 2 (2011): 133 (emphasis in original).

has a physical part, which is a problem if God is supposed to be essentially incorporeal, because he is a spirit [John 4:24].) Second, and as a corollary to this, it requires us to say that there is no meaning to language about Christ preexisting his incarnate state. For many Christian theologians sympathetic to a classical Chalcedonian Christology, this will not be a price they are willing to pay.

But perhaps the most important recent attempt to articulate a version of the Hegelian Thesis is that given in the actualist ontology of those that have followed Bruce McCormack's understanding of Barth. Robert Jenson puts Barth's mature position in *Church Dogmatics* II/2 like this: "According to Barth, God's being is most decisively construed by the notion of *decision*. God is so unmitigatedly personal that his free decision is not limited even by his 'divine nature': what he is, he himself chooses. But that must be to say, God *is* the act of his decision. Thus the doctrine of election, of God's choice 'before all time,' is for Barth the center of the doctrine of God's being."[24] He goes on to add that what is chosen according to Barth is the union of God in the person of Christ with humankind. "But since God *is* his act of choice, God in making this actual choice not only chooses that he *will be* the man Jesus; as the event of the choice, he *is* the man Jesus."[25]

McCormack has taken this way of thinking as a point of departure for a Barth-inspired constructive theological program, which is still being worked out.[26] Part of this debate has to do with how Barth should rightly be interpreted. Though that is also an important theological matter (especially for those theologians who are Reformed), that is not our primary concern here. Our concern is with how McCormack develops a Barth-inspired trajectory in his own work.

Suppose we think of God's act in creation as an expression of his freedom and aseity. He is free to create and refrain from creating. He is also independent of the creation, both psychologically and metaphysically (a matter to which we shall return in the next chapter). According to McCormack, God's eternal decision to elect to be God for us in Christ is not merely what the scholastics would have called a hypothetically necessary divine act. That is, it is not merely the case that God freely ordains the creation of a world in which Christ is the mediator of human salvation. In choosing to be God

---

[24] Jenson, *Systematic Theology*, 1:140.

[25] Jenson, *Systematic Theology*, 1:140.

[26] An interesting, and salient, indication of the influence of Jenson on McCormack in this regard can be found in Bruce L. McCormack's recent editorial, "In Memoriam: Robert Jenson (1930–2017)," *International Journal of Systematic Theology* 20, no. 1 (2018): 3–7.

for us in Christ, the God who saves us by electing (and reprobating) himself, God constitutes himself to be who he is. That constitution is something that, according to this Hegelian Thesis, obtains in history. In other words, it is because God elects Christ—who is who he is because of a particular historic action in his incarnation, life, death, and resurrection—that God is constituted as God for us in Christ. So not only is God's life something that unfolds in the history of Christ's life, but on this way of thinking, the divine life is also made the particular life of Father, Son, and Spirit because God ordains that he will be God for us in Christ.

As we have already had cause to note, this is related to the recent debate about the so-called *logos asarkos,* or word of God without flesh.[27] Both Jenson and McCormack maintain that there is no meaning to the claim that Christ exists without flesh (although they give slightly different reasons for why this is the case). For McCormack there is no Son of God without the flesh.[28] To posit a life of God the Son before or logically prior to his life in the flesh is to posit a God-behind-God, as if there is the God revealed to us in Christ in the economy of salvation and a God behind this economic deity, one whose actions are mysterious but who (it seems) ordains to be the particular God we know in and through Christ once he decides to create the world that he does. Reaching back behind the economic Trinity (that is, God as he is revealed to us in the economy of creation and salvation) to a putative ontological Trinity (that is, God in himself abstracted, as it were, from any economic function in creation and salvation) is not merely useless speculation; it is a theological dead end. "To make Jesus Christ the subject of election," if carried out consistently, says McCormack, conceding that Barth was not always consistent in this respect, "is to bid farewell to the distinction between the eternal Word and the incarnate Word." An eternal Word would be no more than a "metaphysical abstraction," with "no reality attached to it."[29] Is such metaphysical abstraction inappropriate in the way similar to the action of trying to, say, look at the man hiding behind the curtain, working the levers that generate the illusion of wizardry that is Oz the Great and Powerful, as in Frank L. Baum's eponymous American fairytale? Not exactly. It is inappropriate in the

---

[27] I have discussed this matter elsewhere. See Crisp, *The Word Enfleshed: Exploring the Person and Work of Christ* (Grand Rapids: Baker Academic, 2016), ch. 2; and Crisp, *God Incarnate: Explorations in Christology* (London: T&T Clark, 2009), ch. 3.

[28] The importance of this point about the *logos asarkos* is underlined by McCormack in "In Memoriam."

[29] Bruce L. McCormack, "Karl Barth's Historicized Christology," in *Orthodox and Modern: Studies in the Theology of Karl Barth* (Grand Rapids: Baker Academic, 2009), 217–18.

sense that to posit a God-behind-God as he is revealed to us economically is
to look for someone behind the curtain *when there is no one there to be found*.
There is no God-behind-God, on this way of thinking. If we do not see this,
we will not understand just how revolutionary this version of the Hegelian
Thesis is: it is tantamount to claiming that God constitutes himself as he is in
the action of electing to be God for us in Christ. By choosing to be *this* God,
rather than some other, he ties who he is, as it were, to the history of salvation
that unfolds in the life and ministry of God Incarnate. McCormack again:
"God *is* in himself, in eternity, the mode of his Self-revelation in time—God
as Jesus Christ in eternity and God as Jesus Christ in time—thus guarantee-
ing that the immanent Trinity and the economic Trinity will be identical in
content."[30]

In addressing the Hegelian Thesis, we have briefly considered two different attempts to tether God's life to history. Both of these are really species of
Barth-inspired theology. In his fine study of Robert Jenson's thought, Scott
Swain observes, "The story of trinitarian theology 'after Barth' is therefore
not only the story of debates about how to interpret Barth's claim that Jesus
is the electing God. It is also the story of debates about whether and to what
extent Barth's historicizing agenda, and its concomitant metaphysical revisionism, requires affirmation and extension."[31] This seems to me to be spot
on. There is much that is appealing about such revisionism. Placing Christ
at the center of the doctrine of election as the subject of election, is, in many
ways, Barth's greatest contribution to Christian theology, and one that Jenson and McCormack have capitalized upon in rather different ways.

But suppose that instead of worrying about avoiding the bifurcation
of the economic and immanent Trinity by means of a historicized, christologically focused account of election we thought of the economic Trinity
as somehow contained "within" the immanent Trinity. That is, suppose
we think of the relationship between the economic and immanent life of
God rather like we think of our own lives. We have "economic" functions:
how we appear to those around us, with whom we interact on a daily basis.
Yet these are but one aspect of who we are. We don't think that because
we have a rich internal life that is necessarily private and incommunicable
to those around us that there is some worrying bifurcation between our
"immanent" selves and our "economic" selves. Instead, we think that there
is an aspect of our lives that is public facing and accessible to the world

---

[30] McCormack, "Karl Barth's Historicized Christology," 218 (emphasis in original).

[31] Scott R. Swain, *The God of the Gospel: Robert Jenson's Trinitarian Theology* (Downers
Grove, Ill.: IVP Academic, 2013), 63.

around us, and another aspect that is not, and cannot be made accessible by definition, though it may be communicated piecemeal through conversation and dialogue. Transpose this onto the picture of God as timeless. His immanent life is eternal, atemporal. It has richness and depth that are by definition incommunicable to his creatures. Yet he graciously communicates something of himself and his purposes to us in revelation, and supremely in Christ. Is the notion that there is a distinction between the immanent and economic Trinity tantamount to the bifurcation of God into two distinct entities? Not at all. Just as there is a distinction between creaturely economic and immanent functions, so there is a similar distinction that can be ascribed to God. How could there not be if we want to preserve the freedom and aseity of God?

The Eschatological Identity Thesis

We come to our third modern theological concern that pushes against the traditional doctrine of God and, therefore, against the notion of divine eternity. This is the *Eschatological Identity Thesis*. It is not unusual to find theologians agreeing that in the eschaton God will be "all in all" so that his purposes are fully and finally revealed to all of creation. I take it that such language bespeaks an epistemological claim about the eschatological revelation of God's purposes. In other words, in the eschaton all of humanity will finally *know* or *perceive* something important about the purposes of God in creation. However, several recent theologians make a much stronger claim about the relation between God's purposes in creation and the eschaton. They claim that God's purposes are only *actualized* in the eschaton, prior to which God's work is merely anticipatory. Some even go as far as to say that something about the divine nature is only *instantiated* in the eschaton, and not before.[32] We shall consider two such theologians here. The first is Robert Jenson, whom we have already considered in relation to the Hegelian Thesis. The second is Wolfhart Pannenberg.

Let us return to Jenson. In the first volume of his *Systematic Theology* he writes, "The biblical God is not eternally himself in that he persistently instantiates a beginning in which he already is all he ever will be; he is eternally himself in that he unrestrictedly anticipates an end in which he will be all he could ever be." He goes on to say, "It holds also—or rather,

---

[32] See, e.g., Roger Olson's essay, "Trinity and Eschatology: The Historical Being of God in Jürgen Moltmann and Wolfhart Pannenberg," *Scottish Journal of Theology* 36 (1983): 213–27.

primarily—with God: a story is constituted by the outcome of the narrated events."[33] Later, in his discussion of Christology, he goes even further when he writes, "God's eternity is the infinity of a life. For what obtains in *life* always comes from a future; the difference between God and us is that he, as the Spirit, is his own future and so is *unboundedly* lively."[34] And again, "[God] is *temporally* infinite because 'source' and 'goal' are present *and* asymmetrical in him, because he is primarily future to himself and only thereupon past and present for himself."[35] Jenson likes to write with such flourishes. At different times he says that God is an event or a fugue, and here, a narrative, a life that comes from the future, and so on. I am not sure what the function of such tropes is supposed to be in his work; it is just not always clear whether they are being used metaphorically or in a kind of critical-realist way as conceptual pictures or windows onto some reality no one concept can hope to express adequately. In any event, from this catena of passages it certainly looks like Jenson thinks that something about the divine nature is *constituted* by the outcome of salvation history. That appears to be an ontological, not merely epistemic or proleptic, claim about the divine life.[36] Here there is a difference between Jenson and McCormack. For McCormack's proposal is about how making Christ the subject of election has implications for protology or first things, rather than eschatology, or last things. By contrast, Jenson seems to think that the history of God, and of Christ in particular, tells us something about the future of God.

The difference here is rather like that between coming to understand that your friend is in fact the son of a famous author, and the change that takes place when your friend gets married. The first example involves a merely epistemic change: you come into possession of a certain piece of information about your friend that was previously unknown to you. Yet nothing has changed with respect to your friend. In the second example, the change is not *merely* epistemic; a legal change in status is involved as well. Something really has changed with respect to your friend. Whereas most Christian theologians

---

[33] Jenson, *Systematic Theology*, 1:66.

[34] Jenson, *Systematic Theology*, 1:143 (emphasis in original).

[35] Jenson, *Systematic Theology*, 1:217.

[36] Compare Richard Bauckham: "On the one hand, the resurrection of Jesus is enacted promise, promise in the form of anticipation. On the other hand, as anticipation of the end, the resurrection of Jesus is promise, precisely because it is only a proleptic appearance of the end, not the coming of the kingdom universally. What is important is that the resurrection of the crucified Jesus entails the future coming of the kingdom he proclaimed." Bauckham, "Eschatology," in *The Oxford Handbook of Systematic Theology*, ed. John Webster, Kathryn Tanner, and Iain Torrance (Oxford: Oxford University Press, 2009), 309.

have been willing to allow that the eschaton brings about a merely epistemic change "so that at the name of Jesus every knee should bend . . . and every tongue should confess that Jesus Christ is Lord, to the glory of God the Father" (Phil 2:10-11), few have thought that the change the eschaton ushers in alters the status of God himself. Yet this is just what defenders of the Eschatological Identity Thesis claim.

Wolfhart Pannenberg is perhaps the best known recent exemplar of this sort of view, though isolating exactly what he thinks on this matter is not always straightforward. In an early essay on the doctrine of God written in dialogue with the atheist philosopher Ernst Bloch (who was also an early influence upon Moltmann's theology of hope), Pannenberg writes that "the question [about the status of talk about God] must now be concerned exclusively with the possibility of a God 'with futurity as a quality of being,' and therefore a return to the God of [classical] theism must be ruled out at this stage."[37] This is an early indicator of his more developed view in which the future is somehow constitutive of the divine nature. His mature position can be found in his three-volume *Systematic Theology*. There, when discussing divine infinity (which he prefers to discussion of eternity as such), Pannenberg remarks that "there is widespread agreement that eternity does not mean timelessness or the endlessness of time."[38] God's "eternity" is part of an everlasting present moment in which he exists, says Pannenberg. God "has no future outside of himself."[39] Pannenberg insists that, in creating the world, God remained free. He "did not have to create the world out of some inner necessity of his own nature."[40] "Creation cannot be an act in time,"[41] Pannenberg remarks, echoing the Augustinian notion that the world is created *with*, not *in*, time. Nevertheless, "We cannot set God's relations to the world in antithesis to his essence, as though this were unaffected by the relations. . . . The relations of God to his creatures must be thought of as an

---

[37] Wolfhart Pannenberg, "The God of Hope" (originally published as part of a Festschrift for Ernst Bloch in 1965), in *Basic Questions in Theology*, vol. 2 of *Collected Essays* (Minneapolis: Fortress, 1971), 242. Another important early resource is Pannenberg's essay, "The God of History: The Trinitarian God and the Truth of History," trans. M. B. Jackson, *Cumberland Seminarian* 19, no. 2–3 (1981): 28–41; originally published as "Det Gott der Geschichte: Der trinitarische Gott und die Warhead der Geschichte," *Kerygma and Dogma* 23 (1977): 76–92.

[38] Pannenberg, *Systematic Theology*, 1:407.

[39] Pannenberg, *Systematic Theology*, 1:410.

[40] Pannenberg, *Systematic Theology*, 2:19.

[41] Pannenberg, *Systematic Theology*, 2:57.

expression of the freedom of his essence and therefore must be depicted as grounded in it."[42]

So it seems that God is self-contained in one sense, yet not timeless. For futurity is (in some sense) a divine quality. God creates on the basis of a hypothetical necessity; that is, once he freely commits himself to creation, the world must obtain. Yet, despite the fact that futurity is a divine quality and God is not timeless, he creates the world with time, and is really related to the world he generates. These are very puzzling claims, and it is difficult to see how they constitute a coherent whole. For it seems that Pannenberg thinks that God lives a life in something akin to a Boethian eternal present, creates the world with time, and yet is dependent upon the course of history, a history to which he is really related. This latter point is made clearer in a section of his *Systematic Theology* entitled "The World as the History of God and the Unity of the Divine Essence." There Pannenberg writes, "Even in his deity, by the creation of the world and the sending of his Son and Spirit to work in it, he [i.e., the Father] has *made himself dependent on the course of history*."[43] Indeed, it is necessary, on his way of thinking "to take into account the *constitutive significance* of this [eschatological] consummation for the eternity of God."[44] So God's life is not merely dependent upon the unfolding of history, as with the Hegelian Thesis. The unfolding of history is somehow *constitutive* of God's identity. Indeed, the divine identity is in some manner *only complete in the eschaton*. God is only God once the eschaton has arrived.

This is a very peculiar account of God's life and relation to creation and the future. Nevertheless, it is not an eccentric interpretation of Pannenberg's work. A number of his most important recent Anglophone commentators have understood Pannenberg as holding something like the Eschatological Identity Thesis. For instance, Timothy Bradshaw writes, "Pannenberg considers the eternal reality of God itself to be dependent on the outcome of history—although such dependence occurs only on the condition that there is a world, rather than being a necessity binding God, who in fact brings

---

[42] Pannenberg, *Systematic Theology*, 2:85. This is a significant departure from classical theism, according to which God has no real relation to his creation. Thus Aquinas: "Creation signified actively means the divine action, which is God's essence, with a relation to the creature. But in God relation to the creature is not a real relation, but only a relation of reason; whereas the relation of the creature to God is a real relation" (*Summa theologiae* 1a.45.3, ad 1).

[43] Pannenberg, *Systematic Theology*, 1:329 (emphasis added).

[44] Pannenberg, *Systematic Theology*, 1:331 (emphasis added).

creation into being out of freedom."[45] Roger Olson is even more forthright. In a critique of Pannenberg's doctrine of the Trinity, he says this:

> To put it plainly: God does not yet fully exist as who he really is and will be—the "all-determining reality." This is because his deity is his rule. Yet, in the final consummation of universal history it will be made clear that God is and always has been the sovereign Lord of history. On the other hand, before and apart from this eschatological denouement God is not yet fully God. This "somewhat idiosyncratic" idea of God's relation to history is at the root of Pannenberg's concept of the relationship between immanent and economic Trinity.[46]

Similar sentiments are expressed by Christiaan Mostert in his monograph on Pannenberg's understanding of God's relation to the future. He writes,

> Pannenberg is arguing not only that God is affected by time, but that the eternal essence of God is constituted by what happens in time, by the creation, reconciliation and perfection of the world in time. Paradoxically, time is the creature of God, yet God allows what takes place in time to be constitutive of God's own being. . . . There is an important sense, then, in which God depends for God's deity on the historical completion of God's activity in the world. . . . For Pannenberg the eschatological resolution of all questions about God is central, as is God's dependence on history's consummation for the constitution of God's own eternal being.[47]

According to these commentators, Pannenberg really does think that the "eternal reality of God" is "*dependent* on the outcome of history." God "*does not yet fully exist* as who he really is and will be"; indeed, God "*depends for God's deity* on the historical completion of God's activity in the world." But this seems hopeless. God's very being cannot be dependent on the creation or upon the unfolding of history within the created order. His identity as God cannot be dependent upon a particular historical outcome. That would be to cut God down to historical size, making a deity in a kind of Hegelian image—an ontotheological project if ever there was one! For it would mean making God, the creator of all things, dependent for his very existence upon the outcome of history. Far from being an improvement upon a more

---

[45] Timothy Bradshaw, *Pannenberg: A Guide for the Perplexed* (London: T&T Clark, 2009), 115.

[46] Roger Olson, "Wolfhart Pannenberg's Doctrine of the Trinity," *Scottish Journal of Theology* 43, no. 2 (1990): 204.

[47] Christiaan Mostert, *God and the Future: Wolfhart Pannenberg's Eschatological Doctrine of God* (London: T&T Clark, 2002), 156.

traditional theistic account of these things, Pannenberg's position is conceptually murky and requires such radical revision to the doctrine of God that it transpires the Deity is dependent for his very identity upon the creation he brings about.[48] It is difficult to see how the being thus described is worthy of worship.

Coda

At the outset of his programmatic account of social Trinitarianism, the German Reformed theologian Jürgen Moltmann says that although a modern understanding of the Trinity must take account of the voices of the tradition, a "return to the earlier Trinity of substance is practically impossible, if only because the return to the cosmology of the old way of thinking about being has become impossible too, ever since modern times."[49] This is symptomatic of the sort of worries with the classical doctrine of God, and of divine eternity and the doctrine of election in particular, that we have examined thus far. The old way of conceiving the divine nature must be supplanted by a modern one, influenced by Barth's program, and taken in a historicized direction—and in the case of Jenson, with "the ontological priority of the future" in mind. But why must we make such radical revisions to our doctrine of God and of election? Might it be that we can have our proverbial cake and eat it too? That is, can we retain a traditional account of the divine nature, including the notion that God is eternal, and yet have a doctrine of election that is profoundly shaped by christological concerns—the concerns that Barth (I think rightly) drew our attention to? I think we can. The next chapter offers one such account.

---

[48] This is one reason why John Cooper thinks that Pannenberg is a panentheist despite his explicit disclaimers of panentheism. See Cooper, *Panentheism: The Other God of the Philosophers—From Plato to The Present* (Grand Rapids: Baker Academic, 2006), ch. 11.

[49] Moltmann, *Trinity and the Kingdom of God*, 18–19.

6

Incarnation Anyway

The first thing to inquire here is whether the Son of God spoken of in this place would have become man or not even if sin, for which we all die, had not intervened.

Rupert of Deutz[1]

In the previous chapter we set out some of the contemporary systematic-theological options on God's relation to his creation and the closely related matter of the divine purpose in creating the world understood in this particular post-Barthian literature. This chapter follows on from the last. If in the previous chapter we gave some account of three recent ways of thinking about these matters in the Hellenization Thesis, the Hegelian Thesis, and the Eschatological Identity Thesis, in this chapter we provide another way of thinking about these matters. But in this case it does not require us to revise our account of the eternity of God. Nor does it require us to historicize the divine nature in some fashion. Nevertheless, it does preserve one of the most important issues raised by this recent post-Barthian literature—that is, the centrality of Christ in the creative purposes of God.

Introduction

One important and interesting theological question pertaining to the incarnation has to do with whether it is contingent upon human sin. In other words, is it the case that God ordains the incarnation because of human

---

[1] Cited in Brooke Foss Westcott, "The Gospel of Creation," in *The Epistles of St John: The Greek Text with Notes and Essays*, 3rd ed. (London: Macmillan, 1892), 290.

sin, and *only* because of human sin? Or is it that there would have been an incarnation irrespective of human sin? If the latter, why would there need to be an incarnation if there had been no human sin? This is usually called the *incarnation anyway question* in the contemporary literature in Christology.[2]

Sometimes, the incarnation anyway question is treated with suspicion as unduly speculative—a matter about which we have insufficient information to form theological judgments. In this chapter I want to suggest that this is actually a vital theological question that merits scrutiny. I grant that it is speculative, but I deny that it is idle or useless speculation. I want to suggest that a certain sort of theological speculation may be permissible provided it is theologically productive, and it seems to me that the incarnation anyway question is just such a question. In particular, I argue that one version of an incarnation anyway doctrine, which I shall designate *the christological union account*, provides the theologian with a reason for thinking that union with human beings is a fundamental aim in creation independent of any human fall. Such union may not require an incarnation, strictly speaking, though an incarnation is a fitting means of bringing such union about. (It also has implications for what we think about the vexed issue of the image of God, as we shall see.) If this is right, then there is good theological reason to think that had there been no fall, there would still have been an incarnation—which is the central claim of all incarnation anyway arguments.

We proceed as follows. First, and by way of preamble, there is a section outlining supra- and infralapsarianism in relation to incarnation anyway arguments. Then, a second section offers a narrative in which the christological union account is set forth. A final section addresses some of the main strengths and weaknesses of this doctrine.

Supralapsarianism, Infralapsarianism, and Incarnation Anyway Arguments

To begin with, we need to set up the argument. Incarnation anyway reasoning is usually connected to the debate about the ordering of the divine

---

[2] See, e.g., Edwin Christian van Driel, *Incarnation Anyway: Arguments for Supralapsarian Christology,* American Academy of Religion Series (New York: Oxford University Press, 2008); and Marilyn McCord Adams, *Christ and Horrors: The Coherence of Christology,* Current Issues in Theology 3 (Cambridge: Cambridge University Press, 2006), ch. 7. Westcott's essay "Gospel of Creation" offers a useful account of the development of this question, which arose rather late in scholastic theology. His monograph *Christus Consummator: Some Aspects of the Person and Work of Christ in Relation to Modern Thought,* 2nd ed. (London: Macmillan, 1887), esp. part 2, chs. 2–3, develops some of these themes in a constructive case for incarnation anyway. See also the bibliographic note appended to van Driel's monograph.

decrees, one of the quixotic preoccupations of Reformed theologians. There are two broad approaches to the question of the ordering of the decrees. The first is supralapsarianism and the second is infralapsarianism. The difference between the two views is usually said to be a difference about the logical or conceptual distinctions in the order of what God ordains to bring about in creation. Because God is thought to be outside of time on this traditional Reformed way of thinking, these distinctions cannot be chronological ones. It isn't as if at one moment God ponders what sort of world to create, then at a subsequent moment thinks about whether the humans that populate one corner of that creation will fall, and then at a still later moment thinks about whether he will redeem some number of those human creatures that will fall, and so on. God does not sit and cogitate over time, ordering his thoughts one after another as they are formed in his mind. For that presumes God is a temporal being. Instead, God ordains these things eternally, or atemporally. We conceive of these things as distinct because they obtain at different times in the creation. God's act in election has numerous discrete temporal effects. Nevertheless, these effects are actually aspects of one eternal act of God.

Let us presume that this way of thinking about God's relation to time is right. The supralapsarian thinks that the ordering of the decrees are such that God ordains the election of some number of human beings logically prior to the decree to permit the fall. Hence, *supralapsus*: the decree to elect is said to be "above" or before the decree to permit the fall, in the logical ordering of these things. By contrast, the infralapsarian maintains that the ordering of the decrees are such that God ordains the election of some number of human beings logically consequent to the decree to permit the fall. Hence, *infralapsus*: the decree to elect is "below" or after the decree to permit the fall, in the logical ordering of these things in the mind of God.

In fact, these are not two distinct views so much as they are two families of views on the ordering of the divine decrees. For there are different versions of each way of thinking about the order of decrees.[3] Incarnation anyway arguments are often thought to be a species of supralapsarianism. It is certainly true that both incarnation anyway and supralapsarian arguments are concerned with God ordaining the salvation of some number of humanity via the work of Christ independent of sin. As we have just seen, standard versions of supralapsarianism comprise arguments that have to do with divine election independent of any fall to sin, but where sin is a matter to be

[3] This is a fairly standard observation. It is also made by van Driel in *Incarnation Anyway*.

accounted for in the ordering of divine decrees—in which case, if incarnation anyway arguments are a species of supralapsarianism, they are a variety of nonstandard supralapsarianism, having to do with counterfactual considerations about creation of a world where there is no sin.

However, as even this cursory statement indicates, there are crucial differences between these two sorts of argument. The most fundamental difference turns on the function of the incarnation. In standard supralapsarianism the incarnation has what we might call a narrowly salvific role; that is, it is ordained as a means to salvation from sin. But incarnation anyway arguments do not construe the incarnation in such a narrowly salvific manner because they are concerned with counterfactual states of affairs in which no fall takes place. We might say that, unlike standard supralapsarian arguments, incarnation anyway arguments do not presume that human reconciliation is the *only* rationale for incarnation. They postulate an additional, perhaps even more basic, motivation for incarnation irrespective of human sin.[4] It is just such an assumption that informs the christological union version of the incarnation anyway argument, to which we now turn.

The Christological Union Account

In order to cover as much ground as possible in a short space, I shall expound the christological union account in the form of a narrative or "just-so story."[5] Having done this, we shall pause to take stock of its main theological claims and potential shortcomings.

God desires to create a world in which there are creatures with whom he may be united, so that they may participate in his divine life. Indeed, participation of creatures in the divine life is a final goal of creation, perhaps even the ultimate goal (though we need not commit ourselves to that claim for present purposes). To that end, God conceives of human beings as creatures ideally suited to such a relationship. They are ideally suited because they are metaphysically amphibian, being composed of bodies (thereby rooted in the physical world God creates) as well as souls (thereby

---

[4] For discussion of a range of medieval ways of thinking about incarnation anyway rationales for incarnation, see Adams, *Christ and Horrors,* 174–84.

[5] I take this christological union account up in more detail in Oliver D. Crisp, *The Word Enfleshed: Exploring the Person and Work of Christ* (Grand Rapids: Baker Academic, 2016). By "just-so story" I just mean a narrative that attempts to explain the origins of something, as Rudyard Kipling's stories about things like the origin of the leopard's spots did in his eponymous volume of children's tales. See Kipling, *Just So Stories* (London: Macmillan, 1902).

having a part that belongs to the immaterial world of spirits).[6] Such metaphysical composition means that humans have a foot in both the physical world of creation and the spiritual world that includes the angels and God. To enable these human creatures to participate in the divine life, God must take the initiative and unite himself with one of these creaturely natures, assuming it and thereby generating an interface between divinity and humanity so that human beings may have a conduit by means of which they may be united to God. (On the christological union view I am expounding here, it is not possible for sinless human creatures to take the initiative and unite themselves to God independent of an act of divine condescension and accommodation such as that envisaged in the incarnation. Even sinless human beings are not capable of this feat of metaphysical bootstrapping![7])

In a similar manner, a house or office needs a wireless hub in order that the various laptop computers, tablets, and cell phones owned by those who live or work in that space may be able to wirelessly access the Internet. The hub is the conduit by means of which the various pieces of electronic hardware owned by users in the property can interact with, or participate in, the virtual world that the World-Wide Web has brought direct to our living rooms and offices. God's union with human nature provides something like a hub, by means of which other human being can access the divine and participate in union with God.

The incarnation is the way in which this hub or interface between divinity and humanity is achieved. That is why the God-man must be both fully human and fully divine: fully human because it is union with this kind of creature that God desires;

---

[6] "Metaphysical amphibians" is a term used by Eleonore Stump in her study *Aquinas* (London: Routledge, 2003), 17. It is a variation on Norman Kretzmann's notion that humans are best described as metaphysical hybrids in Saint Thomas Aquinas' *Summa contra gentiles*. See Kretzmann, *The Metaphysics of Creation: Aquinas's Natural Theology in "Summa contra gentiles II"* (Oxford: Oxford University Press, 1998), 273. In a similarly Thomist vein, Carlo Leget writes, "From a theological perspective, human beings hold a unique central position in creation. They are the bridge between the material and the spiritual world. This central position is a privileged one. Consequently Aquinas calls a human being 'a little world' (*minor mundus*) and considers humanity to be more perfect—in the sense of containing all dimensions of creation—than, for example, angels who intellectually are far more gifted than the most brilliant human minds" ("Eschatology" in *The Theology of Thomas Aquinas*, ed. Rik van Nieuwenhove and Joseph Wawrykow [Notre Dame: University of Notre Dame Press, 2005], 366).

[7] But why think that sinless humans cannot unite themselves to God independent of divine action? First, because election is according to the good pleasure and will of God, not human desire (Eph 1). What is more, as Marilyn Adams points out in her discussion of medieval incarnation anyway arguments, there may be biblical-theological reasons for thinking this. Ephesians 5:31-32, coupled with Gen 2:24 and related passages like John 17:22, suggests that union with God in Christ is a fundamental goal in creation that is not dependent on human sin (Adams, *Christ and Horrors*, 177–78), in which case one reason for thinking that sinless humans cannot bootstrap themselves into union with God without divine condescension and accommodation is that any such union is a divine gift.

fully divine because it is union with God that is the intended outcome. By analogy, a working hub for wireless connection to the Internet must have the right component parts so that it can interact with signals sent from computers and other devices that are attempting to access the World Wide Web wirelessly. It must have the complete electronic parts necessary to provide this interface, and that includes both the hardware and the electronic connection to the remote servers that together provide the global computer network that is the Internet. Only with both the right hardware and the right electronic connection will the hub function correctly. Similarly, only if the interface between humanity and God is fully divine and fully human, having the relevant component parts that belong to each of these entities, will it be possible to generate the spiritual "hub" by means of which human beings can be united to God in order to participate in his divine life.

So if God desires to create a world in which there are creatures with whom he may be united, in order that they may participate in his divine life as a final end of the creation, then it looks like the incarnation is a fitting means by which to provide for such an outcome. In other words, for human beings to be able to participate in the divine life, we need a hub or interface with the divine, and an incarnation is one way in which God can provide that. The claim is not that the incarnation is a *requirement* for such an outcome. It is only that the incarnation is *a fitting means* of providing for this outcome. It may be that it is the most fitting, all things considered. But there are good reasons for opting for the weaker modal claim instead. (For one thing, it is easier to defend.)[8]

What theological reason do we have for thinking that the incarnation is indeed a fitting mechanism by means of which this hub between God and humanity has been established rather than, as it is more often reported, merely the means by which human salvation is obtained? Here we may appeal to evidence of an inferential or indirect sort. The doctrine of the image of God has long been the subject of theological debate, and there are different views about what that image consists in. However, it is indisputable that alongside biblical passages that make claims about human beings being made in the divine image (e.g., Gen 1:26-27; 9:6; 1 Cor 11:7; 2 Cor 3:15-18; Jas 3:9), there are passages in the New Testament that speak of Christ as the image of God (e.g., Phil 2:6, Col 1:15, 2 Cor 4:4, Heb 1:3). There is a tradition, often associated with the Orthodox Church, of linking these two sorts of biblical passages, generating an account of the image of God that is christological in nature. Let us call this the *christological doctrine of the image of God*. On this way of thinking,

---

[8] It may be that the stronger modal claim is true, in which case defending the weaker claim involves arguing for something that approximates to the truth. Such notions of "fittingness" are familiar to readers of Saint Anselm of Canterbury and Saint Thomas Aquinas, among others.

Christ is the image of God, strictly speaking. We image God as we are conformed to the prototypical image of God in Christ.[9]

Suppose God intends to create a world in which there are creatures with whom he may be united, so that they may participate in his divine life as a final end of the creation. Suppose further that in order to bring about this union God conceives of the incarnation as a fitting means to this end. According to this line of reasoning, God first intends to create a world in which there are creatures with whom he may be united so that they may participate in his divine life as a final end of the creation. He intends humans to be those creatures. And he intends the incarnation as a fitting means to this final end in creation. In other words, it is by means of the incarnation that God brings about the interface between humanity and divinity necessary for his final end to be achieved. On this view it makes sense to think that Christ is ordained as the image of God, being both fully divine and fully human. His human nature is generated for a divine person, to be *his* human nature over which he has metaphysical ownership. That human nature is specially created to be fit for use by a divine person, being without sin. In the hypostatic union that obtains at the first moment of incarnation, God the Son can be seen and interacted with by means of his human nature; and his human nature is, as it were, "impressed" upon the divine life. This means that there is in Christ an interface between divinity and humanity, a hub by means of which human beings can be united to God like the wireless electronic hub in our earlier example. (In other words, the hub as applied to the incarnation is the hypostatic union of Christ's human and divine natures.) Christ is the image of the invisible God, the firstborn over all creation. He is the express image of the Father. But he is also a human being, having all the parts of a human being, including a body and soul, rightly related, that makes his human nature metaphysically amphibious, as are all other human beings.

So far, so good. The christological doctrine of the image of God goes a step further to claim that God ordains that human beings are formed in order that he may be united with them by means of the incarnation. Christ is not just the interface between humanity and divinity. He is in fact the prototypical human, the one after whose image we are all fashioned as human beings. And because his human nature is made in order to be united with God, so also our human natures are made with this capacity. *Not* that we are hypostatically or personally united to God in the way that Christ's human nature is united to God the Son; we are not. Nevertheless, we have the *capacity* to be hypostatically united to God. There is a capacity to interface between divinity and humanity built into human nature, so to speak. It is this very capacity that is utilized by God the Son at the first moment of incarnation so that he

---

[9] For more on this view, see Crisp, *Word Enfleshed*. Taking her cue from the Baptist theologian Stanley Grenz, Suzanne McDonald takes up a similar theme, broadening out a christological model of the image of God so that the church is a community of the divine image in the world. See McDonald, *Re-imaging Election: Divine Election as Representing God to Others, and Others to God* (Grand Rapids: Eerdmans, 2012), ch. 4.

is able to "upload" himself into the human nature formed for him in the womb of the Virgin.[10] For this reason, his human nature is the human nature of a divine person. It never exists independently of a divine person and therefore never becomes a person independent of God the Son. All other human beings (you and me included) are not the subjects of such a divine upload at the first moment of generation. One consequence of this is that we become human persons independent of God because God fails to do something to us that he does in the case of Christ: he fails to upload himself into our human natures at the moment they are generated in utero. For this reason our human natures are not human natures possessed by a divine person.

According to the christological doctrine of the image of God, then, Christ bears the prototypical image of God. His human nature is like the original sculpture from which a mold is taken in order to reproduce copies of the original, with our human natures being the copies. Or, to change the simile, his human nature is like the proto-type automobile from whose blueprints the production-line vehicles are made, with us being the production-line versions of the same model of vehicle.

Transposed into the language of divine election, we can say this: God ordains that he will create a world of creatures with whom he may be united so that they may participate in his divine life as a final end of the creation. Human creatures are those entities conceived for this purpose because they are metaphysical amphibians, having both physical and immaterial parts. God ordains that he will unite himself to human creatures by assuming a particular human nature, the nature of Christ. This assumption brings one human nature into a hypostatic or personal union with a divine person—namely, God the Son. God the Son voluntarily chooses to be Christ, in order to bring about this union between divinity and humanity. He is, in one important sense, the ground or foundation of our election because it is his eternal decision to be the mediator between divinity and humanity that enables the incarnation to take place. And it is the incarnation that enables us to participate in the divine life by means of the secret working of the Holy Spirit uniting us to Christ. So God ordains Christ as the means by which union with God is made possible for human beings. Christ is the first human in terms of the logical priority in God's decrees. God first ordains that Christ will be the hub between divinity and humanity, the means by which union obtains. To be this hub, he must be the image of the invisible God. Presumably, in accordance with Scripture, he must have a sinless human nature (Heb 4:15) in addition to his divine nature, in order for the personal union between God and the natural endowment of a creature to obtain. So his human nature images God by means of the hypostatic union. It is made a fitting vehicle or vessel by means of which the Second Person of the Trinity can act in creation; that is, his human nature

[10] The sort of mechanism I have in mind here is explained in more detail by Brian Leftow in "A Timeless God Incarnate," in *The Incarnation*, ed. Stephen T. Davis, Daniel Kendall, and Gerald O'Collins (New York: Oxford University Press 2002), 273–99; and Oliver D. Crisp, *Divinity and Humanity: The Incarnation Reconsidered* (Cambridge: Cambridge University Press, 2007), ch. 2.

is made to be metaphysically united to a divine person.[11] Other human natures, including those possessed by you and me, are made after the likeness of his prototypical nature. For this reason we image God as we image Christ. So God ordains Christ as the interface between divinity and humanity. Christ's incarnation brings about this interface, enabling union with God to be achieved by the power of the Holy Spirit at work within us, linking or uniting us to Christ in a way analogous to the linking of particular computers or tablets to the wireless hub in the home or office where we work.

This brings us to a vital matter, often misunderstood in theology. The claim here is not that God the Son assumes some sort of universal humanity, so that by becoming human God the Son somehow changes all human natures from the inside out, so to speak.[12] This is to confuse two things: the property that all human beings share in virtue of being human, and the particular instance of a human nature that is assumed by God the Son. God the Son assumes a human nature—that is, a particular human nature, the nature of Jesus of Nazareth. The human nature of Jesus is *his* human nature; it is made *for him* by the miraculous work of the Holy Spirit in the womb of the Virgin. But it is a particular human nature, not some universal human nature (whatever that might mean). The reason why the incarnation brings about union with God is not because in assuming human nature he assumes some universal thing that we all share with him, and that he is able to heal from the inside out. Rather, this union obtains by means of the incarnation acting as an interface between divinity and humanity, enabling us to be united to God in Christ via the secret working of the Holy Spirit. Much theological ink has been spilled trying to get this distinction clear, and not a few important theologians have been confused on this very matter. Clarifying what is meant by this union, and how it is brought about by the incarnation, is vital.

This brings us to a second important consideration. By setting up the doctrine of election in terms of God's desire to be united to his creation via a particular sort

---

[11] Here I assume that the human nature of Christ is specially fashioned for union with God the Son; there are no worlds in which God the Son's human nature exists independent of the hypostatic union as a mere human person. For discussion of this matter, see Alfred J. Freddoso, "Human Nature, Potency, and the Incarnation," *Faith and Philosophy* 3 (1986): 27–53.

[12] See van Driel, *Incarnation Anyway*, 6 and 139, for a helpful explication of this point. See also Crisp, *Divinity and Humanity*, ch. 2. A contemporary instance of this confusion can be found in Kathryn Tanner's otherwise excellent work, *Christ the Key* (Cambridge: Cambridge University Press, 2009), ch. 7. It is also a constituent of Thomas F. Torrance's theology of the vicarious humanity of Christ. For a brief overview of this, see Myk Habets, "The Doctrine of Election in Evangelical Calvinism: T. F. Torrance as a Case Study," *Irish Theological Quarterly* 73, nos. 3–4 (2008): 339. For two historic examples, consider Saint Athanasius, *On the Incarnation*, trans. John Behr (Yonkers: Saint Vladimir's Seminary Press, 2011), §§9, 20; and Gregory Nazianzus, "Oration 30.21," in *On God and Christ: The Five Theological Orations and Two Letters to Cledonius*, trans. Frederick Williams and Lionel Wickham (Yonkers: Saint Vladimir's Seminary Press, 2002).

of creature fitted to this purpose (i.e., human creatures), it should be clear that this reasoning implies incarnation anyway. That is, on this christological union way of conceiving things, union with God is not contingent upon human sin. It is independent of any fall. In fact, it is independent of any creaturely action. On this view, God desires union with his creatures so that they may participate in the divine life. This is the end, or one of the ends, at which God aims in creating this world. But it is an aim that would have been fulfilled if he had created a world in which there was no human sin, and no fall, being instead a world that was populated by unfallen human creatures with whom he desired union. Humans in such circumstances would still need a means by which to be united to God because (on this way of thinking) being a sinless human is not a sufficient condition for such union; it requires some additional special divine action. A mediator between divinity and humanity is one suitable means by which to achieve the goal of union, though not perhaps the only one, all things considered. To put this point slightly differently, on the christological union account, even a sinless creature is not in a position to be united to God. Such union requires both an interface between divinity and humanity, such as the incarnation provides, and a means by which human creatures may be united to God via that interface, which is provided by the secret working of the Holy Spirit.[13]

Strengths and Weaknesses of the Christological Union Account

This completes our exposition of the christological union account and, with it, the constructive part of the chapter. We may now turn to the strengths and weaknesses of the argument embedded in this narrative. Let us begin with the strengths before turning to some potential weaknesses.

Strengths of the christological union account

The first great strength of the christological union account (perhaps, of all incarnation anyway doctrines) is that it does not make God's gracious act of condescension in Christ dependent upon human sin. Union with God in Christ by means of the Holy Spirit is the great triune work in the economy of creation, and on this way of thinking about the matter, it is one of the ends (perhaps the ultimate end) at which God aims in creating the world. Indeed, we might say that this outcome is hardwired into the metaphysics of creation. So this christological union version of an incarnation anyway argument places Christ at the center of creation, and union with God as the end of creation. Indeed, on this way of thinking, a complete theological

---

[13] The pneumatological dimension to union with Christ is explored in Crisp, *Word Enfleshed*.

understanding of creation is impossible without the doctrine of the Trinity (especially, the *opera trinitatis ad extra sunt indivisa* principle), without a high Christology, and without the agency of the Holy Spirit applying the benefits of Christ to the believer.[14] Not only that, but it also draws on a christological doctrine of the image of God that has ecumenical promise (especially with Orthodox Christians).

What is more, despite the fact that it requires a high Christology, and a christologically focused account of God's act and ends in creation, the christological union account also preserves a robust notion of divine freedom. This is the second strength of the view. In contemporary discussion of election, it is Karl Barth's doctrine in *Church Dogmatics* II/2 that casts a long shadow over all other attempts to conceive of divine election. Yet one of the persisting worries about Barth's doctrine is its implications for divine freedom. There is a current scholarly debate about the precise dogmatic shape of Barth's doctrine, and here is not the place to enter into that discussion.[15] However, on one currently influential rendering of his doctrine, Barth's mature views of divine election and the Trinity are in tension, a tension he did not finally resolve. Had he resolved this tension in the direction of his doctrine of divine election, then it would have been clear that his view implies that the very trinity of God is a function of divine election. "Expressed more exactly," says Bruce McCormack, "the eternal act of Self-differentiation in which God is God 'a second time in a very different way' and a third time as well is *given in* the eternal act where God elects himself for the human race." He goes on to say, "In other words, the works of God *ad intra* (the trinitarian processions) find their ground in the *first* of the works of God *ad extra* (viz. election)."[16]

On the face of it, this interpretation of Barth's legacy for contemporary reformulations of the doctrine of election implies that God is somehow constituted as triune in his eternal act of election. Since, on Barth's view, Christ is the subject and object of this electing act, the electing God and the elect (and reprobate) human being, this is tantamount to saying that God is

---

[14] A view common in much of the Reformed Orthodox theology. For a contemporary restatement, see Michael S. Horton, *Covenant and Salvation: Union with Christ* (Louisville: Westminster John Knox, 2007).

[15] A recent collection of papers on the topic can be found in Michael T. Dempsey, ed., *Trinity and Election in Contemporary Theology* (Grand Rapids: Eerdmans, 2011).

[16] Bruce L. McCormack, "Grace and Being: The Role of God's Gracious Election in Karl Barth's Theological Ontology," in *Orthodox and Modern: Studies in the Theology of Karl Barth* (Grand Rapids: Baker Academic, 2009), 194 (emphasis in original). An earlier version of this essay was published in John Webster, ed., *The Cambridge Companion to Karl Barth* (Cambridge: Cambridge University Press, 2000).

constituted who he is as a triune being by the eternal act of divine election whereby he chooses to be God for us in Christ. But this seems a rather Pickwickian sense of "chooses." For if this eternal choice is the very act by means of which God determines his very being as triune, then it is difficult to see how God may refrain from such a momentous choice. In fact, it is very difficult to know what to make of this claim, since it suggests that this eternal act is logically prior to the divine being, which seems very strange indeed. How can anything, God included, *act* logically prior to *being*? It is difficult to see what this means, for it would appear that any agent, God included, must exist in order to act in one way or another.[17] But perhaps the view is less problematic than this. Perhaps McCormack and other like-minded interpreters of Barth only mean to suggest that on this Barth-inspired way of thinking, God decides in the eternal act of election (the election of Christ) that he will be God for us, and therefore that he will be Father, Son, and Spirit in the economy of salvation.

In any case, as I say, on the face of it this interpretation of Barth raises serious questions about the meaning of divine freedom in creation, which is usually taken to mean God may or may not create a world, and God may or may not create this world. He is free to create; and he is free to refrain from creating. What is more, there is nothing to constrain God to act in one way rather than another other than his own nature. The christological union account offered here is consistent with this more traditional way of speaking about divine freedom. This, I think, is a strength rather than a weakness of the view. It is also an important way in which this incarnation anyway account parts company with the Barth-inspired construal of the doctrine of election favored by McCormack, among others.[18]

A third and closely related strength of the view is that it is commensurate with divine aseity. If divine freedom has to do with God being able to create or refrain from creating a world, and this particular world, divine aseity has to do with God being independent of the created order. This has two aspects. He must be metaphysically independent. That is, he is ontologically independent of everything outside himself. But he must also be psychologically independent of the creation. That is, he has no lack or need that requires

---

[17] For a similar line of criticism, See Paul Helm, "Karl Barth and the Visibility of God," in *Engaging with Barth: Contemporary Evangelical Critiques*, ed. David Gibson and Daniel Strange (New York: T&T Clark, 2008), 273–99.

[18] I say this as someone who has learned much from the work of McCormack and others who champion the actualist account of Barth's ontology, and who continues to appreciate the constructive project such theologians are engaged upon.

satisfaction from some source external to himself. Now, on the face of it, the christological union account satisfies the first of these claims about divine aseity because it is consistent with the notion that God may refrain from creating a world. Nor does it imply that the world is something like the necessary product of divine creativity, as, say, Jonathan Edwards does.[19] But does the christological union account satisfy the second aspect of aseity—namely, divine psychological independence? The way I have set it up may suggest that it does not. For if one of the final ends of creation is unitive in nature (i.e., divine union with some number of creatures or some aspect of his creation), then it may seem that God is dependent on creation for the fulfillment of his desire for such union.

However, I think that this worry can be assuaged without too much difficulty if we attend to the detail of the unitive end of creation as set forth in the christological union argument. Recall that the divine creative act is framed in terms of a conditional: *if* God ordains the creation of a particular world, such and such necessarily follows from that. But since God may refrain from creating a world (and, therefore, may refrain from creating *this* world), he does not have a psychological need that is only met by an act of creation. God is not like the artist who must compulsively create in order to satisfy a basic urge or creative impulse. Nevertheless, God is creative. But he is creative because he chooses to be creative. Given that he chooses to create a world, he then is faced with a decision about the ends in creation, and—so the christological union account goes—he decides that union with creatures is a fitting end for creation. None of this implies that God is psychologically dependent on something outside himself for his own happiness. In this way, it seems to me that the christological union account manages to navigate the difficult waters of divine aseity without falling into some of the problems that someone like Jonathan Edwards did, in his assertion that creation is the necessary output of essential divine creativity.

We come to a fourth strength to the view. My earlier remarks about Barth might lead readers to think that the christological union account attempts to make a decisive break with Barth. That would be a mistake. My own thinking about election in general, and this version of the incarnation anyway argument, owes a significant debt to Barth. As McCormack points out in his work on the Swiss theologian, one of the great insights Barth brings to the discussion of election is that it that must be located in the doctrine of

---

[19] For elaboration on this point, see William J. Wainwright, "Jonathan Edwards, William Rowe, and the Necessity of Creation," in *Faith, Freedom, and Rationality*, ed. Jeff Jordan and Daniel Howard-Snyder (Lanham, Md.: Rowman & Littlefield, 1996), 119–33.

God, not elsewhere, in the doctrine of creation.[20] The christological union argument outlined here takes that seriously. For if God creates in order to be united to his creatures so that they may participate in his life, and if Christ is the prototypical metaphysical amphibian that makes such union possible via human creatures, then it looks like creation is itself a function of the doctrine of election, which is (in one sense, at least) located in the doctrine of God. I take this to be an attraction of the view, and one of its strengths, at least in part because it means the incarnation is not fundamentally restorative but unitive. That is, it is not fundamentally a matter of God reconciling us to himself (though it does achieve that in the actual world, of course). It is fundamentally about God providing the means of uniting us to Godself. The human sin that obtains in the actual world, then, complicates this picture by adding to the unitive function of election a redemptive one.

Weaknesses of the christological union account

We come to potential weaknesses. Perhaps chief among these is the worry with which we started: that this doctrine is speculative in the pejorative sense. Scripture speaks of Christ coming into the world to save sinners (1 Tim 1:15), not of Christ coming into the world irrespective of human sin in order to unite us to God. Saint Paul makes it clear that Christ "died for our sins in accordance with the scriptures" (1 Cor 15:3), not that Christ would have come into the world even if there was no need for human redemption from sin. So how is this doctrine consistent with the teaching of Holy Writ? Here I think we must be careful to acknowledge that Scripture speaks in the concrete language of religious faith—the language of proclamation, not of the schoolroom. The biblical material that speaks of Christ's work in the world is concerned only to explain why Christ *actually* came into the world. However, this is perfectly consistent with the christological union view set out here. The issue is not whether Christ Jesus *came* into the world to save sinners. I take it that on that question, Scripture has a view (so to speak). The issue is whether Christ *would have come* into the world if there were no sinners to save. The view expressed here is that he would have done so, because union with God requires some act of divine condescension and accommodation, some interface between God and humanity, in order to unite us to Godself irrespective of human sin. What is more, this function is in one sense more

---

[20] See McCormack, "Seek God Where He May Be Found: A Response to Edwin Chr. van Driel," reprinted in *Orthodox and Modern,* 276.

fundamental than the redemptive function Christ has in the actual world in virtue of human sin.

So it seems to me that the theological issue doesn't turn on whether the incarnation anyway doctrine is consistent with what Scripture says the work of Christ *actually* achieves. It turns on the question of the eternal purposes of God in creation. If his eternal purpose is to be united to the created order by means of human beings, the metaphysical amphibians of creation, then we have an important motivation for seriously considering the christological union version of an incarnation anyway argument.

Are there indications of this in Scripture? I think there are. Consider, for example, the great christological passage from Colossians 1:15-18a, which tells us that "He is the image of the invisible God, the firstborn of all creation; for in him all things in heaven and on earth were created, things visible and invisible, whether thrones or dominions or rulers or powers—all things have been created through him and for him. He himself is before all things, and in him all things hold together. He is the head of the body, the church." The passage goes on to link Christ to redemption, of course. But it is not insignificant that he is here said to be the image of God, the agent of creation, *for whom* all things are created. He is also the one who holds all things together, as well as being the head of the church. Then there is the passage in Ephesians 5 about the union between wives and husbands that is set forth as an analogue to the mystery of the union between Christ and the Church (Eph 5:32). Finally, there is the matter of becoming partakers of the divine nature, as Peter puts it in his second epistle (2 Pet 1:4). Much more would need to be said were we attempting to give a biblical-theological case for a supralapsarian Christology. These passages are merely illustrative of a certain christological priority in certain strands of Scripture that is (so it seems to me) consistent with the sort of christological union account offered here.

A second concern is raised by Jonathan Edwards in his seminal work, *A Dissertation on the End for Which God Created the World.*[21] There he lays out with great penetration and insight a careful analytical argument for the conclusion that God's goal in creation is, in the final analysis, to bring himself glory. There are other ends God aims at in creating the world. But this end is the most fundamental, or, as Edwards puts it, the most ultimate. The christological union account outlined here depends on the claim that one fundamental aim in creation is unitive. On the face of it, it would appear

---

[21] *God's End in Creation*, as it is usually called, can be found in Jonathan Edwards, *Ethical Writings*, ed. Paul Ramsey, vol. 8 of *The Works of Jonathan Edwards*, ed. Perry Miller (New Haven: Yale University Press, 1989).

that Edwards' concern runs in a different direction. Is his position the more biblical and defensible?

Not necessarily. For one thing, as I have been at pains to make clear, the christological union account only requires that the unitive aim is *one* of the fundamental aims of creation, not the only one, not necessarily even the ultimate one. As Edwards points out, there are multiple ends in creation at which God aims. Some are more ultimate than others, however. In this regard it is possible that God aims at union with his creatures, though he has a regard to himself and his own glory in doing so. It may even be that his glory is the ultimate end of his external works, though union is a means to that end—what, in Edwards' nomenclature, would constitute a final end but not an ultimate end.

However, I worry that the Edwardian obsession with divine self-glorification as the ultimate end of all God's creative works makes the creation, including creatures like you and me, merely the instruments by means of which God brings himself glory. This is a problem. For normally we would think that an entity that seeks its own glory over a unitive end is morally deficient. To take a simple example, if a spouse tells her beloved that she married him in order to be united with him according to the Pauline "one flesh" principle, that would be something to celebrate. However, if she told him that she married him in order to be united to him simply because she knew that such union would bring her gratification and happiness, we might worry about her motives. Edwards is at pains to point out that a perfect being would be remiss in not glorifying himself, because there is nothing higher for such a being to aim at, no greater entity that he should seek to glorify in his actions. On the Edwardian scheme it seems that my example of the loving spouse is not to the point because God is significantly unlike the spouse. The spouse is remiss if she aims at her own gratification in marriage, making her partner the instrument by means of which to instantiate that gratification. For it is morally wrong to instrumentalize other agents in that way. But God cannot fail to glorify himself; it is not a moral lack on his part, not a sign of moral dereliction or of vanity but of his being perfect.

My worry is that it is Edwards' response that is not to the point. The issue is not whether God ought to glorify himself in his works, or even whether God ought to aim at this as the ultimate end of creation. The issue has to do with whether, in order to achieve this end, God may create human beings with the express purpose of using them as instruments by means of which he may achieve this end. If one feels the force of this concern (as I do), then it may be that the christological union account must part ways with Edwards at this point, making the unitive function the more fundamental end in creation. Happily, just such a unitive view of God's end in creation can be found elsewhere (e.g., in the work of Saint Thomas Aquinas.)[22] Although Saint Thomas' mature view on these matters was cautiously to eschew speculation on whether the incarnation would have obtained apart from redemption, affirming instead that the fall may be the occasion of God's redemptive work in Christ (in *Summa theologiae* 3.Q.1, art. 3), it is interesting that in discussing the question of the fittingness of the incarnation, he says the following:

> The very nature of God is goodness, as is clear from Dionysius (*Div. Nom.* i). Hence, what belongs to the essence of goodness befits God. But it belongs to the essence of goodness to communicate itself to others, as is plain from Dionysius (*Div. Nom.* iv). Hence it belongs to the essence of the highest good to communicate itself in the highest manner to the creature, and this is brought about chiefly by "His so joining created nature to Himself that one Person is made up of these three—the Word, a soul and flesh," as Augustine says (*De Trin.* xiii). Hence it is manifest that it was fitting that God should become incarnate.[23]

This, it should be clear, is independent of questions of a fall from grace.[24]

Conclusion

The aim of this chapter has been to commend one particular incarnation anyway argument—namely, the christological union account.[25] If the christological

---

[22] Compare Carlo Leget, who writes this about Saint Thomas' eschatology: "According to Aquinas' theological cosmology, the world is at the service of the corporeal dimension of man; the corporeal dimension is at the service of the spiritual one; and the spiritual dimension is at the service of the union with God. Sometimes Aquinas takes the three steps as one, saying that the universe is created for the sake of the beatitude of the saint" ("Eschatology," 367; he refers here to *Summa theologiae* 1.73.1).

[23] Saint Thomas Aquinas, *Summa theologiae,* 3.Q.1, art. 1.

[24] I owe this point to Westcott, whose account of the medieval scholastic debates about incarnation anyway is most helpful. See "Gospel of Creation," 300. It has been suggested to me that this excerpt from Aquinas makes the incarnation somehow necessary. But this is not what Aquinas says. Although what he says here indicates that the communication of God's goodness is necessary (and we might take issue with that), he is careful to say that this means that the incarnation is a *fitting* mode of such communication of divine goodness. Clearly, a fitting mode is not a necessary mode.

[25] We have noted that the christological union argument has some conceptual overlap with the thought of Saint Thomas Aquinas. It also has some parallels with other medieval scholastic thinkers, such as Rupert of Deutz, Alexander of Hales, Bonaventure, and especially Saint Thomas' teacher, Albert the Great. See Westcott, "Gospel of Creation," for a

union account is on target, then union with God—a fundamental aim of creation—is not merely a matter of redemption from sin. It is about the need for some divine action of accommodation and condescension by means of which humanity and divinity are conjoined in order that we may access the divine and participate in the life of God. Although for all we know God could bring this about by some other means, it is fitting that this action be brought about by the incarnation, and, given the structure of the argument, this makes the incarnation independent of the fact of human sin. Along the way we have also seen that this christological union account throws light on other, related themes, such as God's end(s) in creation and the image of God in human beings.[26] I submit that this unitive account provides a theological motivation for one version of the incarnation anyway argument that has much to commend it. After all, it would be odd to think that the spectacular work of divine grace that is the incarnation is merely God's rescue plan, rather than the outcome he intended independent of human sin in order to unite us to Godself.

---

cameo of each of these theologians on this topic. I take it that such conceptual overlap is a good thing that may provide an ancillary reason for thinking it an argument worthy of serious consideration.

[26] Other things being equal, a doctrine that has greater explanatory power is surely to be preferred to one that has less explanatory power. The christological union account certainly has explanatory power, accounting for the fundamental issue of God's aims in creation, as well as the disputed matter of the divine image, in pursuit of a motivation for an incarnation anyway argument. The argument could be expanded further to include other aspects of Christology and soteriology, which is what I have tried to do in *The Word Enfleshed*.

7

Original Sin

In Adam's Fall,
We Sinned all.

The New England Primer[1]

The previous chapter set out an argument for a version of an incarnation anyway approach to God's purposes in creation. Nevertheless, the fact is, human beings are fallen and do require salvation and reconciliation with God. The incarnation in the actual world is a matter of rescuing us from ourselves. So what are we to make of the doctrine of original sin, which is at the heart of Christian teaching on this fundamental theological theme?

This chapter sets out a constructive account of original sin that attempts to take seriously the Christian tradition (particularly, the Reformed tradition) and that avoids the serious theological drawback of the doctrine of original guilt (roughly, the notion that Adam's progeny bear the guilt for Adam's original or primal sin). I dub this account the *moderate Reformed doctrine of original sin*. I also argue that an adequate understanding of original sin must be open textured enough to accommodate some version of the story of evolutionary human development. Although I do not offer an account of how original sin is consistent with evolutionary human development, the doctrine set out here is commensurate with several live options on this controversial theological topic.

[1] Benjamin Harris, *The New England Primer* (Boston: 1688).

Dogmatic Preamble

In his recent monograph *In Adam's Fall,* Ian McFarland eschews any attempt to explain the origins of human suffering while retaining an Augustinian doctrine of sin. On his account, "The proper dogmatic function of original sin is limited to offering a *description of* rather than an *explanation for* the human condition apart from grace." Indeed, "Original sin . . . is rightly used to emphasize God's gracious response to human need and not to provide an etiological explanation for humanity's being in need."[2]

On the face of it, this seems like an odd thing to say about the explanatory scope of original sin. Historic accounts of the doctrine are usually deployed in order to do precisely what McFarland denies—namely, to provide a theological explanation of how it is that human beings are in their current vitiated moral condition. Indeed, it is this very aspect of historic doctrines of original sin at which objections from those working on evolutionary history often take aim. An example will make the point. Scientist and theologian Arthur Peacocke writes,

> Biological death can no longer be regarded as in any way the consequence of anything human beings might have been supposed to have done in the past, for evolutionary history shows it to be the very means whereby they appear, and so, for the theist, are created by God. The traditional interpretation of the third chapter of Genesis that there was a historical "Fall," an action by our human progenitors that is the explanation of biological death, has to be rejected.

He goes on to say, "There was no golden age, no perfect past, no individuals, 'Adam' or 'Eve' from whom all human beings have descended and declined and who were perfect in their relationships and behavior."[3]

It looks like McFarland is denying one of the main planks of the traditional doctrine in order to avoid the sort of hard objections posed by writers like Peacocke. In other words, his approach (even if it is indebted to the Augustinian tradition) depends upon a sort of revisionist strategy with respect to the doctrine of original sin. Other things being equal, it is surely

---

[2] Ian A. McFarland, *In Adam's Fall: A Meditation on the Christian Doctrine of Original Sin* (Oxford: Wiley-Blackwell, 2010), 47–48.

[3] Arthur Peacocke, *Theology for a Scientific Age: Being and Becoming—Natural, Divine and Human* (Oxford: Blackwell, 1993), 222–23. For a recent attempt to restate a doctrine of original sin under the sort of constraints envisaged by Peacocke, see Daryl P. Domning and Monika K. Hellwig, *Original Selfishness: Original Sin in the Light of Evolution,* Ashgate Science and Religion Series (Farnham: Ashgate, 2006).

preferable to avoid significantly truncating the explanatory scope of the doctrine of original sin in order to meet objections like that posed by Peacocke, among others. Nevertheless, there is a certain elegance and parsimony to McFarland's attempt to address such concerns. Denying the explanatory value of original sin as far as the etiology of human suffering is concerned in order to make room for a descriptive account of the doctrine defangs the sort of worry articulated by Peacocke, paving the way for a constructive dogmatic account, the task with which McFarland concerns himself in the larger part of his study.

But perhaps there is a way in which the theological sensibility that informs McFarland's fine work can be adapted for the purposes of a rather different strategy. Here is one such suggestion: concede at the outset the story of human development as told by the sort of evolutionary history presupposed by Peacock and many others while withholding making a final judgment about which version of this story is true (consistent with the commitments of Christian theology). This requires some explanation.

There are various accounts of evolutionary history. Many are metaphysically naturalist in nature. For instance, E. O. Wilson writes, "If humankind evolved by Darwinian natural selection, genetic chance and environmental necessity, not God, made the species."[4] Such versions of the story of evolutionary history are straightforwardly incompatible with Christian faith. As Scottish theologian Alan Torrance observes, "It is simply confused to try and build any kind of theistic teleology onto a naturalistic (and hence, by definition, inherently atheistic) account of the origins of human nature. To build a theistic account of human nature onto a foundationally naturalistic account is to seek to integrate a full-orbed nonteleological account and an explicitly and foundationally teleological account."[5] On these terms it appears that the theologian cannot be expected to offer a doctrine of original sin that appeals to *any old version* of evolutionary history. It has to be one that is at least not inconsistent with a teleological theological understanding of that history, and that means one that is not metaphysically naturalist.[6]

---

[4] E. O. Wilson, *On Human Nature* (Cambridge, Mass.: Harvard University Press, 1978), xiii, cited in Alan J. Torrance, "Is There a Distinctive Human Nature? Approaching the Question from a Christian Epistemic Base," *Zygon* 47, no. 4 (2012): 904.

[5] Torrance, "Is There a Distinctive Human Nature?" 910.

[6] Note, the claim is not that the scientist should set aside *methodological* naturalism, only *metaphysical* naturalism. One can adopt methodological naturalism and still hold the metaphysical supernaturalism, as is the case with most scientists who are persons of religious faith. But metaphysical naturalism is inconsistent with orthodox Christian faith; it entails the denial of supernaturalism.

No doubt there will be other constraints in a properly Christian theological account as well, having to do with the particular etiology of human suffering given in Scripture. Suppose one thinks of Scripture as the normal means by which God speaks to his church. Then, the etiology of human suffering and human origins given in Scripture will have a direct bearing on the version of evolutionary history that is acceptable to the theologian. The assumption here is that the theologian must pay attention to different sorts of testimony in making judgments about how to frame a constructive account of original sin. This includes appeals to both the testimony of Scripture (and tradition) and to the views of the scientific community on matters pertaining to evolutionary history.

Now, as I have already indicated, there are various versions of the evolutionary history story, various variations upon it, some of which are metaphysically naturalist in nature and some of which are not. It seems to me that the Christian theologian concerned to accommodate some version of the sort of evolutionary history to which Peacocke refers may want to provide an account of original sin that is consistent with a range of views on the precise character and shape of this history, but that prescinds from approving any one of this range of views. The reason for doing so should be fairly obvious: although the story of evolutionary history articulated by Peacocke is widely agreed upon, the precise contours of evolutionary history are still, to some extent, the subject of dispute. We might put it like this: The broad outline of human descent from earlier hominid groups is regarded by the consensus of the scientific community as a settled matter. But which groups, how that came about, when and where—these are matters that are still being ironed out by ongoing research.[7] Suppose that is right. Then theologians wishing to give an account of original sin would be well advised to ensure that their version of the doctrine is conceptually open textured enough to accommodate a range of different views on those aspects of evolutionary history that bear upon original sin, such as the evolution of human beings from earlier hominid populations.

Naturally, this approach precludes certain options. We have already noted some of the constraints that will apply to the versions of evolutionary history to which the accommodation-minded theologian can appeal: a non-metaphysically naturalist version of the story commensurate with the truth

---

[7] See, e.g., the special issue of *Perspectives on Science and Christian Faith* 62, no. 3 (2010), in which there are a number of articles devoted to the historicity of Adam and Eve, genomics, and theological reflection in the light of evolutionary science: http://www.asa3 .org/ASA/PSCF/2010/PSCF9-10dyn.html.

contained in the testimony of Scripture (and, therefore, consistent with a teleological theological understanding of the story). There will be further matters of a theological nature to take into account as well, including how one construes the biblical testimony, what it is said to teach, and so on, in addition to the question of which sort of nonmetaphysically naturalist, teleology-friendly story of evolutionary development one adopts. But there are also theological issues that are precluded by this sort of approach. In other words, there are constraints that apply to the theological aspects of this strategy of accommodation and constraints that apply to the range of views about evolutionary history that are acceptable. To take an obvious example, the theologian attracted to such a strategy is unlikely to be sympathetic to the notion that the primeval prologue of Genesis 1–3 provides a complete, historical record of human origins that can simply be unproblematically read off the surface of the text.[8]

Let us take stock. There may be good prudential reasons for the theologian pursuing a strategy that accommodates evolutionary history to ensure that the account of the doctrine of original sin in question is consistent with a range of evolutionary views. However, such an approach is constrained: by the need for a nonmetaphysically naturalist account of evolution, by the need for a theological (and, therefore, teleological) understanding of the place of human beings in creation, and by the teaching of Scripture. Divines from particular churches may well add to this list the need to ensure their conclusions are consistent with the teaching of a particular confession, creed, or tradition (e.g., the magisterium of the Roman Catholic Church, or the doctrines stated in the Westminster Confession, or the Augsburg Confession, or whatever). Nevertheless, this still leaves open a range of possible positions on evolutionary history relative to matters theological.[9] It is my view that a

[8]   Recently, Hud Hudson has provided an account of the doctrine of original sin that is underwritten by the metaphysics of hyperspace and that delivers (on one rendition, at least) a way of thinking about hyperspace and hypertime consistent with what is often euphemistically called a "literal" reading of Gen 1–3. See Hudson, *The Fall and Hypertime* (Oxford: Oxford University Press, 2014). I shall not presume Hudson's account here, though his essay is a powerful and illuminating piece of analytic metaphysics from which I have learned a great deal. We shall return to Hudson's understanding of hyperspace in the final chapter.

[9]   Some confessional and catechetical documents clearly teach monogenism, e,g., the Westminster Confession or the *Catechism of the Catholic Church*, in which case theologians in, say, Presbyterian churches that have the Westminster Confession as a subordinate standard, or Roman Catholics that pay heed to the *Catechism of the Catholic Church*, must find ways of understanding their confession or catechism that do not preclude some version of evolutionary history. This is not impossible. But it does present certain confessional-hermeneutical problems that Christians in such traditions must navigate.

doctrine of original sin that leaves open as wide a range of possible positions on evolutionary history relative to some cluster of theological constraints is all the better for doing so. For given the current state of human knowledge about paleoanthropology, it is surely wise to withhold acceptance of one particular view of human origins if that is feasible.

Moreover, it seems to me that such an option is indeed feasible. In the next section I shall provide one such account. It is tradition specific, so that it has to deal with the theological constraints I have already outlined. But it is so structured that it does not commit its defender to one particular version of the story of evolutionary history.

Outline of a Doctrine of Original Sin

There is no single agreed-upon definition of original sin in the Christian tradition—no hamartiological analogue to the famous "definition" of the person of Christ given in the canons of the Council of Chalcedon. Instead, there are various versions of the doctrine that attend to a common set of theological themes, though they differ among themselves about the precise dogmatic shape of original sin. Nevertheless, all versions of the doctrine that are theologically orthodox must avoid the heresy of Pelagianism, according to which human sinfulness is a matter of imitation, not imputation, and is not in principle a foregone conclusion for any particular individual. Also to be avoided is the error of semi-Pelagianism, according to which human beings are able to exercise their free will independent of divine grace in order to cooperate with divine grace in bringing about their own salvation. But as to what original sin is, theological opinion divides along the lines of particular theological traditions. For instance, Roman Catholics argue that original sin is essentially a privative state, wherein fallen human beings lack the original justice and righteousness with which our first parents were created.[10] Without

---

[10] "Although it is proper to each individual, original sin does not have the character of a personal fault in any of Adam's descendants. It is a deprivation of original holiness and justice, but human nature has not been totally corrupted: it is wounded in the natural powers proper to it, subject to ignorance, suffering and the dominion of death, and inclined to sin—an inclination to evil that is called concupiscence" (*Catechism of the Catholic Church*, part 1, §2, ch. 1, par. 7, 405). I shall not refer to the Orthodox concept of ancestral sin here in detail, though this represents an important alternative to the Roman version of a privative account of original sin. A helpful account of the Orthodox view is given in John S. Romanides, *The Ancestral Sin* (Ridgewood, N.J.: Zephyr, 2002). He writes, "In the East, the fall is understood to be a consequence of man's own withdrawal from divine life and the resulting weakness and disease of human nature" (34).

this moral property, fallen humans are constitutionally incapable of pleasing God. However, by and large, historic Protestant traditions think of original sin in rather more gloomy terms as a corruption of human nature consequent upon the primal sin of an original human pair. This corruption is said by some (especially those in the Reformed tradition) to include the ascription of original sin as a moral deformity to all human beings after Adam and Eve. It also includes the notion of original guilt. That is, the guilt incurred by Adam (and Eve) for their primal sin is imputed or otherwise transferred to all their descendants. On this way of thinking, fallen human beings not only possess the sinful condition bequeathed them by their first ancestors but also possess the guilt of the primal human sin, and for this reason are said to be generated in a culpable, not merely privative, moral state.

Having said that, there are three core tenets common to all historic, orthodox doctrines of original sin. These are as follows. *First*, that there was an original pair from whom we are all descended; *second*, that this pair committed the primal sin that adversely affects all their offspring; and *third*, that all human beings after the fall of the original pair are in need of salvation, without which they will perish. Note that the doctrine of original sin as some property possessed by all human beings post-fall is not part of this dogmatic core, though it is important in Western theology (both Roman Catholic and Protestant).[11] This is because it is not a doctrine universally agreed upon by the Orthodox. Nor is original guilt part of this dogmatic core. It is an addition to the doctrine made by many, though not all, Protestant theologians—especially, though not exclusively, those in the Reformed tradition.[12]

Now, clearly it would be morally inappropriate to commit oneself to a doctrine that has consequences that are obviously unjust or immoral. Yet on the face of it, the conjunction of the three dogmatic tenets of the historic doctrine plus the notion that original sin and original guilt are properties possessed by fallen human beings appears unjust and immoral because on this view Adam's sin and guilt are ascribed to me. Such a state of affairs seems unjust because I suffer for the sin of an ancestor from long ago with whose action I did not agree or concur. It is immoral because it is necessarily

[11] Of course Christ does not possess original sin, and for Roman Catholic theologians, neither does Mary Theotokos.

[12] Many free evangelicals and Baptists seem to hold to a doctrine of original guilt, e.g., the 1689 Baptist Confession of Faith, which reads, "They being the root, and by God's appointment, standing in the room and stead of all mankind, the guilt of this sin was imputed, and their corrupted nature conveyed, to all their posterity descending from them by ordinary generation" (article 6.3).

morally wrong to punish the innocent, and I am innocent of Adam's sin (I did not commit his sin or condone it). It is also immoral because the guilt of one person's sin does not transfer to another (I am not guilty of committing Adam's sin).

In analogous mundane circumstances, we would think it a travesty of justice were an innocent person to suffer a penalty because of the sin of another whose sin they did not consent to and could not have prevented from occurring. And we would think it inconceivable that the guilt of one individual could be transferred to another. There are situations in which we allow the transfer of certain penalties from one agent to another, such as the paying of fines. But in such circumstances guilt and culpability are prized apart from the notion of penalty, so that it is possible for, say, my friend to pay for my parking fine instead of me. I am the one culpable for the fine. But as long as the fine is paid, the law is satisfied. Who pays it is not legally salient, provided the fine is remitted by an appropriate substitute. The same does not apply to crimes of a criminal rather than pecuniary nature, however. For instance, a murderer may not avoid the hangman's noose by asking for a friend to take his or her place, even if the friend is willing and able to do so. At least part of the reason why this is not judged appropriate in most human legal systems is that there is an assumption that crime must fit punishment, and that culpability for such crimes attaches to the culprit, is nontransferable, and *is* legally salient in determining the penalty.

It does not seem for many historic Protestant theologians enamored of original sin plus original guilt that human sin is analogous to the pecuniary rather than criminal cases just mentioned: fit between crime and punishment, along with culpability and the nontransferability of guilt, are salient in determining the penalty, which, in the case of original sin, is exclusion from the presence of God. For these reasons I suggest that the doctrine of original guilt is such a significant obstacle to contemporary restatements of the doctrine of original sin that it would be prudent to remove it from the doctrine. It is not at all clear to me that the biblical warrant for this notion is a strong one, and there appear to be good moral reasons for excising it.[13]

---

[13] I have dealt with these matters in more detail in Crisp, *The Word Enfleshed: Exploring the Person and Work of Christ* (Grand Rapids: Baker Academic, 2016), ch. 7; and "Sin," in *Christian Dogmatics*, ed. Michael Allen and Scott Swain (Grand Rapids: Baker Academic, 2015), 194–215. My own views on this topic have changed in the last decade. It now seems to me that the biblical warrant for original guilt is thin. The oft-touted Adam Christology of Rom 5:12-19 does not yield anything like a clear and unambiguous doctrine of original guilt. N. P. Williams' critique of the claim that original guilt is implicit in the Pauline corpus

Nevertheless, in keeping with many Protestant theologians, it also seems to me that original sin is a real moral corruption or deformity of soul that affects all human beings with the exception of Christ. It is not merely a privation of original justice or participation in the divine life consequent upon primal sin. This is a common Protestant notion that can be found in a number of Reformation symbols. For instance, article 9 of the Thirty-Nine Articles of Religion of 1563, which form the dogmatic bedrock of Anglicanism, states,

> Original sin . . . is the fault and corruption of the Nature of every man, that naturally is engendered of the offspring of Adam; whereby man is very far gone from original righteousness, and is of his own nature inclined to evil, so that the flesh lusteth always contrary to the Spirit; and therefore in every person born into this world, it deserveth God's wrath and damnation. And this infection of nature doth remain, yea in them that are regenerated; whereby the lust of the flesh, called in Greek, *phronema sarkos* . . . is not subject to the Law of God. And although there is no condemnation for them that believe and are baptized; yet the Apostle doth confess, that concupiscence and lust hath of itself the nature of sin.

Similarly, article 15 of the Belgic Confession of 1561 states that original sin

> is a corruption of the whole human nature—an inherited depravity which even infects small infants in their mother's womb, and the root which produces in humanity every sort of sin. It is therefore so vile and enormous in God's sight that it is enough to condemn the human race, and it is not abolished or wholly uprooted even by baptism, seeing that sin constantly boils forth as though from a contaminated spring.

It goes on, "Nevertheless, it is not imputed to God's children for their condemnation but is forgiven by his grace and mercy."[14]

Both of these confessions, from two Magisterial Reformation traditions, Anglicanism and the continental Reformed, respectively, clearly teach that

---

repays study. See his *The Ideas of the Fall and Original Sin* (London: Longmans, 1927), 156–57.

[14] Compare the Scots Confession (1560), the third chapter of which states, "By which transgression, commonly called Original Sin, was the image of God utterly defaced in man; and he and his posterity of nature became enemies to God, slaves to Satan, and servants to sin; insomuch that death everlasting has had, and shall have, power and dominion over all that have not been, are not, or shall not be regenerated from above: which regeneration is wrought by the power of the Holy Ghost, working in the hearts of the elect of God an assured faith in the promise of God, revealed to us in his word; by which faith we apprehend Christ Jesus, with the graces and benefits promised in him." Note the absence of a doctrine of original guilt.

original sin is a corruption of human nature. Notice, however, that there is no clear, unambiguous doctrine of original guilt in either of these symbols, though this is a staple of later Reformed thought (e.g., the Westminster Confession of Faith 6.3). Note also that the Belgic Confession speaks of an inherited depravity, which is, as the Articles of Religion says, "naturally engendered."

The fact that neither symbol teaches original guilt might be thought a weak reason for claiming that original guilt is not an essential component of Reformed confessionalism—a kind of argument from silence. Where an argument for a particular conclusion x does not imply or deny some further claim y, one cannot use the argument for x as the basis for denying y or implying y. To claim that the argument either implies y or denies it is to argue from silence. However, that is not quite the issue in view here. Suppose one were to offer a comprehensive account of x. Suppose further that x neither implies y nor denies y. At some later date, some of those that hold to the conclusion of argument x come to think that y *is an additional component that should be included with x,* whereas others come to think that y *is not an additional component that should be included with x.* What has changed is that further reflection has uncovered an issue that was previously unaccounted for in the arguments for x—namely, y. One might wonder whether y is an implication of x after all, for it is not unusual to find historic claims for one sort of thing that turn out to imply further claims not envisaged by those who articulated the historic claim in the first place. A good example is the principle that equality of political rights implies that women be enfranchised. My claim is that original guilt is not an implication of the doctrine of original sin expressed in the Anglican Articles of Religion or in the Belgic Confession. The framers of these documents give no indication that they had a doctrine of original guilt in mind when explaining their particular understanding of original sin, though they do not deny it, either. I do not think that they simply did not see that original guilt is an implication of their views, for I think that original guilt is neither implied nor denied by their accounts of original sin—in which case original guilt is a concept that is distinct from the doctrine *as expressed in* these documents. It may be consistent with the documents. But it is not an implication of them, just as it may be consistent to uphold the Constitution of the United States along with the Bill of Rights that have passed into federal law, though we do not think that the amendments that make up the Bill of Rights are *implications* of the Constitution as such.[15]

---

[15] The U.S. Constitution was passed in May 1787; the Bill of Rights was not ratified until September 1789. It was not introduced because such a bill was thought to be an

In keeping with these confessional documents, suppose original sin is a moral corruption that is inherited. It arises early in the development of a first human population and is passed down by both parents to each successive generation. How does this happen? Here we may turn to the story of Eden as a template. Early in human development, in (say) a first human community, there is some moral breach with God, some primal act of dereliction that introduces a moral corruption to human beings that is inheritable. Call this action the *primal sin*. On this way of thinking, inheriting a state of sin is not a condition for which the person born in this morally vitiated condition is culpable because (we suppose) a person cannot be held morally responsible for a condition with which he or she is born. It is not the fault of individuals that live diachronically downstream of the first human community that they are generated in a state of moral corruption.

It should be fairly obvious that what obtains with respect to the corruption with which fallen human beings are generated also obtains, mutatis mutandis, with original guilt. That is, fallen humans can be no more guilty of the sin of a putative human pair or aboriginal human community than they can be culpable for inheriting a state of sin. How could it be otherwise? For surely the ascription of moral properties and responsibility to a particular agent requires the agent in question to be the proper subject of such properties. But to be the proper subject of culpability for the primal sin or the guilt of that sin one would have to be the person who committed the primal sin. If a person inherits a vitiated condition, like the child born a heroin addict because its mother is a heroin addict, we do not blame the child for being in this state as we do the parent. For plainly an agent cannot be culpable for being generated and born in a state with which it did not concur. Similarly, if a person is born with a disposition to alcoholism, we would not think that agent morally responsible or culpable for possessing such a disposition, though we would normally think the agent is morally responsible for taking the steps that lead toward alcohol dependency because in the latter case the agent chooses to act on the basis of a disposition. It seems to me that something similar can be said for fallen human beings. They all possess the moral corruption inherited from their parents, and their parents, and so on, going back through the generations to some original human community. Being born in such a state is not something for which one can reasonably be said to be responsible or culpable. But acting upon such a disposition (if, indeed, it

---

implication of the Constitution, but rather to assuage worries about federalism and over-weening central government felt by the Anti-Federalists.

is a disposition) is something for which a person may be morally responsible and culpable.

There is, in other words, a distinction to be made between original sin and actual sin. Whereas original sin is that inherited moral corruption with which we are all generated, and for which we are not responsible or culpable, actual sins are those particular things we are disposed to do because we are born in a morally vitiated state. The person born with a disposition to substance abuse is liable to become an alcoholic; the fallen human being is liable to commit actual sin. Does this mean only that it is *very likely* that those born with the moral corruption of original sin will commit actual sin? Is it possible to *avoid* actual sin as (we might think) it is possible for the person disposed to alcoholism to avoid becoming an alcoholic? Following others in the Reformed tradition, I do not think so. Rather, the moral corruption of original sin makes it inevitable that all fallen human beings will actually sin on at least one occasion *if they live long enough and are the proper subject of moral states and properties.* This condition is important: some human beings born with original sin will not live long enough if they die prematurely. Others may not be the proper subject of moral states and properties, in which case they cannot commit actual sins for which they are responsible and culpable. For instance, babes in arms are not capable of actual sin because they are not moral agents, strictly speaking. Similarly, those who are born severely mentally impaired may not be the proper subjects for the ascription of moral states and properties.

This condition may be thought too strong. For it may be thought babies may have moral states for all we know, just as at least some individuals who are mentally impaired may have moral states as well (though perhaps not the *severely* mentally impaired). If that is right, then we can weaken our condition to something like this: babes in arms and at least some that are mentally impaired are not the *appropriate* subjects for the ascription of moral responsibility and culpability. Then we could run the claim about the inevitability of actual sin (other things being equal) with the relevant change thus: *the moral corruption of original sin makes it inevitable that all fallen human beings will actually sin on at least one occasion, if they live long enough and are appropriate subjects for the ascription of moral responsibility and culpability.* The underlying assumption is something like this: where we are not clear that an entity is the subject of moral states and properties, it is a good idea to give such an entity the moral benefit of the doubt. This means not ascribing to such entities moral responsibility and culpability for their actions—something we often do when interacting with nonhuman animals.

But this leaves open the question of why it is that those who possess original sin but do not actually sin are condemned. For if, on this view, possession of the moral property of original sin is not a state that entails culpability or original guilt, it is difficult to see why those like babes in arms or the severely mentally impaired would be condemned for possession of original sin alone.

There are actually two issues here, and it is important not to conflate them. The first one is the matter of why, on this view, possession of original sin yields condemnation irrespective of actual sin. The answer to this issue is that possession of original sin will lead to death and exclusion from the presence of God without the application of the relevant treatment—in this case, salvation through Christ.

The Swiss Magisterial Reformer Huldrych Zwingli held this sort of view. He writes, "Original sin, as it is in the children of Adam, is not properly sin . . . for it is not a misdeed contrary to law. It is, therefore, properly a disease and condition—a disease, because just as he fell through self-love, so do we also; a condition, because just as he became a slave and liable to death, so also are we both slaves and children of wrath . . . and liable to death."[16] The language of "disease" may be unhelpful and has often led to misunderstanding, as if Zwingli's view is tantamount to a denial of original sin as moral corruption. That seems to me to be a mistaken interpretation of his doctrine.[17]

---

[16] Huldrych Zwingli, *"Account of the Faith to Charles V,"* in *On Providence and Other Essays*, ed. Samuel Macauley Jackson (1922; repr., Durham, N.C.: Labyrinth, 1983), 40. I discuss this in greater detail in Crisp, "Retrieving Zwingli's Doctrine of Original Sin," *Journal of Reformed Theology* 10, no. 4 (2016): 1–21. Calvin defines original sin as a "hereditary depravity and corruption of our nature, diffused into all parts of the soul, which first makes us liable to God's wrath, and then also brings forth in us those works which Scripture calls 'the works of the flesh' [Gal 5:19]. And this is properly what Paul often calls sin" (*Institutes of the Christian Religion*, ed. John T. McNeill, trans. Ford Lewis Battles, Library of Christian Classics 20–21 [1559; repr., Philadelphia: Westminster, 1960], 2.1.8, 251). Though different from Zwingli, Calvin's position is much closer in tone than some later Reformed writings on the subject. What is more, Calvin, like Zwingli, denies that we bear original guilt. See also R. Michael Allen's treatment of Calvin's "restrained" doctrine of original sin in "Calvin's Christ: A Dogmatic Matrix for Discussion of Christ's Human Nature," *International Journal of Systematic Theology* 9, no. 4 (2007): 382–97, in which he corrects several misconceptions regarding other Reformed accounts of the doctrine—including some of my earlier work on the topic.

[17] I argue this at length in "Retrieving Zwingli's Doctrine of Original Sin." A classic example of someone who thinks Zwingli's view on original sin is unorthodox is the great nineteenth-century historian of doctrine Philip Schaff. He writes, "Zwingli departed from the Augustinian and Catholic system, and prepared the way for Arminian and Socinian opinions. He was far from denying the terrible curse of the fall and the fact of original sin; but he regarded original sin as a calamity, a disease, a natural defect, which involves no

But, in any event, irrespective of whether Zwingli's position on the topic is theologically problematic, the comparison between possession of original sin and being born into slavery is instructive. What is more, like Zwingli, it seems to me that original sin makes a person "liable to death" without the interposition of the benefits of Christ's saving work.

This leads me to the second issue, concerning the condemnation of babes in arms and the severely mentally impaired. It is perfectly consistent with the foregoing, and with Augustine and a number of other theologians who follow him in this regard, to say that there may be certain individuals who are passed over by divine grace and finally excluded from the presence of God in the eschaton—including some babes in arms and severely mentally impaired individuals. Original sin would then be the mechanism by means of which God's decision in preterition is brought about in time. However, I find such a view morally repulsive. With theologians like the nineteenth-century Presbyterian divine William Shedd, I think that God can elect babes in arms that die in infancy and the severely mentally impaired as a class and absent faith, so that the possession of original sin, which would normally lead to condemnation without the interposition of the benefits of Christ's saving work, does not lead to this conclusion in these limit cases.[18] It does not lead to this conclusion because such individuals are incapable of faith as well as being incapable of acting in a way that is consistent with the ascription of moral responsibility and culpability. So there is good reason for God to elect them without faith, as a class, and on the basis of Christ's work.

Coda

This completes the constructive section of the chapter, and the presentation of the *moderate Reformed doctrine of original sin*. We can sum up our findings as follows:

(1) All human beings after the first primal sin (barring Christ) possess original sin.
(2) Original sin is an inherited corruption of nature, a condition that every fallen human being possesses from the first moment of generation.

---

personal guilt, and is not punishable until it reveals itself in actual transgression." Schaff, *History of the Christian Church*, vol. 8, *Modern Christianity. The Swiss Reformation*, 3rd ed. (1910; repr., Grand Rapids: Eerdmans, 1976), §29.

[18] See William G. T. Shedd, *Dogmatic Theology*, ed. Alan Gomes, 3rd ed. (1888; repr., Philipsburg, N.J.: Presbyterian and Reformed, 2003). I discuss Shedd's views in greater detail in *An American Augustinian: Sin and Salvation in the Dogmatic Theology of William G. T. Shedd* (Milton Keynes: Paternoster; Eugene, Ore.: Wipf and Stock, 2007).

(3) Fallen humans are not culpable for being generated with this morally viti-
    ated condition.

(4) Fallen humans are not culpable for the primal sin, either. That is, they do
    not bear original guilt (i.e., the guilt of the sin of some putative first human
    pair or human community being imputed to them along with original sin).

(5) This morally vitiated condition normally inevitably yields actual sin. That
    is, a person born with this defect will normally inevitably commit actual sin
    on at least one occasion provided that person lives long enough to be able
    to commit such sin. (The caveat "normally" indicates that there are limit
    cases that are exceptions to this claim, including the limit cases discussed
    above—e.g., infants that die before maturity and the severely mentally
    impaired.)

(6) Fallen human beings are culpable for their actual sin and condemned for it,
    in the absence of atonement.

(7) Possession of original sin leads to death and separation from God irrespec-
    tive of actual sin.[19]

More would need to be said in a complete account of this version of the
doctrine. I have only been able to give an outline of it here. Nevertheless,
this dogmatic sketch should provide some understanding of the form and
theological implications of this moderate Reformed doctrine of original sin.

Some may worry that this reasoning seems entirely philosophical and
without biblical warrant. That is a good worry to have when doing Christian
theology. But it is to mistake the kind of reasoning presented here. I am not
offering a biblical warrant for a particular doctrine of original sin, though
I think the doctrine I have outlined can be supported from Scripture. We
might say that this is an instance of a chapter on doctrinal criticism, not in
biblical theology or exegesis. To this end, I have attempted to provide a moderate account of original sin that is consistent with one strand of the Christian tradition (the Reformed tradition, broadly construed), though it is not
the sort of view often reported as the Reformed doctrine of original sin. It is
a minority report, though, as I have tried to indicate, not without theological
support from at least one of the Magisterial Reformers (Zwingli) and several
Reformed symbols (the Belgic Confession and the Articles of Religion, as
well as the Scots Confession). I am also concerned with finding an account
of original sin that avoids some of the significant drawbacks to those versions of the doctrine that presume original sin is imputed from Adam to me,

---

[19] Recall that possession of original sin renders the bearer unfit for the presence of God
and liable to be disbarred from the goods associated with the life to come in the presence of
God, without the interposition of some act of atonement.

and that I am guilty of Adam's sin—doctrines common among Reformed divines. Finally, I am interested in finding a doctrine that has ecumenical promise. Both Roman Catholic and Orthodox accounts of original sin do not include a doctrine of original guilt and are privative in nature: original sin is described as the privation of a state of original justice or righteousness, or as the loss of some morally exalted state with which the aboriginal human pair were created. The doctrine outlined here is much closer to this sort of view than those versions of the doctrine that conceive of original sin as a moral corruption that is imputed to all humanity post-Adam, alongside the imputation of original guilt. For those concerned to find theological convergence between the different communions of the body of Christ, this may also be a reason for taking seriously the argument I have presented.

In closing, two things remain to be done: first, and picking up on some remarks in the first section of the chapter, to give some account of how the argument I have set out is commensurate with a (circumscribed) range of views on evolutionary history; second, to provide some account of the bearing of my argument upon the three core dogmatic claims of traditional doctrines of original sin given at the beginning of the constructive part of the chapter.

As to the first matter, as I have summarized it, the moderate Reformed doctrine withholds judgment about whether there is a specially created aboriginal human pair from whom all subsequent human beings are descended. So it does not *presume* monogenism, the view that humans are descended from an aboriginal pair, which is a worry raised by a number of those working on evolutionary history today—though it is consistent with it. It also prescinds from any judgment about the origin of human suffering and misery, and whether nature is created "red in tooth and claw." This is the first worry contained within the objection from evolutionary history. In other words, the doctrine is consistent with more than one story about both these worries, and that (it seems to me) is a strength rather than a weakness.

We come to the second matter, which was to provide some account of the bearing of my argument upon the three core dogmatic claims of traditional doctrines of original sin given at the beginning of the constructive part of the chapter. Recall that the three claims in question were: *first*, that there was an original pair from whom we are all descended; *second*, that this pair committed the primal sin that adversely affects all their offspring; and *third*, that all human beings after the fall of the original pair are in need of salvation, without which they will perish.

To my mind it is the third of these claims that is dogmatically most fundamental. Human beings are sinners in need of salvation in Christ. Without this claim the gospel is lost. The first two claims have to do with a particular construal of the Eden story of Genesis 1–3, and the echoes of this in New Testament Adam Christology in places like Romans 5 and 1 Corinthians 15 that are common in precritical accounts of original sin. Although I have used the language of an original human community rather than an aboriginal pair, there are human origins scenarios that provide for a pair from whom all modern humans are descended that is consistent with the objection from evolutionary history.[20] The doctrine presented here is consistent with either of these views, for—to repeat—it prescinds from judgment on these matters. That is, it is consistent with either an evolutionary history that provides for some first human community from which all modern humans are descended, or an evolutionary history that provides for some aboriginal human pair from whom all modern humans are descended. This, it seems to me, is one important benefit of having an open-textured doctrine of original sin commensurate with a range of views on evolutionary history, which is the sort of view I have been trying to commend.

[20] See, e.g., Keith B. Miller, ed., *Perspectives on an Evolving Creation* (Grand Rapids: Eerdmans, 2003), esp. the papers in section 2; and Robin Collins' essay, "Evolution and Original Sin," 469–501. See also the contributions by John Walton and Denis Lamoureux in *Four Views on the Historical Adam*, ed. Matthew Barrett and Ardel B. Caneday (Grand Rapids: Zondervan Academic, 2014). At a more popular level, see the different views outlined by Deborah Haarsma and Loren Haarsma in *Origins: Christian Perspectives on Creation, Evolution, and Intelligent Design*, rev. ed. (Grand Rapids: Faith Alive Christian Resources, 2011).

8

Virgin Birth

Very Flesh, Yet Spirit too;
Uncreated, and yet born;
God-and-Man in one agreed;
Very-Life-in-Death indeed,
Fruit of God and Mary's seed;
At once impassible and torn
By pain and suffering here below;
Jesus Christ, whom as our Lord we know.

Ignatius of Antioch[1]

In this chapter we turn from diagnosing the problem of human sin, given the actual state of affairs God has created, to considering the solution to this malaise in Christ's reconciling work, beginning with the doctrine of the incarnation. We shall consider several key issues in setting forth such an account. The first of these has to do with the event by means of which God the Son becomes incarnate—namely, the virginal conception of Christ. This has been the subject of sustained criticism in modern theology, though it is a tenet of the catholic faith expressed in the ecumenical creeds and in the confessions of particular branches of the church as well. In my earlier work I offered a defense of the traditional doctrine of the virginal conception of Christ.[2] This has been challenged by the British New Testament scholar Andrew Lincoln in an essay and subsequent monograph on the doctrine.[3] In this chapter I shall offer a sustained response to Lincoln's work.

---

[1] *Epistle to the Ephesians 7*, in *Early Christian Writings: The Apostolic Fathers*, trans. Maxwell Staniforth and Andrew Louth (1968; repr., Harmondsworth: Penguin Books, 1987), 63.

[2] Oliver D. Crisp, *God Incarnate: Explorations in Christology* (London: T&T Clark, 2009), chs. 4–5.

[3] Andrew T. Lincoln, *Born of a Virgin? Reconceiving Jesus in the Bible, Tradition, and Theology* (Grand Rapids: Eerdmans, 2013). See also his earlier essay "'Born of the Virgin

Preamble

In an intriguing essay about the methodology of historical biblical criticism, the Reformation historian David Steinmetz writes that an important difference between historical-critical exegesis of the Bible and the traditional exegesis of the church is that "traditional exegesis is quite willing to read earlier parts of the Bible in light of later developments, while historical criticism is very reluctant to do anything of the kind."[4] Whereas historical biblical critics are concerned to set texts into their own time and place in order to avoid anachronism, traditional exegetes do the opposite, presuming "no one can properly understand earlier developments in the biblical story unless one reads them in light of later."[5] What one guild treats as anachronism, the other treats as appropriate reflection on earlier material in light of further data.

Steinmetz goes on to say that historians are always engaged in writing what he calls "second narratives." In detective fiction readers are often treated to a plot in which the clues are uncovered piecemeal as the story unfolds. This is what he calls the "first narrative." It is usually only in the final denouement of the first narrative that we come to understand how the different, apparently inconsequential, and disparate pieces of information explained in passing in the course of the evolving mystery add up to one whole account. In this closing act, the detective reveals the truth about how the crime was perpetrated and by whom. This is what Steinmetz means by the second narrative, which makes sense of the first, providing meaning and coherence to the diverse bits of evidence uncovered along the way.

In his recent work on the virgin birth, the British New Testament scholar Andrew Lincoln treats us to a "second narrative" reading of the relevant biblical and postbiblical texts that have to do with this important Christian doctrine.[6] In his second narrative, Lincoln purports to show that a revisionist account of the incarnation, one that does not include a concept of virgin birth, is to be preferred to the traditional way of thinking about this

---

Mary': Creedal Affirmation and Critical Reading," in *Christology and Scripture: Interdisciplinary Perspectives*, ed. Andrew T. Lincoln and Angus Paddison (London: T&T Clark, 2008), 84–103, which showcases some of the themes developed more fully in his subsequent monograph.

  [4] David C. Steinmetz, "Uncovering a Second Narrative: Detective Fiction and the Construction of Historical Method," in *The Art of Reading Scripture*, ed. Ellen F. Davis and Richard B. Hays (Grand Rapids: Eerdmans, 2003), 54.

  [5] Steinmetz, "Uncovering a Second Narrative," 54.

  [6] Lincoln, *Born of a Virgin?* and "Born of the Virgin Mary."

doctrine. As he puts it at the close of his study, "It would be a great pity to get so caught up in debate over the means of incarnation that we lose sight of the still astonishing and potentially life-changing truth claim that in the fully human life of Jesus of Nazareth, son of Joseph and Mary, and for the sake of humanity and the world God became incarnate."[7]

In this chapter I will argue that the theological reasons Lincoln gives for revising the traditional doctrine of the virgin birth are insufficient. He has not demonstrated that the traditional doctrine of the virgin birth should be overturned in favor of his second narrative. The argument has four sections. In the first I outline a version of the traditional doctrine of the virgin birth, drawing on my own previous work on the topic. Then in a second section I assess what I take to be the most significant theological reasons Lincoln provides for departing from this traditional view of the virgin birth. Section three offers an assessment of Lincoln's strategy. Finally, I provide some reflections on the wider issues Lincoln's second narrative raises for those working in biblical studies and theology.

On the Traditional Doctrine of the Virgin Birth

Let me begin by giving some account of the traditional doctrine of the virgin birth. [8] It is a theological commonplace to incorporate within the notion of "the virgin birth" the virginal conception, gestation, and birth of Christ by means of synecdoche. I will follow this convention here. I will also refer to *the traditional doctrine of the virgin birth*, or TVB for short, and *the dogma of the virgin birth*. By the TVB, I just mean the historic Christian view of the virgin birth expressed in places like the Nicene Creed: "For us and for our salvation he came down from heaven; he became incarnate by the Holy Spirit and the virgin Mary, and was made human."[9] This creedal expression is one way in which the dogma of the virgin birth has been confessed by the church catholic. I take it that dogmas are particular doctrines that have a formal definition or that have a particular canonical form as they are expressed in creedal and confessional documents of the church. Dogmas have a normative status in Christian theology that mere Christian doctrines do not. They rise above mere doctrine, so to speak, being part of the confession of the church.

---

[7] Lincoln, *Born of a Virgin?* 302.

[8] This section draws on arguments first presented in my earlier work in *God Incarnate*, chs. 4–5.

[9] This translation can be found on the website of the Christian Reformed Church: https://www.crcna.org/welcome/beliefs/creeds/nicene-creed.

Although not all churches have a place for formal creeds and confessions, it is true to say that the vast majority of Christian churches do have a place for dogma (or something very like it) and do treat certain doctrines as part of the conceptual core of the faith, such as the Trinity, incarnation, and atonement.[10] The virgin birth is a doctrine that has such a dogmatic form. It is universally confessed among the churches of the catholic faith as part of the Nicene Creed and is, in fact, a very ancient doctrine that can be traced back to the subapostolic period (see, for example, the hymn fragment cited as the epigram to this chapter, from the work of Ignatius of Antioch) and into the New Testament itself (in the birth narratives of Matthew and Luke).

That said, the contentious issue at the heart of the traditional doctrine of the virgin birth is not the manner of Christ's gestation or parturition, but his generation. More specifically, the thing that is theologically remarkable about Christ's generation is that his human nature is said to be generated by means of a miracle—the bringing about of the zygote of Jesus of Nazareth in the womb of the Virgin via the agency of the Holy Spirit.[11] In contemporary biological terms, the major theological issue facing defenders of the TVB is the generation of new genetic material, specifically the Y chromosomes requisite to the production of a human male.[12] It is no part of the traditional doctrine that the Holy Spirit is the male parent of the human nature of Christ, for, to put it bluntly, the Holy Spirit does not impregnate the Virgin. Nor is it the case according to the traditional doctrine that the Virgin is merely the conduit by means of which God brings about a whole human male zygote *ex novo*, and without any genetic contribution from the Virgin. Instead, the

---

[10] Thus, Orthodox, Roman Catholic, Lutheran, Reformed, Anglican, and at least some Baptist churches (e.g., those who subscribe to the 1689 London Baptist Confession of Faith).

[11] For present purposes I shall not enter into debate about whether zygotes are human natures or human beings, or whether they are the matter from which human natures or human persons develop. I have discussed this elsewhere in *God Incarnate*, ch. 5.

[12] There is theological debate about the gestation of Christ's human nature. Thomas Aquinas thinks Christ's human nature is fully formed in the womb of the Virgin from the get-go yet gestates for nine months. Thus, Aquinas: "The body's very formation [i.e., Christ's body] in which conception principally consists, was instantaneous, for two reasons. First, because of the infinite power of the agent, viz. the Holy Ghost, by whom Christ's body was formed. . . . Secondly, on the part of the Person of the Son, whose body was being formed. For it was unbecoming that He should take to Himself a body as yet unformed. . . . Therefore in the first instant in which the various parts of the matter were united together in the place of generation, Christ's body was both perfectly formed and assumed" (*Summa theologiae* 3a.Q.33, art. 1, trans. Brothers of the English Dominican Province). However, those who are not committed to Aquinas' Aristotelian biology may be less enthusiastic about his reasons for thinking that Christ's human body must be fully formed prior to its assumption.

traditional doctrine is that the Virgin is *Theotokos*. As the God Bearer, she is the one whose gamete is miraculously fertilized by the action of the Holy Spirit so that her womb may bear God Incarnate. Normally, the Y chromosome necessary for the act of syngamy by which the fused male and female gametes produce a genetically unique male zygote is supplied by the male seed. In the case of Christ, there was no male gamete as such because no male seed was involved. Nevertheless, the genetic material that would normally be supplied by a male gamete was miraculously introduced to the ovum of the Virgin, resulting in syngamy, and the generation of the zygote that is or becomes Christ's human nature.[13] How this "missing" genetic material was provided by the Holy Spirit is unknown, although it is possible that he generates it specifically for the purpose of the virginal conception.[14]

Of course, the modern biological construal of the virginal conception of Christ just sketched is entirely speculative; the precise biological conditions necessary for the virginal conception of Christ are no part of the TVB, and, unsurprisingly, much premodern theologizing about the virgin birth that attempts similar speculation does so in accordance with the deliverances of premodern biology.[15] Sometimes much is made of this point. (Lincoln's study is no exception in this regard.) However, given that the doctrine of the virgin birth is primarily concerned with demarcating the virginal conception of Christ's human nature as a miracle brought about by the Holy Spirit, and not with the biological story that explains how that may have occurred (for all we know), it is immaterial from the point of view of dogmatic theology[16]

---

[13] There is an interesting literature that bears upon this topic. See, for example, R. J. Berry, "The Virgin Birth of Christ," *Science and Christian Belief* 8 (1996): 101–10; Norman M. Ford, *When Did I Begin?* (Cambridge: Cambridge University Press, 1988); David Albert Jones, *The Soul of the Embryo: An Enquiry into the Status of the Human Embryo in the Christian Tradition* (London: Continuum, 2004); Arthur Peacocke, "DNA of Our DNA," in *The Birth of Jesus, Biblical and Theological Reflections*, ed. George J. Brooke (Edinburgh: T&T Clark, 2000); and Joseph Donceel, "Immediate Animation and Delayed Hominization," *Theological Studies* 31 (1970): 76–105.

[14] Is the "missing" genetic material needed to produce a human male zygote generated out of nothing by the Spirit? Is it formed from existing matter? I have no idea. I have already noted that the traditional doctrine precludes the option of the introduction of a human male gamete by means of normal reproductive processes. But on the question of the manner in which the Holy Spirit actually introduces the "missing" genetic material required to generate the human nature of Christ in the Virgin's womb, the dogmatic tradition is silent.

[15] David Albert Jones provides an interesting account of premodern biology in this regard. See *Soul of the Embryo*.

[16] That is, with respect to the dogma, or the formal, confessional aspect of the doctrine of the virgin birth of Christ.

what the ancients thought about human conception or about the miraculous generation of Christ's human nature in particular. For the dogma of the virgin birth is consistent with more than one biological story about how the virginal conception of Christ came about.

The doctrine of the virgin birth has historically been thought to be a bulwark against docetism (the notion that Christ only appeared to be human) and adoptionism (the view that the Word took possession of an existing human person), as well as being a way of reinforcing commitment to Christ's sinlessness (for in the virginal conception, the Holy Spirit ensures that the zygote formed in the Virgin's womb is without sin). However, none of these reasons for holding to the TVB seem to me to be decisive. Here is why: God could bring about an incarnation without the virginal conception of Christ by means of normal human reproductive processes. There is nothing to prevent God from bringing this about—no lack of power, no obstacle to his doing so. He can ensure that the self-same result obtains by means of an incarnation without virgin birth as occurs in the incarnation by means of a virgin birth. For in each case what happens is that a human nature is formed in the womb of Mary Theotokos that is assumed by a divine person. The only relevant difference is the manner in which the human nature is generated, whether by normal biological reproduction or by means of a miracle.

Well then, suppose Jesus of Nazareth was the product of the union between Joseph and Mary, as Lincoln believes. Nothing could be more "fleshly," more "real," than the generation of a human being through normal human reproduction. This would seem to be sufficient to rebut docetism. What about adoptionism? Suppose that the Holy Spirit ensures that the zygote formed through the fusion of Joseph and Mary's gametes is a suitable candidate for assumption by a divine person. Add to this the idea that at the very moment when a human being would normally be formed in utero (whenever that may be), the human nature of Christ is assumed by the Word. That seems to be sufficient to safeguard against adoptionism. We could apply similar reasoning to the case of the sinlessness of Christ. The Holy Spirit ensures the zygote formed by the union of the gametes of Joseph and Mary is without sin so that the Word may assume it.

Although what we might call a No-Virgin-Birth version of the doctrine of the incarnation (hereinafter NVB doctrine) could meet these ancient worries about the human nature of Christ, like Anselm of Canterbury, I think that the doctrine of the virgin birth is a fitting or suitable means by which

Christ's human nature is generated.[17] It is a sign that indicates this particular individual is marked out in the purposes of God (as happened in a similar fashion with John the Baptist and other Old Testament characters like Isaac). I have already indicated that God *could* have brought about the incarnation without a virgin birth. That does not seem to me to be particularly controversial. However, the dogma of the virgin birth that is confessed by catholic Christians conveys that *in point of fact* this is not how God did bring about the incarnation.

A doctrine that has the status of a dogma, such as the virgin birth, has deep roots in the Christian tradition. Indeed, as has already been intimated, it is often thought that dogma is part of the conceptual core of the faith. Whether we think that the virgin birth is part of the conceptual core of the faith might be disputed, of course, and I take it that this is part of Lincoln's point. However, it seems at the very least that the virgin birth is a doctrine that has a long history, going back to the earliest times in the life of the church. It is also indisputably part of the confessional deposit of the church catholic that all Christians (or almost all) confess. That is, it is a dogma in the sense I am using that term, whether or not one thinks that all dogmas are part of the conceptual core of the faith.[18] For these reasons it seems to me that there must be very good theological reasons for entertaining the idea that such a doctrine should be discarded. Andrew Lincoln thinks he has provided such reasons; it is his argument to which we turn next.

Lincoln's Revisionist Account of the Incarnation

At the heart of Lincoln's critique of the TVB is the claim that there are different and incommensurate accounts of the incarnation in the biblical texts. He maintains that later church tradition takes one of these accounts—the virgin birth story—and canonizes it, effectively writing out of church history the alternative position. This alternative presumes Christ's human nature was

[17] See Anselm, *On the Virginal Conception and Original Sin,* in *Anselm: Basic Writings,* ed. and trans. Thomas Williams (Indianapolis: Hackett, 2007), 327–60.

[18] How could a dogma not be part of the conceptual core of the faith? I suppose Lincoln's defenders might suggest something like this: the conceptual core of the faith may not entirely overlap with what has in fact been deemed dogma in this history of the church. It may be that some church council has mistakenly canonized a doctrine, or given it a formal dogmatic status that it should not have because it is not in fact part of the conceptual core of the faith. This is like saying a particular society may make slavery legal although, in fact, it is a great injustice. The society in question has passed into law something that is not just, though the lawmakers of the time thought it was just.

generated via the sexual union of Joseph and Mary. It is his contention that this NVB doctrine is a better and more plausible understanding of the incarnation than that offered by the TVB.[19]

Over the course of the first half of his study, Lincoln develops the aspect of his "second narrative" that focuses on the biblical tradition. Here is a précis of some of the main elements: The birth narratives are the only clear reference to a virgin birth in the New Testament. They appear similar in structure to the miraculous birth stories of other ancient heroes or gods and appear to be given in order to provide Christ with a suitably supernatural etiology, which is why they are unlike much Jewish literature in this respect. Like other such ancient birth stories, the birth narratives contain elements that are clearly fictional—the miraculous birth being the most important of these. It is often asserted that the rest of the New Testament is silent on the matter of Christ's virgin birth. Lincoln denies this. He maintains that there is evidence of a NVB account of the incarnation elsewhere in some of the earlier material of the New Testament. Thus Paul in the Epistle to the Romans indicates that Christ had a normal human birth. He is said to be the seed of David "according to the flesh," who was "declared to be Son of God with power according to the spirit of holiness by resurrection from the dead" (Rom 1:3-4). There is even evidence of this NVB tradition in Luke-Acts alongside the birth narratives. Although Luke's narrative begins with an account of the virgin birth, Lincoln offers a critical analysis of elements in the story that seem at odds with this. (In this connection he mentions things like the emphasis on Joseph's credentials as a descendant of David when he is not the biological father of Jesus, and the way in which the birth narrative is ignored in other elements of the story, such as the inclusion of both Mary and Joseph as the "parents" of Jesus to whom Simeon addresses himself in Luke 2:26-27.) He goes on to suggest that the reference to Joseph in Luke's genealogy is also suspicious. The text reads, "He was the son (as was thought [ἐνομίζετο]) of Joseph son of Heli" (Luke 3:23b). But, says Lincoln, the parenthetical remark in this passage is sufficiently ambiguous to leave doubt in the reader's mind.[20] Lincoln concludes by saying, "It is insufficient simply to conclude that the non-historicity of the virgin birth cannot be proven. The

---

[19] This is not the only possible alternative explanation of Christ's generation, of course, and Lincoln discusses other views. One of these is the widely reported notion that Christ was the son of the union between the Roman soldier Panthera and Mary. Lincoln thinks that the story of Christ being the natural biological son of Joseph is a more likely explanation than the story of Panthera, however.

[20] Lincoln, *Born of a Virgin?* 117–18.

issue is not one of proof but of probabilities." It is his judgment that "the balance of probabilities appears to be against the virgin birth belonging to the earliest stratum of Christian memories about Jesus' life and for it being an elaboration of affirmations about Jesus based on belief in the resurrection."[21]

I do not propose to enter into detailed debate about the merits of Lincoln's argument in favor of the view that the NVB material he purports to find in the New Testament should be privileged over the TVB material of the birth narratives. Suffice it to say, it is not at all obvious to this reader that the story of Christ's miraculous birth recorded in Matthew and Luke should be understood to be a piece of creative fiction. Nor is it clear to me that one must understand references to the "seed of David" as offering a NVB alternative to the birth narratives. It does not appear to me contrived to see the designation "seed of David" merely as a way of identifying Christ with the Davidic line, as the messiah, much as one might see the designation "Son of Adam" or "Daughter of Eve" in the *Chronicles of Narnia* as a way of identifying a person as a human, rather than satyr, faun, or beaver. The designation "Son of Adam" or "Daughter of Eve" doesn't mean that Edmund or Lucy, of whomever, is *literally* a son or daughter of some putative first human pair. The idea is that they are descendants of Adam and Eve; they belong to the genealogical lineage of Adam and Eve. I suggest one could understand the designation "seed of David" in a similar manner as it is applied to Christ. Moreover, the supposed minority report preserved in Luke's narrative suggests a very odd arrangement, where the author has preserved a NVB account alongside a TVB account without indication of this tension aside from hints and insinuations. Is it not a simpler explanation of this particular narrative, whose author is often thought to be very particular in his recording of other historical events, to suppose that he is simply registering the fact that Joseph was widely understood to be Jesus' biological father though in fact he was not?[22]

Rather than focusing in detail on whether Lincoln is right in his account of the New Testament data—that is, rather than weighing in on the question of whether or not he has made a sound hermeneutical case for his particular reading of the New Testament materials—let us focus on the theological upshot of his position. What theological reason does Lincoln provide for his

---

[21] Lincoln, "Born of the Virgin Mary," 95.

[22] In Charles Dickens' classic tale *Great Expectations*, Pip believes his sponsor is Miss Havisham, though it transpires the convict Magwitch is his secret benefactor. The novel turns on this case of mistaken identity. I suppose something like this is conveyed by Luke. Jesus was supposed to be the biological son of Joseph, but the Lukan narrative explains how we know he was not; it is another case of mistaken identity.

second narrative? There are at least six reasons that I can find in his study. These are as follows: the question of the genre and history of the biblical birth narratives, whether the virgin birth is necessary for the incarnation, problems with the metaphysical assumptions underpinning the traditional doctrine, the biological continuity of Christ with the rest of humanity, the changing function of the doctrine of the virginal conception, and Lincoln's "critical loyalty" to the church's creedal tradition. We will consider each of these in turn.

The question of the genre and history of the birth narratives

Lincoln maintains that the New Testament is "the word of God through the words of humans."[23] Nevertheless, he inveighs against theologians (like the present writer) who think that the virgin birth should be accepted on the grounds that it is taught in Scripture because this "confuses what is at stake. That they [the birth narratives] are part of canonical Scripture tells us nothing about their literary genre and therefore what sort of history they may or may not contain."[24] What is more, trusting them "as divine revelation entails trusting their witness to the significance of Jesus and does not necessarily mean taking them literally as straightforward, historically accurate accounts."[25] Interestingly, Lincoln goes on to indicate that he does not want to concede ground to those who think that "whether the account is reliable history or not, it still would be expressing a truth about Christ."[26] On his way of thinking, that would be to split the Bible into two parts, dealing with spiritual religion on the one hand and matters of science and history on the other. This he deems unacceptable.[27] Yet he is quite prepared to contemplate the prospect that the birth narratives are not reporting on historical events but are largely works of fiction constructed to resemble ancient birth stories of other heroic figures, such as Moses or Caesar.

This indicates an underlying concern with the way in which Lincoln's second narrative addresses matters of theological authority. In short, he does not provide the reader with a clear account of how his treatment of the text is consistent with a view of it as Scripture. More specifically, it does look like his treatment of the birth narratives is an instance of the view that "whether the account is reliable history or not, it still would be expressing a truth about

[23] Lincoln, *Born of a Virgin?* 244.
[24] Lincoln, *Born of a Virgin?* 244. In this course of this section of the work, Lincoln takes issue with my presentation of the virgin birth in *God Incarnate*.
[25] Lincoln, *Born of a Virgin?* 244.
[26] Lincoln, *Born of a Virgin?* 245.
[27] Lincoln, *Born of a Virgin?*

Christ." So it is difficult to resist the conclusion that he is speaking out of both sides of his mouth on this matter.

This is only underlined when he says things like this: "By holding together both the notion of a virginal conception and the assumption that Joseph was Jesus' biological father, Luke reinforces the dialogical and polyphonic nature of scriptural truth about the significance of what God has done and is doing in Christ."[28] It is difficult to know what Lincoln means by the "dialogical and polyphonic nature of scriptural truth" here. For the TVB and the NVB doctrines are not two sides of one truth, or two aspects of one philosophical dialectic. They are two incommensurate explanations of the same event— namely, the incarnation. Unless Lincoln thinks that ancient writers had no problem with denying the law of the excluded middle, according to which either a proposition is true or its negation is true, then it is difficult to see how his claim can be an accurate account of the biblical material. I suppose the author of Luke and the fathers of the early church could have failed to see that Luke's gospel preserves both a TVB and NVB account, just as the early church could have failed to see that there are traces of a NVB doctrine elsewhere in the New Testament. But that does not seem to be very likely, and certainly less likely than the prospect that after two thousand years of church history, Lincoln has uncovered what so many before him have missed.

Whether the virgin birth is a necessary means for incarnation

A second theological reason for Lincoln's revisionist second narrative is found in his argument that the virgin birth is not necessary for an incarnation. The two doctrines can be prized apart so that we may speak of an incarnation independent of a virgin birth. It is a mistake to conflate these two matters.[29] I have already indicated that I am in full agreement with this claim. The incarnation did not have to be brought about by a virginal conception. However, the TVB states that this is, as a matter of fact, how God ordained things. We might say that it is a fitting but by no means necessary means of incarnation.[30] In and of itself, the idea that a virgin birth is not necessary for

---

[28] Lincoln, *Born of a Virgin?* 250. This is not an isolated text but reflects a concern that informs the argument of the book as a whole.

[29] He writes of the "theological mistake" of "treating the virgin birth as the necessary mechanism for the incarnation." Lincoln, *Born of a Virgin?* 251.

[30] In dealing with what he calls Crisp's "olive branch" on this matter (that is, my claim that the incarnation does not require a virgin birth, all things considered), Lincoln says that there is a significant difference between my view, which assumes the authority of Scripture and the creeds, and "a theological perspective that pays greater attention to the historical

the incarnation does nothing to show that there was, in fact, no virgin birth. Lincoln thinks that he has shown the TVB is not viable for Christian theology today on other grounds. But since all sides can agree that a virgin birth is not necessary for the incarnation, it is not clear what (if any) advantage this line of reasoning gives him.

Problems with the metaphysical assumptions underpinning the traditional doctrine

This brings us to matter of the philosophical categories that undergird the TVB as it is expressed in the creedal tradition. In the course of his comments on the need to distinguish the TVB from the doctrine of the incarnation construed along NVB lines, Lincoln has something to say about the metaphysics used by defenders of the TVB.[31] On the sort of TVB envisaged by theologians like the present author, the doctrine of the incarnation and virgin birth has "such questionable assumptions as that if Christ is a divine person, he cannot be a human person, though he has a human nature, and that a human nature is itself composed of two substances, body and soul, the former generated from its parents, the latter created out of nothing by God."[32] He goes on to say this:

> Given contemporary understandings of personal identity and given that "person" as applied to members of the triune God is at best analogical, how much sense does it make to insist on the basis of such problematic ancient assumptions that the human Jesus was not a person, because that would be incompatible with him also being the person of the Word of the Son, and then to struggle to indicate how Jesus had sufficient genetic traits to be somehow human without being a person?[33]

What is needed, Lincoln believes, is an approach "that is not dismissive of serious contemporary biblical criticism" and that takes account of contemporary knowledge without being "restricted to its particular categories

---

conditionedness of both the Bible and the credal traditions" (*Born of a Virgin?* 273–74.) In fairness, my earlier work on this topic may have been a bit too flat-footed in this regard. But it is difficult to see how Lincoln's alternative is a better one when he does not appear to have provided his readers with a clear way of understanding the Bible's authority in this matter.

[31] Once more, it is the present author that Lincoln is addressing at this juncture. See *Born of a Virgin?* 274–75.

[32] Lincoln, *Born of a Virgin?* 274.

[33] Lincoln, *Born of a Virgin?* 274.

and formulations, following Chalcedon's attempt to safeguard the mystery of Christ being both fully human and fully divine."[34]

Lincoln is right to suggest that there are a number of different ways of thinking about the metaphysics of the incarnation, and I do not propose to enter into debate about which of the ways of thinking about this matter are the most appropriate, or most helpful, at this particular juncture.[35] However, that is not what is troubling about Lincoln's remarks. Rather, what concerns me is that he seems to be unaware that his comments betray a rather superficial understanding of the TVB, as well as a rather odd view about the metaphysics of human persons. This is all the more surprising given the fact that a stated aim of Lincoln's project is to take account of the theological and historical issues pertaining to the TVB.

On the face of it, Lincoln seems to be saying that Christ is a human person and a divine person. But that is straightforwardly unorthodox: it implies Nestorianism. Of course Christ is a person—that is not in dispute. The issue is whether he is (let us say) *merely* a human person, or a human person *possessed by a divine person*, or a divine person *with a human nature*. Only the last of these three claims is consistent with orthodoxy. So it is difficult to see how a view that endorses this understanding of the two natures doctrine of Chalcedonian Christology can be termed a "questionable assumption."

He also asks how much sense it makes to insist on the basis of these "problematic ancient assumptions" about divine and human personhood as applied to the incarnation "that the human Jesus was not a person, because that would be incompatible with him also being the person of the Word of the Son." It is difficult to know what to say about this aspect of his worry. For it seems to suggest either that Lincoln has a rather cloudy understanding of the two natures doctrine of Chalcedonian Christology, or that he thinks the two natures doctrine is numbered among the "problematic ancient assumptions" to which he refers. The latter explanation seems more likely, and there are numerous modern theologians who are suspicious of the two natures doctrine or even reject it.[36] It may not be surprising that a scholar recommending

---

[34] Lincoln, *Born of a Virgin?* 274.

[35] As they say, "I have views on the matter." But my views are a matter of public record, so I won't repeat myself here.

[36] One of the chapters of Lincoln's study is warm in its praise of Friedrich Schleiermacher in just this respect. There Lincoln characterizes Schleiermacher's contribution to the doctrine of the incarnation as a "helpful case study." In his judgment, Schleiermacher "shows the need for reformulating theology and Christology in light of the problems with the language of earlier doctrinal statements, such as nature, substance and person, and with the traditional metaphysical assumptions behind them" (*Born of a Virgin?* 238). There are

a revisionist account of one important Christian doctrine—namely, the TVB—also recommends a revisionist account of other, related doctrines, including the two natures doctrine. But it is difficult to know how to argue against Lincoln's position at this point because it seems to depend largely on a preference for a different way of approaching the incarnation—including not just the virgin birth but also the two natures doctrine of classical Christology, along with its language of substance, nature, and persons, and the traditional metaphysical assumptions that lie behind these concepts. Labeling some undesirable theological notion a "problematic ancient assumption" provides those with a stake in these matters no reason to abandon the assumptions in question.

On the matter of substance dualism—the view that, as Lincoln puts it, a human nature is itself composed of two substances, body and soul—we may be more brief.[37] Although this is not the only feasible view of human nature, it continues to be a live option in the philosophical literature and has been the mainstay of much historic Christianity up to the present. Lincoln may object to this particular metaphysical view of human nature. But in my judgment the TVB only requires that Christ has a complete human nature—whatever that may be. It doesn't require a version of substance dualism, although arguably some species of this position has been the default traditional view of the matter.[38]

The question of biological continuity with humanity

It may be thought that the genes supplied by miracle in the TVB do not count as "human," in the sense that they are not in continuity with the human race. They are not the product of human evolution, like Mary's ovum. Nevertheless, on the TVB Christ's human nature is in sufficient continuity with the human race to be counted as a member of the race on the basis of the genes he acquires from his mother, which (for all we know) provides a threshold

---

those who would concur with this judgment. But it is by no means the only live option in contemporary systematic theology!

[37] It seems to me that substance dualism is better described as the view according to which a human person is a soul that normally has metaphysical "ownership" over a particular human body. But since this does not affect the point being made here, I leave it to one side.

[38] This is something I argue in *God Incarnate*, ch. 7, where I defend those who wish to adopt a materialist Christology, according to which Christ's human nature has no soul because no human being has a soul distinct from the body.

of genetic material sufficient to be considered human.[39] Let us call this *the threshold condition.*

Lincoln does not like the threshold condition.[40] In a footnote he says, "Apart from the problems of any consensus on determining what such a genetic threshold might be, on this view we would be talking not, as the doctrine of the incarnation does, of the humanity of a specific person, Jesus of Nazareth, who needed a Y chromosome to be a human male, but of an abstract and speculative category of 'humanity' into which he is made to fit."[41] This is puzzling because in the case of the TVB threshold condition, both the Virgin's ovum and the missing genetic material supplied by miracle are ultimately the product of the same divine agent. It is not as if Mary's ovum was inseminated by some nonhuman creature or by means of some nefarious laboratory experiment. The missing genes are a product of divine action just as the generation of the human race is ultimately the product of divine action. If God decides to provide the requisite Y chromosome to generate a human male by means of a miracle as the threshold condition allows, why think that this new genetic material coupled with the genes supplied by the Virgin do not add up to a new human individual after the moment of syngamy? There is no "abstract speculative category" of humanity at work here, just a particular condition that (I suppose) needs to be met in order for the divine agent who brought about the human race to bring about a new human individual by means of a miracle.

The changing function of a virginal conception—from underlining to undermining the doctrine of the incarnation

Worries related to the threshold condition are developed by Lincoln in his claim that the TVB has become a theological liability. When the virgin birth was understood against the background of a premodern understanding of human biology, it served the purpose of *underlining* that the origins of Christ's human nature were miraculous. However, given a modern understanding of

---

[39] This is the view I develop in *God Incarnate.*

[40] Lincoln also thinks that believing Christ was sinless from the moment of generation on the basis of a TVB fails to take with sufficient seriousness the need for Christ to overcome sin through a real historical struggle (*Born of a Virgin?* 283–84). But this quickly runs into theological difficulties. For if Christ's sinlessness is not guaranteed from the moment of generation, how is it guaranteed? And how can God, who is not merely without sin but also incapable of sinning (i.e., is impeccable), be united to a human nature that is not sinless from the get-go?

[41] Lincoln, *Born of a Virgin?* 260n37.

human biology, the virginal conception *undermines* the doctrine of incarnation. Not only does it imply that the normal process of procreation was not appropriate for Christ (which Lincoln regards as a problem rather than an advantage of the traditional doctrine), but it also implies Jesus cannot be fully human because "he had no normal male chromosome, and therefore is not fully at one with the humanity that is to be redeemed."[42]

According to Lincoln, this problem can be traced back to the Council of Chalcedon, which in affirming the TVB introduced a confusion of humanity and divinity—the very thing the council wished to avoid. It "replaces an aspect of normal human existence for Jesus with a divine property." He goes on to say that, unlike other humans, Jesus' "entire being is assumed by and subsists in the Word, the Second Person of the Trinity. That does not mean that the one subject of the life of Jesus is the Word as such but that it is the incarnate Logos who is both divine and human. . . . Because the Word chooses to be identified with this particular human life, Jesus' entire life is divine."[43] But it is this affirmation that the TVB occludes or obscures in its conflation of incarnation with virginal conception. So we are better off preserving the spirit of Chalcedon's two natures doctrine and denying the letter of the TVB.

Aside from the not-insignificant confusion about the nature of the incarnation—for a one-subject account of the incarnation is surely an entailment of the two natures doctrine—it is not clear that Lincoln's way of conceiving the incarnation is consistent with Chalcedon. The two natures doctrine is not merely concerned with the Word *identifying himself* with the particular human life of Jesus of Nazareth. It surely includes this, but as it stands this is insufficient for a two natures doctrine. For it is consistent with a much weaker view of the relation between the Word and Jesus, one according to which the Second Person of the Trinity merely approves or endorses the life, ministry, and actions of Christ.

However, let us set this to one side. The more important issue here is Lincoln's claim that the TVB implies Jesus cannot be fully human because "he had no normal male chromosome, and therefore is not fully at one with the humanity that is to be redeemed." It is not clear to me why possession of a normal male chromosome is a *requirement* for Christ to be included within humanity, for the reasons given above in response to Lincoln's fourth reason. That is, the threshold condition stipulates that possession of the chromosomes from the Virgin may be sufficient (for all we know) to establish

---

[42] Lincoln, *Born of a Virgin?* 264. See also 270, 280–81.
[43] Lincoln, *Born of a Virgin?* 280.

Christ's connection to the human race. The missing genetic material is provided by the same divine agent ultimately responsible for the human race; so it is not clear why Christ is not a member of the human race.

"Critical loyalty" to the church's creedal tradition

The final piece in Lincoln's second narrative is perhaps the most contentious. Taking his cue from debates about the *filioque* clause in discussions of the Trinity, and the way in which our understanding of creation has changed in light of modern cosmology and evolution, Lincoln suggests that theological tradition is a living thing that changes over time according to the needs of new generations of Christians. It is not that doctrinal truth is relative, but that "the Church in succeeding generations through its theologians and teachers, through its worship and practice, is inevitably involved in the hard work of interpretation of the truths that shape its life. It should not be surprising that advances in knowledge throw up problems that require rethinking the tradition."[44]

So far, so good. But by what criterion are such changes to be judged? How are we to ensure that a change is within the bounds of a tradition and not a departure from it? Lincoln suggests that modifications to tradition must "express more adequately the witness of Scripture taken as a whole, and have a place in the proper summary of the gospel."[45] Such changes must cohere with other doctrines and make the explication of the gospel today less problematic than the traditional alternative. It is Lincoln's contention that removing the TVB meets these informal "criteria of discernment."[46]

How are we to square this revisionism about the TVB with confessing the creed? Lincoln's response, like his response concerning the birth narratives, is a kind of sympathetic revisionism that seeks to preserve the spirit, not the letter, of the creeds. We cannot believe the TVB any longer. But we can retain the conviction that God is fully present in Christ's life from its beginning and is the one whose action ultimately explains Christ's life.[47] Given

---

[44] Lincoln, *Born of a Virgin?* 294.

[45] Lincoln, *Born of a Virgin?* 295.

[46] "What has been proposed here is that the virgin birth part of the tradition is under severe pressure both from the recognition of Scripture's diversity on the matter of Jesus' conception and the place of the annunciation stories in the literary conventions of ancient biography and from our contemporary understanding of the biological make-up of the human male. No longer making it an essential doctrine or credal element meets the criteria of discernment suggested above" (Lincoln, *Born of a Virgin?* 295).

[47] Lincoln, *Born of a Virgin?* 297.

that the creeds are political documents, the result of debate and discussion, of interpretation and diplomatic language, we can reinterpret them for our own times.

It might be objected that confessing a tenet of the creed that one does not believe in any straightforward sense is more than a little disingenuous. But this, Lincoln maintains, is confused.[48] It is to conflate creed and doctrine, and to fail to distinguish between the confession of the church as a whole and the assent of the individual believer to every line of what is being confessed. Affirming the creed is a "badge of belonging,"[49] a way of identifying oneself with the whole church. It is not a way of ensuring we all believe exactly the same thing. Such "critical loyalty" to the creeds is, Lincoln maintains, the official stance of the Church of England in several reports of the church's Doctrine Commission going back to 1938.[50]

There are several different issues that need to be teased out here. First, Lincoln is wrong if he thinks that confessing the creed is not a way of ensuring Christians believe the same thing. That is exactly the purpose of the creeds: they are catechetical instruments, which is why they have historically been embedded in the liturgies of the churches. The point of the creeds and confessions of the church is to ensure that believers do not have a mistaken view of the doctrine in question, and hold to the right form of doctrine. That is why the issue of the *filioque* is such a running sore in the life of the church; it is a clause added unilaterally by one branch of the church to an ecumenically agreed upon instrument of catechesis—namely, the Nicene Creed. The doctrine of creation is not like the *filioque* in this respect because the ways in which our understanding of creation have changed over the past two hundred years are not obviously at odds with the confessional tradition. So Lincoln's attempt to drive a wedge between assenting to the creed and believing a particular tenet of the creed is troubling. Couldn't an Arian do something like this? "I assent to the creed taken as a whole as a way of identifying myself with the life of the church, and, in broad terms, with what the creed affirms," says the Arian. "However, I do not believe every tenet of the creed. In particular, I deny that Christ is fully divine."

Second, although there is a hermeneutical task that each new generation must take up, it is not at all clear that this includes reinterpreting the conceptual core of the faith as expressed in an ecumenical dogma like the virgin

---

[48] Lincoln, *Born of a Virgin?* 298–99.

[49] Lincoln, *Born of a Virgin?* 299.

[50] Lincoln, *Born of a Virgin?* 300–301. The reports of the Doctrine Commission in question do not sit well with article 2 of the Articles of Religion.

birth. Granted, the creeds are the result of political upheaval and debate—but so what? That says nothing about their truth value. After all, a diplomatic resolution may be a political solution *as well as* expressing the truth of the matter.

Third, Lincoln's criteria for discernment are so vague as to be of no real practical benefit for the task at hand. For Lincoln's criteria are not sufficient to make a judgment about whether the TVB or NVB is the right way to understand the doctrine of the incarnation. Nor are his criteria fine grained enough to exclude certain undesirable views. Just plug in the recent American evangelical debate about the eternal generation of the Son, or recent Christian philosophical arguments in favor of neomonothelite views of Christ's human nature. In both cases protagonists for revision have made arguments similar to Lincoln's criteria for discernment. They claim that their revisions "express more adequately the witness of Scripture taken as a whole, and have a place in the proper summary of the gospel." They claim that their revisions cohere with other doctrine, and that retaining the traditional position hinders the explication of the gospel today such that a revision will make this less problematic.

Assessing Lincoln's Second Narrative

Let us take stock. Of the different elements that make up what I take to be the main load-bearing theological structures of Lincoln's second narrative, the first raises worries about the consistency with which Lincoln approaches the biblical texts as Scripture and what he thinks the texts themselves affirm. The second reason, concerning the necessity of a TVB for the incarnation, can be conceded by defenders of the TVB. So it is rather weightless. The third, concerning problems with the metaphysical assumptions underpinning the TVB, trades on what might charitably be termed an underdeveloped grasp of the metaphysics of the incarnation, coupled with a sympathy for the sort of classical liberal Christology set forth by the likes of Schleiermacher—Christology that is contentious.[51] Lincoln's fourth reason, concerning the biological continuity of Christ with the rest of humanity, is perhaps the most troublesome for a modern defender of a TVB doctrine. But even here it is

---

[51] Lincoln's warmth toward Schleiermacher's degree Christology, according to which Christ was simply more "God-conscious" than other human beings, does seem to be in tension with his insistence upon a NVB version of the doctrine of the incarnation. Of course, he may align himself with a Schleiermacher-inspired Christology. But there is no reason why his readers should follow him in this regard.

not clear that his objection does significant damage if God can be said to supply the missing genetic material requisite to the production of a human male. And it is difficult to see why this would be theologically objectionable since the same divine agent is ultimately responsible for all of Christ's genetic inheritance. Against his fifth reason, I have argued that the TVB is only a theological liability if one adopts Lincoln's view that modern biology provides us with a defeater for the TVB. However, I can see no reason provided by Lincoln for thinking this is the case. The TVB is consistent with more than one biological story about the virgin birth, including modern biological accounts—as I argued in the opening section of this chapter. Lincoln's sixth reason trades on a mistaken view of the role of the creeds and confessions, and fails to offer criteria for discerning when it is appropriate to revise doctrines that are inadequate.

In short, on the basis of the theological reasons scrutinized here, I judge that Lincoln has not shown that the TVB needs to be rejected in favor of a NVB account of the incarnation.

Coda: Anachronism and Lincoln's "Second Narrative"

Despite my criticisms of the letter of Lincoln's revisionist account of the doctrine of the virgin birth, I am in sympathy with the spirit of his project. By that I mean that I am in sympathy with his ambition to provide a second narrative that takes seriously both the biblical and theological issues that this doctrine raises. In fact, the virgin birth is a good case study of how scholars of biblical studies and theologians might find common cause. Here is a doctrine that is embedded in the tradition and is part of the witness of the catholic church but that has been the source of historic controversy. Here, too, is a doctrine that is founded upon particular biblical texts but whose provenance is contested in the biblical studies guild.[52] How are we to make constructive progress in assessing such matters? Surely a dialogical and collaborative attempt to do so is the most efficient way forward, for none of us has expertise that covers all these different areas comprehensively.

---

[52] Typical in this regard is the judgment of Marcus Borg. He thinks that the birth narratives of Matthew and Luke are not historical, nor is the virginal conception of Christ. "I do not see these stories as historical reports but as literary creations," he writes. "They are not history remembered but rather metaphorical narratives using ancient religious imagery to express central truths about Jesus' significance" (Borg, "The Meaning of the Birth Stories," in *The Meaning of Jesus: Two Visions*, by Marcus Borg and N. T. Wright [San Francisco: HarperCollins, 2000], 179).

A generation ago in a well-known essay entitled "Fern Seeds and Ele-phants," C. S. Lewis bemoaned the narrow, unliterary, and downright theologically revisionist views of biblical scholars. A great gulf existed (so it seemed) between people of Christian faith in the pews and the views expressed in much mainstream biblical scholarship of the era.[53] Happily, we live in very different times. One can still find old-school biblical crit-ics whose second narratives do sometimes seem, like the sons of Anak, to be remnants of a bygone age. But today there is a large and sophisti-cated body of work in biblical scholarship that is theologically informed and that attempts to bridge the gulf between biblical study and systematic theology—often with very impressive results.

Although I have reservations about Lincoln's second narrative and the conclusions he reaches, I welcome his attempt to engage seriously with the theological and biblical tradition, refusing the old binary of nonconfessional biblical scholarship *or* Christian theology. One might think of Lincoln's work as a case study of such cross-disciplinary scholarship from which sub-sequent work on the doctrine of the virgin birth can certainly learn. Natu-rally, the ambition to straddle these two disciplines does not in and of itself mean theologians and biblical scholars suddenly find themselves in greater agreement than before, as the conclusions of this chapter demonstrate. Nev-ertheless, the attempt to address the cultural drift that has pushed these two disciplines apart in the past two centuries is an endeavor that should (I think) be embraced.

As I intimated earlier in this chapter, one important question going for-ward is how the biblical and postbiblical traditions are weighted in making theological judgments and in the writing of our various "second narratives." Lincoln's position gives primacy to the biblical texts as understood by histor-ical biblical criticism. On his way of thinking, the postbiblical tradition is, in principle, revisable in light of new ways of looking at the biblical material—even if the topic in question is deeply embedded in the creedal and con-fessional tradition of the church. Although he seriously engages important figures in the Christian tradition, a persistent worry throughout the book is that theological accounts of the virgin birth are anachronistic. But I wonder whether his own account is able to escape this objection. Although Lincoln

---

[53] C. S. Lewis, "Fern Seeds and Elephants," in *Fern Seeds and Elephants, and Other Essays on Christianity* (London: Fontana, 1975). A very helpful recent reflection on the changing times in biblical scholarship that engages Lewis' classic essay can be found in Richard Bauckham, *The Bible in the Contemporary World: Hermeneutical Ventures* (Grand Rapids: Eerdmans, 2015), ch. 2.

presents his view as a more secure interpretation of the biblical material, and a "critically loyal" reading of the postbiblical tradition, he does seem motivated by worries that the virgin birth is a kind of theological embarrassment we could do without. But what is this if it is not an anachronism—just anachronism of a different sort? The biblical writers and the theologians of the patristic period felt no such embarrassment; why should theologians today? Perhaps, as David Steinmetz recommends, "Biblical scholars who are also Christian theologians," or who are wanting seriously to engage theology, as Lincoln surely does, "should worry less about anachronism and more about the quality of the second narratives they have constructed."[54]

---

[54] Steinmetz, "Uncovering a Second Narrative," 65.

9

Christ's Two Wills

Then he withdrew from them about a stone's throw, knelt down, and prayed, "Father, if you are willing, remove this cup from me; yet, not my will but yours be done."

Luke 22:41-42

Having considered the virginal conception of Christ in the previous chapter, we turn now to think about one important implication of the historic two natures doctrine according to which Christ is one divine person subsisting in two natures—one divine, the other human. The focus of our attention will be upon the doctrine of *dyothelitism*. This is the view that Christ has not just two distinct natures (one divine, the other human) but also two distinct wills (one divine, the other human). It is the position of Christian orthodoxy developed in the fires of controversy in the first seven centuries of the Christian era—or what I shall call *classical Christology*. It was canonized at the Third Council of Constantinople in AD 681. The fathers of the council maintained that the two natures doctrine of Chalcedonian Christology, according to which Christ has two complete, distinct natures, one human, the other divine, implies that Christ has two distinct wills, one belonging to his human nature and the other belonging to his divine nature. If he has only one will, then (according to classical Christology) either his divinity or his humanity is incomplete, depending on whether the will in question is a divine or human one. One deliverance of the two natures doctrine (as understood by the fathers of Constantinople III and—as they saw it—in continuity with Nicene Christianity) is that his two natures are complete and personally united. So he must have a complete human nature, including a human will and principle of action that is distinct, and a complete divine nature, including a divine will and principle of action that is distinct.[1] As well as affirming dyothelitism as orthodox, the fathers of the council rejected the major alternative, monothelitism. This is the view according to which Christ has only one will that is shared between his two natures.

In this chapter I will offer a defense of dyothelitism against several of its recent detractors. In the first section I set the scene for what follows, outlining the puzzle of dyothelitism. Then, in a second section, I turn to consider some metaphysical distinctions that will help make some sense of the theological context in which the puzzle of dyothelitism arises, paying particular attention to some issues in the two natures doctrine that I have tackled at greater length elsewhere. The third section gives an account of the neomonothelite position of J. P. Moreland and William Lane Craig, with some help from Garrett DeWeese. This is followed in the fourth section by a discussion of Jordan Wessling's attempt to offer a qualified defense of a neomonothelite position in conversation with the Christian tradition. The fifth section offers my assessment of neomonothelitism. I argue that although these scholars raise some important issues for classical Christology and the dyothelite view, on balance their case is not preferable to the classical view. The conclusion draws these threads together.

Setting the Scene

For modern thinkers the doctrine of dyothelitism is one of the most puzzling aspects of classical Christology. We normally think that the will of a person is just a way of speaking about the agency of that person. The person is said to will one thing or another, but the will is not some sort of faculty belonging to the nature of the person. Rather, it is a way of speaking about the person who is willing a particular thing. But if that is right, then it seems that the will goes with the person, not the nature, so to speak, which is contrary to classical Christology. As Christian philosopher Garrett DeWeese puts it, "Since mental properties inhere in persons and not natures, it follows that the mind and will are faculties or capacities of

---

[1] The text of the canon in question reads, "We proclaim equally two natural volitions or wills in him and two natural principles of action which undergo no division, no change, no partition, no confusion, in accordance with the teaching of the holy fathers. And the two natural wills are not in opposition, as the impious heretics said, far from it, but his human will following, and not resisting or struggling, rather in fact subject to his divine and all powerful will." Norman P. Tanner, S.J., ed., *Decrees of the Ecumenical Councils*, 2 vols. (Washington, D.C.: Georgetown University Press, 1990), 1:128.

persons and not of natures. Persons are conscious, natures are not; persons have the capacity of making choices and exercising active power, natures do not."[2] We can put this worry in terms of an axiom (to which we shall return in the course of the argument of this chapter). Elsewhere, I have called this the *Chalcedonian Axiom*.[3] It is this:

(CA) Christ has one of whatever goes with the person and two of whatever goes with natures.

The concern that CA generates for defenders of classical Christology is that the will of Christ should go with the natures. That is, there should be *two* wills in Christ according to classical Christology, hence dyothelitism. But modern psychology and philosophy presume that it is persons that will things and that are centers of operation, in which case there should only be *one* will in Christ, the will of God the Son, which is equivalent to monothelitism. However, monothelitism is unorthodox. This raises a significant concern with respect to the classical Christological account. Let us call this *the puzzle of dyothelitism*.

This puzzle has given rise to a recent debate in contemporary analytic theology, which includes the work of DeWeese, about the human and divine will of Christ. On the one side, there are those analytic theologians who want to defend the classical christological consensus.[4] On the other side are several prominent evangelical Christian philosophers (most of whom are associated with Biola University) who maintain that because the will goes with the person, not the nature, it makes little sense to speak of Christ having a human will distinct from his divine will. It might be better, say these philosophers, to speak instead of the one will of the theanthropic person of Christ than to

---

[2] Garrett J. DeWeese, "One Person, Two Natures: Two Metaphysical Models of the Incarnation," in *Jesus in Trinitarian Perspective*, ed. Fred Sanders and Klaus Issler (Nashville: Broadman & Holman Academic, 2007), 142.

[3] The Chalcedonian Axiom is due to DeWeese's work, though he does not call it this. For discussion of the matter, see Oliver D. Crisp, *The Word Enfleshed: Exploring the Person and Work of Christ* (Grand Rapids: Baker Academic, 2016), ch. 5, esp. p. 85. It is only a rough rule of thumb, of course. Christ has only one left hand, but that "goes with the human nature," not the person, of Christ. But he has two hands, and that goes with his human nature. And so on.

[4] Examples include the work of the present author, James Arcadi, Sarah Coakley, Richard Cross, Thomas Flint, Alfred Freddoso, Timothy Pawl, and Eleonore Stump, among others.

persist with the rather strained language of dyothelitism.[5] This latter view is sometimes referred to in the literature as neo-Apollinarianism. For, like the historic Apollinaris, these philosophical theologians maintain that there is one will in Christ—namely, the will of God the Son who is the only person "in" Christ, so to speak. (For, according to the two natures doctrine of classical Christology, Christ is a divine person with a human nature, not a divine person united with a human person.)

Nevertheless, I shall refrain from referring to this view as neo-Apollinarian because such terminology is potentially inflammatory. (Designating an opponents' view as heretical at the outset is clearly a piece of *ad hominem* guilt by association.) What is more, calling this view neo-Apollinarian may actually be misleading, for reasons we shall come to presently. (To anticipate: there are ways of construing this position that don't seem to be *straightforwardly* Apollinarian.) Given these considerations, I shall refer to this view as neo-monothelitism instead, since the central claim being made by these authors is that the monothelite position repudiated by the fathers of Constantinople III has more merit than the tradition has thought, and should be reconsidered for both biblical and philosophical reasons.

Some Metaphysical Distinctions

Before going any further, it will be helpful to set out some terminological distinctions that will inform our discussion of neomonothelitism. A good place to start is Alvin Plantinga's short essay "On Heresy, Mind, and Truth."[6] There Plantinga outlines two accounts of Christology that have informed much of the recent discussion of the incarnation in analytic theology. According to

---

[5] Examples include Garrett DeWeese in the aforementioned essay, "One Person, Two Natures"; and J. P. Moreland and William Lane Craig in *Philosophical Foundations for a Christian Worldview* (Downers Grove, Ill.: IVP, 2003), 597–614. Jordan Wessling offers a cautious assessment of this debate, arguing that the case against neomonothelitism is not proved. See Wessling, "Christology and Conciliar Authority: On the Viability of Monothelitism for Protestant Theology," in *Christology Ancient and Modern: Explorations in Constructive Dogmatics*, ed. Oliver D. Crisp and Fred Sanders (Grand Rapids: Zondervan Academic, 2013), 151–70. Andrew Tern Loke's essay, "On Dyothelitism Versus Monothelitism: The Divine Preconscious Model," *Heythrop Journal* 57, no. 1 (2016): 135–41, is also worth reading in this connection. Much of the substance of this work overlaps with his discussion in his monograph *A Kryptic Model of the Incarnation* (Farnham, Surrey, UK: Ashgate, 2014; repr., London: Routledge, 2016), 58–64. I shall consider Moreland, Craig, and Wessling in more detail later in this chapter.

[6] Alvin Plantinga, "On Heresy, Mind, and Truth," *Faith and Philosophy* 16, no. 2 (1999): 182–93.

the first view, in assuming human nature the Word acquired the property of human nature—a property necessary and sufficient for being a human being, as Plantinga puts it at one point. This is *the abstract nature view* of the incarnation. I will refer to those who take this view in what follows as *abstractists*. By contrast, according to the second view, in assuming human nature the Word acquired a specific—that is, concrete—human nature. As Plantinga puts it, on this view "what he [the Word] assumed was *a* human nature, a specific human being."[7] On this second view, "In the incarnate Christ there were two wills, one human and one divine, and two intellects, one human and one divine."[8] This is *the concrete nature view* of the incarnation.[9] Let us call those who defend this view *concretists*. There are different ways of construing abstractism and concretism in the literature, depending on whether one thinks about the "parts" that compose Christ. But for our purposes we need not enter that discussion here. It will be sufficient to refer to the broad distinction between abstractists and concretists, since, as I shall argue, this is the salient issue that differentiates neomonothelites from their opponents.[10]

Using these two ways of thinking about the metaphysics of the incarnation, Plantinga sketches his own (perhaps idiosyncratic) account of the history of classical christological debate. The canons of the Council of Chalcedon in AD 451 seem to fit better with an abstract nature view, he surmises, although the canons of the Third Council of Constantinople in AD 681 seem to be a better fit with the concrete nature view. For according to Chalcedon, Christ is composed of a divine nature essentially and a human nature accidentally. But according to Constantinople III, Christ has a human will and divine will. Much turns on what we make of the wills in question, as Plantinga makes clear:

Shall we say that duothelitism [*sic*] is the idea that the will of Christ had both the nature of a human will and the nature of a divine will, in the

---

[7] Plantinga, "On Heresy, Mind, and Truth," 183 (emphasis in original).

[8] Plantinga, "On Heresy, Mind, and Truth," 184.

[9] I have dealt with this at greater length in Oliver D. Crisp, *Divinity and Humanity: The Incarnation Reconsidered* (Cambridge: Cambridge University Press, 2007), ch. 2.

[10] For discussion of "parts" Christology, see Crisp, *Divinity and Humanity*, ch. 2. A helpful overview of the debate is given in Jonathan Hill's introduction to *The Metaphysics of the Incarnation*, ed. Anna Marmadoro and Jonathan Hill (Oxford: Oxford University Press, 2011). A sophisticated account of the terms "hypostasis," "person," and "nature" as applied to the incarnation can be found in Tim Pawl's monograph *In Defense of Conciliar Christology: A Philosophical Essay*, Oxford Studies in Analytic Theology (Oxford: Oxford University Press, 2016), ch. 2.

abstract sense of "nature"? The partisans of the abstract view would happily accept that. Or shall we say that duothelitism is the idea that there are two distinct concrete wills (supposing that in fact a will is a concrete object of some kind)? The concretists would happily accept *that*, and then it looks as if it's the abstractists that are tugging the laboring oar.[11]

The moral of this christological tale, according to Plantinga, is that stipulating what counts as an orthodox doctrine (in this case, an orthodox doctrine of the incarnation) is not an easy task. I think he is right about this. The incarnation is a deep and difficult matter. If one holds to something like an abstract nature view of the incarnation, does that imply monothelitism? Perhaps not. If one holds to a concrete nature view of the incarnation, does that imply Nestorianism? Again, perhaps not. Yet an initial assessment of this matter might lead one to think so.[12]

Let me explain. Suppose Smith is an abstractist who is committed to classical Christology. And suppose Jones is a concretist who is also committed to classical Christology. Smith thinks that in becoming incarnate God the Son acquires a property, the property of human nature. "Human nature" is a rich property that includes in its conjuncts all those things necessary and sufficient for being human. Naturally, this includes a human will (whatever a human will turns out to be). So in becoming incarnate, God the Son acquires the property of human nature that includes a human will. What does that mean? Well, on one way of thinking about this, it means that from the first moment of incarnation onward, God the Son is able to act as a human being in addition to acting as a divine person. In order to act as a human being he must be able to will as a human being. Because he has a human nature from the first moment of incarnation, he is able to will as a human being. Notice on this view that the subject here is God the Son. To put it more carefully, we might say that from the first moment of incarnation onward, God the Son is able to will as a divine person and also able to will as a human being. For from the first moment of incarnation onward, God the Son exemplifies human nature (he has acquired the property of human nature) so that he is able from that time onward to will as a human being.

At first glance this seems like a strange thing to say. But according to the abstractist, the reason it seems strange is that we are used to talking about the

---

[11] Plantinga, "On Heresy, Mind, and Truth," 185 (emphasis in original).

[12] In my earlier work on this topic (in *Divinity and Humanity*), I was more sure that the metaphysical story one tells about the human nature of Christ has certain implications about monothelitism and dyothelitism. These days, as a result of subsequent conversation on the topic, I am slightly more cautious about drawing such conclusions.

nature of a person in terms of the one individual nature a person instantiates that is essential to that person. Smith is a human being, and exemplifies a human nature. Her human nature—that is, the human nature of Smith—is essentially human. Indeed, Smith is a fully human person; she is also *merely* a human person. Christ is not like that. As Thomas Morris reminds us in *The Logic of God Incarnate,*

> the kind-nature exemplified distinctively by all human beings is that of humanity. To be a human being is to exemplify human nature. An individual is fully human just in case he fully exemplified human nature. To be merely human is not to exemplify a kind-nature, a natural kind, distinct from that of humanity; it is rather to exemplify humanity without also exemplifying any ontologically higher kind, such as divinity.[13]

God the Son exemplifies human nature, but he is not *merely* human. He is a divine person with a human nature. In acquiring human nature he acquires the capacity to will as a human being in addition to being able to will as a divine person. He—a divine person—is able to will to do things as a human being because he exemplifies human nature.

Such distinctions are helpful. They usually go hand in hand with what is known as a reduplicative strategy in order to avoid the conclusion that the abstractist position is monothelite. Reduplication involves speaking of Christ *qua*, or "as," human or divine. So we parcel out certain tasks to one or other of the natures of Christ in order to be able to shield the other nature from certain claims that would otherwise seem to be metaphysically damaging. For instance, classical Christology claims that Christ is omnipotent *qua* divine but not *qua* human; and he is limited in power *qua* human but not *qua* divine. Here the claim is that Christ can will certain things *qua* human and other things *qua* divine. So a reduplicative strategy involves attempting to deploy reduplication in the incarnation in order to avoid embracing certain significant problems that would appear to be implied by commitment to the doctrine.

In my earlier discussion of this matter I said that the problem with this abstractist attempt to avoid the implication of monothelitism is that it seems like a metaphysical sleight of hand.[14] Consider the example I used on that previous occasion.[15] Clark Kent is a mild-mannered newspaper reporter.

---

[13] Thomas V. Morris, *The Logic of God Incarnate* (Ithaca, N.Y.: Cornell University Press, 1986), 66.

[14] Crisp, *Divinity and Humanity*, ch. 2.

[15] Crisp, *Divinity and Humanity*, 60.

Superman is the Man of Steel. Yet one person is both Kent and Superman. He wills certain things *qua* Kent, and other things *qua* Superman. Yet one person wills both as Kent and as Superman. But this only shows why the abstractist position seems dubious. The attempt made by the abstractist to parcel out the two wills of Christ ends up looking very like the Kent-Superman example, and in the case of Kent-Superman, we don't suppose that there are two distinct wills being employed by one person. Rather, we think that Kent-Superman wills certain things in his guise as a mild-mannered reporter and wills other things in his guise as Superman. But one person wills these things, and willing them under the guise of Kent or Superman is not sufficient for Kent-Superman to have two distinct wills in the manner that was understood by the fathers of Constantinople III. For they spoke of two natural wills (*duo physikas theleseis*) and two natural operations (*duo physikas energieas*) subsisting "indivisibly, incontrovertibly, inseparably, and inconfusedly" in Christ.[16] It seems to me that this way of construing dyothelitism most naturally suggests a differentiation between the two wills of Christ that is deeper, or more pronounced, than the abstractist position can allow.

Let us return to Jones, who I said was a concretist enamored of classical Christology. On this view, the incarnation involves the assumption by God the Son of a human being. This human being begins to exist and at that very moment is assumed by the Second Person of the Trinity. So adoptionism does not obtain on this view. Nor does Nestorianism straightforwardly follow from the view—that is, it does not imply or entail Netorianism. Although God the Son and his human nature are concrete particulars, there are not two persons present in the incarnation. For on this version of concretism (a version that Jones hopes is consistent with classical Christology), in assuming a human nature God the Son brings it into union with his person, making it something like his instrument. At no time is it a human nature independent of assumption by God the Son, so it never forms a fundamental substance independent of God the Son. It is always *his* human nature. This is strange, but it is a familiar enough view for those conversant with medieval theology and more recent mereological accounts of the incarnation that draw upon this medieval debate.[17] Although on the face of it Jones seems to

---

[16] The text can be found in Henry R. Percival, ed., *The Seven Ecumenical Councils of the Undivided Church: Their Canons and Dogmatic Decrees* (New York: Edwin S. Gorham, 1901), 345.

[17] See, e.g., Brian Leftow, "A Timeless God Incarnate," in *The Incarnation*, ed. Stephen T. Davis, Daniel Kendall, and Gerald O'Collins (Oxford University Press 2002); Leftow, "The Humanity of God," in Marmadoro and Hill, *Metaphysics of the Incarnation*; and

find it easier to give some account of Christ's willing certain things along the lines of classical dyothelitism, the worry is that in embracing concretism Jones has embraced a view that strongly suggests Nestorianism, though it does not imply or entail it. This much may be true. But it is insufficient to push concretism beyond the bounds of classical christological orthodoxy. (A comparison will make the point: smelling of tobacco and ale *strongly suggests* that a person is a smoker and drinker, but it may be the case that this person has just been in the company of members of the Inklings group—a band of notorious smokers and drinkers!—and is not in fact a smoker or drinker. Sometimes theologians are too quick to assign a view to a person on the basis of such circumstantial evidence.)

It is very difficult to see how a concretist could end up with monothelitism unless the version of concretism in question is straightforwardly Apollinarian. That is, if the concretist is committed to an idea that Christ's human nature lacks a distinct human will and center of operation, the lack being supplied by the divine person who assumes the human nature in question, then the concretist is a monothelite—but only because he or she is an Apollinarian about Christ's human nature. Provided Christ's human nature is complete, including a human will and center of operation, the concretist position implies dyothelitism. As just mentioned, it may seem to press beyond this to Nestorianism, but that is another matter. The point here is that concretists who endorse an orthodox two natures doctrine in accordance with classical Christology are neither Apollinarian nor monothelite. The concretist position that is consistent with classical Christology is clearly dyothelite.

The Moreland-Craig Proposal

With these distinctions in mind, we can turn to the case for neomonothelitism. One of the clearest and most theologically and historically nuanced accounts to date is given by the Biola University philosophers J. P. Moreland and William Lane Craig.[18] They propose a constructive monothelite Christology that endorses the two natures view of Chalcedon but that postulates

---

Thomas P. Flint, "Should Concretists Part with Mereological Models of the Incarnation?" in Marmadoro and Hill, *Metaphysics of the Incarnation*; Crisp, *Word Enfleshed*, chs. 5–6; and Eleonore Stump, "Aquinas on the Metaphysics of the Incarnation," in Davis, Kendall, and O'Collins, *Incarnation*, 197–220.

[18] DeWeese's paper "One Person, Two Natures" is also worth considering, as is Loke's work, esp. his study *Kryptic Model of the Incarnation*. But both of these have been subjected to thorough criticism by Tim Pawl. Interested readers are directed to his discussion in *In Defense of Conciliar Christology*, ch. 9.

with Apollinaris that the Logos was the rational soul of Christ.[19] On their view God the Son contained archetypically within his divine nature all the properties requisite for being human prior to the incarnation with the exception of being embodied.[20] So their account of human nature is an abstractist one, but with an interesting Apollinarian twist: God the Son possesses human nature independently of the incarnation because he is a divine person. All that was required in the incarnation in order for Christ to be "fully human" was the acquisition of a human body:

> God himself is personal, and inasmuch as we are persons we resemble him [in virtue of possessing the image of God]. Thus God already possesses the properties sufficient for human personhood even prior to the Incarnation, lacking only corporeality. The Logos already possessed in his preincarnate state all the properties necessary for being a human self. In assuming a hominid body, he brought to it all that was necessary for a complete human nature. For this reason, in Christ the one self-conscious subject who is the Logos possessed divine and human natures that were both complete.[21]

Later in the same discussion Moreland and Craig admit, "The model here proposed implies monothelitism, since the Logos, as the mind of Jesus of Nazareth, has but a single will." However, this is an implication that is "in our view unobjectionable, since dyothelitism, despite its conciliar support, finds no warrant in Scripture."[22] As evidence of this claim, the authors cite Christ's agony in the garden of Gethsemane (Luke 22:42), where Christ prays "Yet, not my will but yours be done." The fathers of Constantinople III, following the teaching of Maximus the Confessor, understood this passage to mean something like, "Yet, not my *human* will but *your divine will* be done." This is consistent with Nicene Christianity and the idea that the divine persons of the Godhead are subsistent relations—the extrapolation of Nicene teaching found in the theology of Thomas Aquinas. Moreland and

---

[19] "We postulate with Apollinarius that the Logos was the rational soul of Christ" (Moreland and Craig, *Philosophical Foundations*, 608).

[20] They write, "The Logos contained perfect human personhood archetypically in his own nature. The result was that in assuming a hominid body the Logos brought to Christ's animal nature just those properties that would serve to make it a complete human nature. Thus the human nature of Christ was complete precisely in virtue of the union of his flesh with the Logos. As a result of the union Christ did, indeed, possess a complete, individual human nature comprised of body and soul; for that nature was made complete by the union of the flesh with the Logos, the archetype of humanity" (Moreland and Craig, *Philosophical Foundations*, 608).

[21] Moreland and Craig, *Philosophical Foundations*, 609.

[22] Moreland and Craig, *Philosophical Foundations*, 611.

Craig think this is mistaken. They interpret the same passage in a way that implies a social account of the Trinity, thus: "Yet, not my [i.e., God the Son Incarnate's] will but yours [i.e., God the Father's] be done."[23] They conclude, "The will of the Logos had in virtue of the Incarnation become the will of the man Jesus of Nazareth. This implication of the model is, in our view, one of its advantages, since it is extraordinarily difficult to preserve the unity of Christ's person once distinct wills are ascribed to the Logos and to the individual human nature of Christ."[24]

But it is not obviously a strength of a theological position that one revisionist doctrine (concerning the incarnation) requires another revisionist doctrine (concerning the Trinity) to prop it up. Moreland and Craig think that the agony of Christ in Gethsemane is best understood against the conceptual backdrop of a social view of the Trinity, or at least against the backdrop of a view according to which there are distinct wills allocated to distinct divine persons in the Godhead—which I take to be a constituent of social accounts of the Trinity. But this is not the traditional view of the Trinity, which defends the claim that there is but one will in God shared between the divine persons, whose personhood is at best analogous to human personhood. Now, the advocate of neomonothelitism is perfectly free to hold a view of the Trinity at odds with the majority voice of the tradition. This in and of itself is not necessarily problematic or unorthodox. Nevertheless, it does point to several closely related theological issues that are worth pausing to note.

First, as I have already indicated, the neomonothelite view adopted by Craig and Moreland is more revisionist than it appears at first glance. For it requires a particular view of the Trinity as well as a particular view of the incarnation, and in both cases the view in question is not the traditional one. So the revisionism involved in adopting their position is greater than it might at first appear. For some theologians that might be regarded as a cost of the view.

Second, the Craig-Moreland proposal assumes a particular strategy for reading the salient biblical passages that is not necessarily obviously better than the traditional alternative. It is true that the alternative reading strategy adopted by the fathers of Constantinople III (under the influence of Maximus the Confessor) is not necessarily the *only* way to read passages such as

---

[23] This is my own extrapolation of what they say about Christ's agony in the garden, not a direct quotation from Moreland and Craig.

[24] Moreland and Craig, *Philosophical Foundations*, 611.

the Gethsemane narratives of the canonical Gospels.[25] Nevertheless, it is a strategy that has informed how the vast majority of the tradition has read these passages, and how they have been understood in terms of their implications for the doctrine of the incarnation. Why should we prefer the reading strategy adopted by Moreland and Craig over that preferred by the fathers of an ecumenical council if both strategies have some merit in terms of their exegesis of the passages in question, neither are incoherent, and yet only one has the imprimatur of the catholic church?[26]

Wessling on Neomonothelitism and Tradition

This brings us to the work of Jordan Wessling. In a recent essay, he offers a qualified defense of neomonothelitism, arguing that the case against neomonothelitism depends in important respects upon the weight given to different sources of theological authority, which may be challenged.[27] The neomonothelite position relies on what he calls the *Conciliar Undercutting Principle* (CUP):

(CUP) The (evangelical) Christian is free to reject an ecumenical conciliar pronouncement if this pronouncement is not taught or implied by Scripture.[28]

[25] This point is made by Wessling, "Christology and Conciliar Authority," in Crisp and Sanders, *Christology Ancient and Modern.*

[26] It is worth noting that the biblical texts we have are themselves the product of ecclesiastical tradition in a very real sense: they were collected together and approved by the fathers of the early church, who included certain texts and excluded others. So a way of reading a particular textual tradition that derives from the reading strategy adopted by the natural heirs of such ecclesiastical leaders is something that (I suggest) theologians do well to take very seriously. For a recent discussion of the role of tradition in theologizing relevant to this point see Steven Nemeş, "On the Priority of Tradition: An Exercise in Analytic Theology," *Open Theology* 3 (2017): 274–92.

[27] See Wessling, "Christology and Conciliar Authority," in Crisp and Sanders, *Christology Ancient and Modern.*

[28] *Caveat lector:* here, and in considering the CAT below, I have amended Wessling's version of the principles so that the conciliar decisions in question are those of an ecumenical council only. I think most Protestants would be less concerned if their views diverged from a Roman Catholic council because they are unlikely to regard such councils as *ecumenical* councils. Plausibly, they are councils of a particular branch of the church, not the whole church, despite Roman Catholic claims to the contrary. (For one thing, a council that does not have full participation from Eastern and Western Christian communions that stand in continuity with previous ecumenical councils cannot be an ecumenical council; Roman Catholic councils do not have full participation from Eastern and Western Christian communions in continuity with previous ecumenical councils; therefore, Roman Catholic councils are not ecumenical councils.)

We have already seen this at work in passing, in the version of neomonothelitism outlined by Moreland and Craig. But it can be found in Garry DeWeese's version of the doctrine as well. He writes, "While most evangelicals should and do regard the deliverances of the ecumenical councils as weighty in defining the orthodox faith, they would agree that the councils cannot be accepted uncritically but must themselves be judged by the authority of Scripture."[29] The CUP needs to be distinguished from the *Conciliar Abrogation Thesis* (CAT):

(CAT) The (evangelical) Christian should reject an ecumenical conciliar statement if and only if it either: (1) contradicts what is taught in or implied by Scripture, or (2) is incoherent.

Defenders of CAT will be much more cautious about overturning the judgment of an ecumenical council than advocates of CUP. Unlike Wessling, I want to press the case for CAT against the CUP of neomonothelitism found in the work of philosophers like DeWeese, Moreland, and Craig. It seems to me extremely implausible that God would allow the vast majority of the church to be led into error on a matter central to the faith.[30] It also seems to me that questions canonized by an ecumenical council of the church are matters that are promulgated and believed by the vast majority of the church. Further, doctrinal questions pertaining to the incarnation are surely matters that are central to the faith. (An aside: this seems true even if we don't have a set of necessary and sufficient conditions for what counts as "central to the faith." I don't have a set of necessary and sufficient conditions for adjudicating what counts as "central to the game of chess," but I do know that a knight can move in certain directions a certain number of places per move, and has the unusual property of being able to "leap over" other pieces on the board. And I know that these qualities possessed by the knight are central to the playing of the game, and in some ways set it apart from other similar games, such as checkers. Similarly, what is believed concerning the incarnation surely touches upon matters that are central to the faith in a way that does not apply to, say, what is believed about the posture one should adopt in prayer.[31])

[29] DeWeese, "One Person, Two Natures," 148.

[30] This is a matter I have touched upon previously. See Crisp, *God Incarnate: Explorations in Christology* (London: T&T Clark, 2009), 14.

[31] Lest the reader think this is a trivial matter, consider the variance of practice in the liturgies of the Free Presbyterian and Associated Presbyterian churches of Scotland on the one hand, and the Church of Scotland on the other. In the first two communions, the congregation stands to pray, whereas in the Church of Scotland the congregation sits to pray.

Consequently, if an ecumenical council promulgates a teaching about the incarnation, it promulgates a teaching about something that is central to the faith. Given that it is extremely implausible that God would allow the vast majority of the church to be led into error on a matter that is central to the faith, and given that the teaching of an ecumenical council is promulgated to the vast majority of the church as a teaching that Christians should embrace, it seems to me that something like CAT is on target. Constantinople III promulgated an important teaching about the incarnation, one that the fathers of that council thought was an implication of the canons of Chalcedon and that was consistent with the apostolic teaching. Their doctrine does not contradict what is taught or implied in Holy Writ, and it is not incoherent. So I think that there is a very good theological reason for holding to the doctrine of this particular ecumenical council, which endorses dyothelitism.

The burden of Wessling's essay is to show that there is some doubt about this—or at least, sufficient uncertainty that the case against the neomonothelites remains unproven. His strategy involves arguing that it is not clear that the doctrine of dyothelitism promulgated by Constantinople III represents a teaching that is central to the faith. He writes, "God allows all kinds of negative states of affairs that surprise us—misguided theological systems, moral evil, animal and human suffering, and so on—states of affairs that appear as bad as, or nearly so, as conciliar error, at least on peripheral doctrines."[32] But, he reasons, if God allows states of affairs that seem almost as bad as conciliar error, why think that conciliar error is that unlikely? It is (he thinks) but a short step from "almost as bad as conciliar error" to "conciliar error."

The addition of the phrase "at least on peripheral doctrines" that appears at the end of the quotation from Wessling just given seems misplaced. The issue is not whether God permits states of affairs almost as bad as mistaken conciliar views about peripheral doctrines, but whether God would permit states of affairs almost as bad as mistaken *ecumenical* conciliar canons about doctrines *that are central to the faith*. These are important qualifiers. It is the decisions of ecumenical councils that are in view—not some local or regional synod but a gathering of the leaders of the church catholic. And it is a question about a matter that is central to the faith, not something peripheral, a matter of adiaphora, such as the posture one adopts in prayer. God does

---

Historically, these liturgical differences have not been thought trivial by members of these different Presbyterian communions. Nevertheless, such difference of practice can hardly be said to be "central to the faith."

[32] Wessling, "Christology and Conciliar Authority," in Crisp and Sanders, *Christology Ancient and Modern*, 163.

indeed permit all sorts of bad states of affairs that are deeply puzzling to people of faith, such as moral evil and animal and human suffering. However, such things are rather different from God allowing a serious doctrinal error to creep into the canonical decision of an ecumenical council—a decision that has become part of the fabric of Christian belief for the vast majority of Christians down through the ages. For this is tantamount to God permitting the vast majority of Christians down through the ages to believe a falsehood about the manner in which he brought about human salvation in Christ.

At the close of his essay, Wessling remarks "many evangelical theologians will remain deeply skeptical about the acceptability of monothelitism. Given the wide reception of the two wills doctrine by Catholics, the Orthodox, and conservative Protestants, these theologians will think that a tremendous burden of proof is placed on the monothelite."[33] But isn't that just because these theologians, and Christian theologians enamored of classical Christology more generally, think that the teaching of the fathers of Constantinople III on dyothelitism *is* a matter that is central to the faith, one that is consistent with the apostolic teaching, and that is coherent? Far from establishing that there is some theological wiggle room for the neomonothelites, Wessling's essay only underlines the fact that monothelitism does indeed stand outside the orthodox mainstream of Christian teaching precisely because it is repudiated by an ecumenical council—a matter that the vast majority of Christians are agreed upon.

Assessing Neomonothelitism

From the foregoing it seems to me that the strength of the neomonothelite position does not lie in its appeal to a supposed biblical tradition over and against the accretions of later, postbiblical Christian tradition. For, as I have tried to indicate, there seems to me to be a very good case for the conclusion that monothelitism is not a traditional, orthodox Christian doctrine, and Wessling's closing remarks about the skepticism of most Christians concerning monothelitism only reinforce this claim. At the very least, the notion that the monothelite position is more securely located in the text of Scripture is, I think, a case that is very difficult to sustain independent of particular interpretive strategies for reading the relevant biblical material, which are contested in the tradition.

[33] Wessling, "Christology and Conciliar Authority," in Crisp and Sanders, *Christology Ancient and Modern*, 170.

Instead, the strength of the neomonothelite position lies in its criticism of the conceptual underpinning of the traditional dyothelite position, which we have called the puzzle of dyothelitism. To recap, this puzzle is motivated by the Chalcedonian Axiom, given earlier:

(CA) Christ has one of whatever goes with the person and two of whatever goes with natures.

The puzzle is that persons have wills, not natures. So the will(s) of Christ should go with the person(s) in Christ, not the natures of Christ. In short, *persons* have wills but natures do not, in which case it seems like dyothelitism rests on a metaphysical mistake.

In one respect, undercutting the metaphysical plausibility of dyothelitism is a much more fundamental problem than the one Wessling attempts to address (important though that is). It is rather like pointing out to a defender of a Ptolemaic cosmology that even if their view is the traditional one, and has been believed by many important thinkers of the past, it is nevertheless a view that is predicated on a way of thinking about the orbital relationships between different celestial bodies that we now know to be false. Similarly, we now think that it is a mistake to assign wills to natures. Instead, we think that wills belong to persons. Christians should not be bound to mistaken ancient psychology just because it was adopted by important church fathers in order to make sense of what they read in Scripture. Their understanding of the text of Scripture may be wrong *because they misconstrued the metaphysics of the incarnation*.

Because this represents a deeper conceptual problem for dyothelitism, it is also more difficult to defeat. In fact, I do not think there is a clear, unambiguous case in favor of dyothelitism and against monothelitism independent of appeal to theological authority. Instead, I think the theologian must engage in a kind of cost-benefit analysis, paying attention to issues pertaining to the witness of Scripture, to the tradition, and to issues of metaphysics. I have already given some reason for thinking that the direct appeal to Scripture made by defenders of neomonothelitism as expressed in CUP is not obviously superior to the more cautious approach of privileging the views of an ecumenical council expressed in CAT. Although I concede that the language of will in relation to nature given by Constantinople III is initially puzzling, there may be good theological reasons for retaining it. But, as we have already noted, it is easier to retain if one is a concretist rather than an abstractist about human nature. Although there may be abstractists who wish to defend dyothelitism, it is much easier to do so given concretism.

To see this, consider the following reasoning: Suppose we presume concretism is true for the sake of argument. Then "human nature" refers to a concrete particular, not merely a property. As I have already explained, although concretism does press in the direction of Nestorianism, and is often accused of being Nestorian, it does not necessarily imply Nestorianism, nor does it entail Nestorianism. So it is not necessarily beyond the bounds of orthodoxy as expressed in classical Christology. It is difficult to see how neomonothelitism is able to sustain the claim made by classical Christology to the effect that Christ is fully but not merely human. The abstractist may claim that all that is required for orthodoxy (that is, orthodoxy that includes dyothelitism as expressed in the canons of Constantinople III) is that Christ is able to will *qua* human, which is consistent with the abstractist's metaphysical commitments about the human nature of Christ. But it is not at all clear (to me, at least) that the reduplicative strategy adopted by abstractists at this juncture is successful. Although the Kent-Superman example does not demonstrate that the abstractist position implies or entails something unorthodox, it does illustrate the fact that the reduplicative strategy is sufficiently conceptually ambiguous on this point that defenders of dyothelitism will remain suspicious that the abstractist is not really able to predicate a distinct human will of Christ in a way analogous to the Kent and Superman example. So, *pace* Craig, Moreland, and DeWeese, it does seem easier to see how the claims of classical Christology can be sustained if the human nature of Christ is understood in terms of concretism rather than abstractism. Concretism is a good fit with dyothelitism, in which case there is at least one plausible approach to the incarnation that is consistent with classical Christology, is orthodox, and is consistent with dyothelitism—namely, concretism.

But does the will go with the nature or the person? That is the fundamental christological question neomonothelitism raises. To this matter I think the concretist has a response that is able to agree with the findings of classical Christology as well as the substance of DeWeese's point about mental properties belonging to persons. The concretist can say that Christ's human nature, a concrete particular, is the natural endowment of a human person, though it is not a human person.[34] That is, it is composed of all the parts requisite to a complete human nature (whatever they turn out to be) but does not form a fundamental substance independent of a divine person because the human nature of Christ is assumed by God the Son at the

---

[34] The term "natural endowment" is borrowed from Brian Leftow. See his "Timeless God Incarnate," in Davis, Kendall, and O'Collins, *Incarnation*.

moment it begins to exist. God the Son makes his human nature his own by assuming it such that the only person "in" Christ, so to speak, is God the Son. This sort of concretism has been spelled out in the recent literature in much more detail than we need to go into here.[35] It is sufficient for our purposes that we see that concretism of this sort means Christ's human nature includes a distinct human will and center of operation and a distinct divine will and center of operation.

Moreover, it is also consistent with this view that the will is something *normally* possessed by a person, not by a nature. Normally, the concrete particular that is a complete human nature forming in utero becomes a human person distinct from a divine person because it is not assumed by a divine person. God does not normally "upload" himself into a particular human nature, taking possession of it from the get-go. In such cases it is natural to think that the will of the mere human person belongs to that person and not to the nature of that person. Christ is unique in that before his human nature can form a person independent of God the Son, it is assumed by a divine person. So it has all the qualities that a normal human nature would have, including a will. This is what I mean by Christ having the natural endowment of a human person. However, in the case of Christ, a human person does not obtain because the nature in question is assumed by God the Son. He assumes the concrete particular of Christ's human nature and in the process acquires the will and center of operation that belong to Christ's human nature. But this very act of acquisition blocks the formation of a person independent of the divine person assuming the human nature in question. In this way the concretist can agree with classical Christology about dyothelitism, and also agree with DeWeese and other neomonothelites that the mental properties of Christ that would normally belong to a person are in this case the property of God the Son who literally "personalizes" his human nature in assuming it.[36]

Let me end the assessment of neomonothelitism with a comment that applies to the Moreland-Craig version of the doctrine in particular. We have seen that their version of neomonothelitism has the consequence that the

---

[35] See, e.g., Crisp, *Word Enfleshed;* Flint, "Should Concretists Part with Mereological Models of the Incarnation?" in Marmadoro and Hill, *Metaphysics of the Incarnation;* Leftow, "Timeless God Incarnate," in Davis, Kendall, and O'Collins, *Incarnation;* Leftow, "Humanity of God," in Marmadoro and Hill, *Metaphysics of the Incarnation;* and Stump, "Aquinas on the Metaphysics of the Incarnation," in Davis, Kendall, and O'Collins, *Incarnation.*

[36] This is one way of construing the ancient doctrine of the an-enhypostatic nature of Christ, which I deal with in more detail in *Divinity and Humanity*, chs. 2–3.

divine persons of the Trinity possess human nature apart from a human body independent of the incarnation. They want to claim that the divine image in human beings reflects an archetype that already exists in the Godhead as a property of the divine nature possessed by the divine persons of the Trinity. But is the *imago Dei* a property of Christ's divine nature alone? Do divine persons have the property of human nature (barring a human body) independent of the incarnation? Does incarnation merely add a human body to God? As Biola theologian Jason McMartin puts it, "If we only have reason to think that Christ bears the image in virtue of his divine nature, then a major motivation for connecting anthropology and Christology will be lost."[37] This, it seems to me, is an important consideration. The divine image in human persons is not the ectype of an archetype in Christ's *divine nature*. Rather, Christ is the archetypical image to which we are conformed (as per Pauline theology) because he possesses a complete and sinless human nature that is hypostatically united to God the Son. On this way of thinking, a way of thinking that owes much to certain strands of patristic theology, the divine image is had through conformity to God in Christ, the second Adam (Rom 5:12-19), the perfect human being, not in virtue of some property God possesses archetypically, and independent of incarnation, as a divine person.[38]

Conclusion

In this chapter I have argued that the neomonothelite view favored by several evangelical Christian philosophers like Garry DeWeese, J. P. Moreland, and William Lane Craig, though theologically sophisticated, is nevertheless problematic. I have also argued that Jordan Wessling's attempt to offer a qualified defense of the neomonothelite position is not successful in attempting to show that there is theological wiggle room for the doctrine in terms of its appeal to theological authority. Nevertheless, the neomonothelites have shown that there are conceptual problems that defenders of the dyothelite alternative must address. And these are problems that are not easily rebutted. I have offered several reasons for thinking that dyothelitism is still worthy of serious theological consideration (independent of explicit appeals to theological authority) that depend upon a different model of the hypostatic union, one that is concretist rather than abstractist. On balance it seems to me that there is sufficient conceptual reason for holding to the dyothelitism

---

[37] Jason McMartin, "The Theandric Union as *Imago Dei* and *Capax Dei*," in Crisp and Sanders, *Christology Ancient and Modern*, 143.

[38] I have dealt with this in more detail in Crisp, *Word Enfleshed*, ch. 4.

of classical Christology given concretism, and sufficient authority for it in the tradition for us to maintain the doctrine. For these reasons it seems to me that dyothelitism is to be preferred to these modern monothelite alternatives.

We have now given some account (and defense) of two key classical christological claims—namely, the virginal conception of Christ and dyothelitism. This completes our discussion of the incarnation, which is the first aspect of Christ's reconciling work. In the next chapter we turn to consider an important theme in the discussion of the other aspect of Christ's reconciling work—that is, the atonement. Rather than giving an account of the mechanism of atonement (something I have done elsewhere),[39] we shall focus instead upon the broader theme of how it is that we are reconciled to Godself by means of participating in the divine life in theosis.

---

[39] See Crisp, *Word Enfleshed.*

Salvation as Participation

*See what love the Father has given us, that we should be called children
of God; and that is what we are. The reason the world does not know us
is that it did not know him. Beloved, we are God's children now; what
we will be has not yet been revealed. What we do know is this: when he
is revealed, we will be like him, for we will see him as he is. And all who
have this hope in him purify themselves, just as he is pure.*

1 John 3:1-3

Once upon a time, respectable academic theologians did not spend much
energy thinking about the doctrine of theosis as a way of conceiving the
nature of salvation in Christ. It was regarded as a sort of Eastern affectation,
a Byzantine curiosity that few Western thinkers took seriously. Today, there
is a thriving cottage industry devoted to the exposition and application of the
doctrine in Western as well as Eastern theological traditions.[1] In this chapter
I shall outline one version of theosis, and then attempt to provide some conceptual framework for thinking about what I take to be the central concern
of all doctrines of theosis—namely, participation in the divine nature. The
aim is a modest one: to make some progress toward a clearer picture of the

[1] See, for example, Roger E. Olson, "Deification in Contemporary Theology," *Theology
Today* 64 (2007): 186–200; Paul L. Gavrilyuk, "The Retrieval of Deification: How a Once-
Despised Archaism Became an Ecumenical Desideratum," *Modern Theology* 25 (2009): 647–
59; and Gösta Hallonsten, "Theosis in Recent Research," in *Partakers of the Divine Nature:
The History and Development of Deification in the Christian Traditions*, ed. Michael J. Christiansen and Jeffrey A. Witting (Grand Rapids: Baker, 2007), 281–93. (The literature is large
and expanding.) See also these representative examples of engagement with the topic from
within my own Reformed tradition: Gannon Murphy, "Reformed *Theosis?*" *Theology Today*
65 (2008): 191–212; Myk Habets, "'Reformed *Theosis?*' A Response to Gannon Murphy,"
Theology Today 65 (2009): 489–98; and Kyle Strobel, "Jonathan Edwards's Reformed Doctrine of Theosis," *Harvard Theological Review* 109, no. 3 (2016): 371–99.

two theologically interrelated notions of theosis and participation—notions that are often touted in the current theological literature but seldom analyzed with the sort of care that they warrant.

We shall proceed as follows: In the first section, I set out one way of thinking about theosis. Then, in a second section, I consider the vexed matter of human participation in the divine life, which is integral to the doctrine of theosis. In a final section, I consider Tom Flint's Theory of Final Assumptions as one way of thinking about human eschatological participation in the divine life. I conclude with some reflections on the upshot of the foregoing.

On Theosis

To begin with, we need to have some idea of the doctrine of theosis. For present purposes I shall treat theosis as a synonym of theopoiesis (being made divine), deification, and divinization. By my lights, the doctrine of theosis is the notion that somehow human beings become partakers of the divine nature by means of union with Christ via the power of the Holy Spirit.[2] Often, theosis is thought to be closely related to the process of sanctification in the Christian life, not as a change that radically alters the moral state of fallen human beings in an instant. The language used connotes some sort of transformation that occurs over time.

However, as it stands, this way of thinking about theosis is sufficiently conceptually fuzzy that it could be misunderstood or misconstrued in important respects. So let us attempt to clarify matters a little further. The "clarifications" offered here may not be agreed upon by all parties. But I think that they reflect some of the important ways in which recent theological work in this area has sought to understand theosis for the purposes of constructive theology. Let me begin by ruling out two common misunderstandings of the doctrine before providing some content to the doctrine.

The first common misunderstanding is that becoming partakers of the divine nature means losing one's individual identity in the divine, as a drop of water is "lost" in the ocean. This is a mistake that is still sometimes found in the literature and that motivates some theologians to steer clear of the doctrine.[3] Yet theosis is not equivalent to some sort of merging with the divine.

---

[2] This is not the only way to construe theosis, of course. See Habets, "Reformed *Theosis?*" for more on this.

[3] See, for example, the discussion of Jonathan Edwards's theology in Robert Caldwell III, *Communion in the Spirit: The Holy Spirit as the Bond of Union in the Theology of Jonathan Edwards* (Milton Keynes: Paternoster Press, 2006), 116–18, and 192. For a critical account

It is not that defenders of theosis expect human beings to eventually cease to be human, or to lose their humanity in some experience of union with the divine. (We shall see that Thomas Flint thinks human beings could lose their personhood in the eschaton in order to be united to God, but that is not the same thing as being assimilated to the divine, or losing one's humanity or even ceasing to be human.)

A second common misunderstanding of theosis is that the doctrine implies that redeemed humans become divine as God is divine. Some of the remarks made by patristic authors and their modern interpreters may mislead the reader into thinking this is what is envisaged by these early theologians. For instance, Athanasius famously remarks that Christ "assumed humanity that we might become God."[4] And in recent times, Metropolitan Kallistos Ware has written, "Such, according to the teaching of the Orthodox Church, is the final goal at which every Christian must aim: to become god, to attain theosis, 'deification' or 'divinization.' For Orthodoxy our salvation and redemption mean our deification."[5] However, human beings are not transmuted into additional deities according to the doctrine of theosis, which would be a metaphysical bootstrapping of a monumental sort. Sometimes incautious remarks made by defenders of theosis might lead one to think that the doctrine implies the transmutation of human beings into divinities, but this is not in fact what it entails.[6] One traditional way of fending off this concern is to point out that theosis does not imply the claim that human beings are transformed so as to share the divine *essence*. Instead, they come to share the divine *nature*.[7] The idea seems to be this: The divine essence is

---

of deification from a Protestant perspective, see Bruce L. McCormack's essay "Participation in God, Yes; Deification, No: Two Modern Protestant Responses to an Ancient Question," in *Orthodox and Modern: Studies in the Theology of Karl Barth* (Grand Rapids: Baker Academic, 2008), 235–60.

[4] Saint Athanasius, *On the Incarnation*, trans. John Behr (Yonkers: Saint Vladimir's Seminary Press, 2011), 54.

[5] Timothy [Kallistos] Ware, *The Orthodox Church*, new ed. (1963; repr., London: Penguin, 1997), 231.

[6] This is consistent with Ware's remarks about becoming "gods." The idea is not that redeemed humans become divine as God is divine but rather that redeemed humans participate in the divine nature in an intimate relation by means of which they acquire certain divine qualities—becoming like little "gods" (compare Ps 82).

[7] Sometimes Orthodox and patristic writers say that theosis means that what God is by *nature* redeemed humans become by *grace*. But I'm not clear how helpful this distinction is without a lot of further qualifications. For it cannot be the case that human beings become divine by an act of grace. The metaphysical bootstrapping issue would still obtain if this were the claim being made, and I'm not sure what it means to say an entity of one sort or kind is

what is shared between the divine persons of the Trinity, is essential to the triune persons, and is incommunicable to creatures. The divine nature is some quality or qualities that the divine persons possess that may or may not be essential to the divine persons, but that are communicable to creatures. For modern analytic metaphysicians, this may be less than clear. For on at least one way of carving these things up, "essence" and "nature" are synonyms, both referring to the properties or attributes God has necessarily, so that to "participate" in a nature (whatever that means) is just to participate in an essence—in which case this would be a distinction without a difference.[8]

But perhaps what is meant is something more like this: There are communicable attributes God possesses that he may share with creatures like humans. Humans may exemplify these attributes and may come to express those attributes in ways that reflect the divine in important respects. Here is an example: Perhaps human beings may exemplify, say, love in a fragmentary and imperfect manner. Yet through prolonged exposure to, and experience of, the divine nature, and through performing certain spiritual practices, human beings may come to exemplify love in a more complete manner— one that better approximates divine love, though it may never be identical to divine love. This is a matter to which we shall return presently.[9]

However one understands the nature/essence distinction, it should be clear from the foregoing that becoming "participants of the divine nature" (2 Pet 1:4) does not necessarily imply becoming divine as God is divine. It does not imply the reduction or removal of the massive ontological gulf that exists between God as the creator of all things and human beings as creatures. One might put it like this: Although the doctrine of theosis presumes that redeemed humanity become partakers of the divine nature, the doctrine does not imply that this relation of participation is symmetrical. Nor does it necessarily presume that the sort of exalted existence enjoyed by the

---

transmuted to another kind by an act of divine fiat. So I have left out discussion of this oft-cited distinction here.

   [8] At one point John Calvin suggests that the distinction has to do with what some contemporary metaphysicians would call a kind essence and an individual essence: "The word *nature* does not denote essence but kind" (John Calvin, *The Epistle of Paul the Apostle to the Hebrews and the First and Second Epistles of St. Peter*, ed. David W. Torrance and Thomas F. Torrance, trans. William B. Johnston [Edinburgh: Oliver & Boyd, 1963], 330).

   [9] It has been suggested to me that the Palamite distinction between the incommunicable divine essence and communicable divine energies might be a better way to carve this distinction because it does not raise the worry of a distinction without a difference. I invite the reader who agrees with this to make the relevant mental adjustment in what follows.

redeemed involves the transmutation of the redeemed into some metaphysically exalted state, making of them little deities.

With these two misunderstandings cleared away, let me say something by way of clarifying the conceptual content of theosis. As I have already mentioned, theosis is fundamentally concerned with participation in the divine life. The notion of participation, union with Christ, and other related concepts are very much in vogue in contemporary theology and biblical studies. But what does this amount to? What is meant by participation in the divine? According to the New Testament scholar and theologian Carl Mosser, "It is this: what is presently true about the incarnate Son will be made true of the redeemed. Redemption in the fullest sense is simply for a human person to become everything Jesus presently is in his glorified, ascended, fully flourishing humanity enthroned at God's right hand."[10] This is a strong claim that begs for further explication. Mosser seems to think that participation in the divine life for the redeemed means coming to exemplify the qualities and properties had by the human nature of Christ in his glorified state. Presumably, this includes some rather odd qualities, such as the ability to appear in locked rooms and physical immortality. But it does not mean that redeemed human beings are somehow made divine, thereby effacing the creator/creature distinction. On this view, participation in the divine involves exemplifying certain qualities had by the glorified human nature of Christ that are not currently enjoyed by fallen human beings. But it also involves a relation of intimate union with Christ, though one that (so it seems to me) stops short of hypostatic union. It is, I think, closer to the notion of a mathematical asymptote, where a curve is on a trajectory toward a line, though the two never finally intersect.

I like much of what Mosser says here. However, his claim that theosis "is simply for a human person to become everything Jesus presently is in his glorified, ascended, fully flourishing humanity enthroned at God's right hand," while consistent with much patristic theology on this matter, may need some finessing. For it is not clear to me that the humanity of the glorified, ascended Christ is significantly different than his humanity during his earthly ministry. To my way of thinking, the difference between Christ's humanity in his earthly ministry and in a glorified, ascended state has more to do with the manifestation of the divine nature "in" or "through" his human nature than it does with some significant (perhaps ontological) change to the human

---

[10] Carl Mosser, "The Metaphysics of Union with God," unpublished paper presented at Fuller Theological Seminary, May 4, 2017, 4.

nature in question. For Christ's human nature is already without sin (Heb 4:15) and is already capable of sustaining hypostatic union with a divine person (John 1:14). This rather different way of thinking about the humanity of the glorified, ascended Christ is consistent with a krypsis Christology, according to which Christ's divine nature is in a sense "hidden" or "concealed" in his incarnate state—a sort of weak functional kenoticism. On this way of thinking, the difference between Christ before his resurrection and Christ in his glorified, ascended state after the resurrection has much more to do with the way in which his divinity is no longer concealed in the same way, so that it is made manifest in his human nature.[11] So being conformed to the image of Christ who is the image of God in theosis is not (in my judgment) a matter of being conformed to the likeness of Christ's glorified humanity—as if that is significantly different from being conformed to the image of his preresurrection humanity. Rather, it is about coming to approximate to the way in which the divine nature is manifest through the human nature of Christ in his glorified, ascended state. Think of the difference between the coil of an electric light that shines dimly with a reduced electrical current running through it, and much more brightly when a stronger current is passed through it. The coil has not changed; the amount of electricity passing through it has. In a similar way, I am suggesting that the glorified, ascended humanity of Christ has not changed in any significant ontological sense. What has changed is not his humanity but the way in which his divinity "shines through" his human nature. So participation in the divine life in theosis does mean that (as Mosser has it) "what is presently true about the incarnate Son will be made true of the redeemed." Moreover, he may be right that redemption in the fullest sense on a theosis-compatible doctrine of participation means "simply for a human person to become everything Jesus presently is in his glorified, ascended, fully flourishing humanity enthroned at God's right hand." But in my view this does not mean that the human nature to which we are conformed is somehow significantly different from that of the preresurrection Christ.[12]

[11] A full explication of this point would take up much more space. Interested readers may consult Oliver D. Crisp, *Divinity and Humanity: The Incarnation Reconsidered* (Cambridge: Cambridge University Press, 2007), ch. 4, where I give some account of a krypsis Christology. This is also related to my argument in *The Word Enfleshed: Exploring the Person and Work of Christ* (Grand Rapids: Baker Academic, 2016) for the conclusion that we are made in the image of Christ, who is the image of God.

[12] Thanks to Christa McKirland for raising this worry about conformity to the glorified human nature of Christ.

Let us take stock. We have seen that theosis does not mean losing one's individuality in the divine. Nor does it mean becoming divine as God is divine. Instead, it is about participation in the divine life and about union with Christ by the power of the Holy Spirit. I presume that this participation is an ongoing thing that will continue into the eschaton. It has a first moment but no last moment because, as Jonathan Edwards puts it in his dissertation *God's End in Creation*, "God, in glorifying the saints in heaven with eternal felicity, aims to satisfy his infinite grace or benevolence, by the bestowment of a good infinitely valuable, because eternal: and yet there never will come the moment, when it can be said, that now this infinitely valuable good has been actually bestowed."[13]

Participation in the Divine Life

The notion of participation is doing a lot of the conceptual heavy lifting for the doctrine of theosis. But, as has already been intimated, what is meant by participation in the divine life in the context of doctrines of theosis is rather unclear. There is much gesturing in the direction of theosis in recent biblical studies and systematic theology. But there is much less by way of explanation of the notion of participation. Thus Princeton theologian Bruce McCormack asks,

> What is finally meant by the well-worn phrase *participation in the life of God*? The phrase is ambiguous on the face of it. Does it mean "participation in the life that is God's own, the life that is proper to him as God, that life that is his *essentially*?" If so, how is it possible to participate in it without participating in the divine essence? . . . To put a finer point on it: is the "life of God" in which we are said to participate *uncreated* life or *created* life?[14]

These are important theological questions. But, as we saw in the previous section, theosis doesn't imply reducing or removing the creator/creature distinction. Nor does it necessarily mean that the sort of participation redeemed creatures enjoy is tantamount to participation in uncreated life— for that would be to participate in divinity as God is divine, which would seem to be metaphysically impossible for creatures. Nor does it necessarily

[13] Edwards, *God's End in Creation*, in *Ethical Writings*, ed. Paul Ramsey, vol. 8 of *The Works of Jonathan Edwards*, ed. Perry Miller (New Haven: Yale University Press, 1989), 527.

[14] Bruce L. McCormack, "Union with Christ in Calvin's Theology: Grounds for a Divinization Theory?" in *Tributes to John Calvin: A Celebration of His Quincentenary*, ed. David W. Hall (Phillipsburg, N.J.: Presbyterian & Reformed, 2010), 505 (emphasis in original).

mean participation in that which is essential to the divine life. But then, as per McCormack's comment, some account of what is meant by participation in the divine life is still wanting.

However, before attempting to address that concern, it is worth noting that some theologians may be wary of even embarking on such a project. One worry is that attempting to get a clearer picture of the notion of participation at work in the doctrine of theosis may be tantamount to attempting to plumb the depths of a mystery the resolution of which is beyond our ken. Similarly, one might worry about an attempt to provide an explanation of, say, the Trinity or the incarnation that such projects are in principle futile because the explanation of these doctrines is simply beyond our human cognitive abilities. Such concerns need not arise where what is being attempted is not an explanation as such but a theological model or picture that may provide some insight into the matter at hand on analogy with scientific models of complex data. It is just such an approach I favor. Explaining human participation in the divine life may be a rather tall order; providing a model or models for thinking about this is both conceptually less demanding, because more theologically modest, and, as a consequence, more likely to make some theological headway. Let us turn to provide some content for such a model by means of a kind of metaphysical just-so story about human reconciliation with, and participation in, the divine.

Suppose we begin by taking up Eleonore Stump's Thomist-inspired account of love, according to which a loving relation between two persons comprises the desire to see the beloved flourish and the desire to be united with the beloved. God has such love for his creatures. So God desires that we flourish and that he be united with us. To that end God seeks union with his beloved creatures. We see this supremely in the case of Christ, where a divine person unites himself to a human nature in order to bring about human reconciliation with God. But in addition to this, this union with human nature in Christ is the means by which fallen human beings can be united to God as well. Christ is a kind of metaphysical bridge between divinity and humanity. As I said in chapter 6, he is a kind of hub, like a wireless hub, that connects us as fallen human beings to God.[15] Just as my personal computer is connected to the Internet by means of radio signals that are transmitted from the hub to my computer and from my computer to the hub, which is hardwired to a cable connection that links it to remote servers, so fallen human beings may be connected to the hub that is Christ by the power of the Holy Spirit.

[15] See also Crisp, *Word Enfleshed*.

This link connects fallen human beings with the divine via Christ's human nature, which is an interface between divinity and humanity.

However, although by means of a wireless connection my personal computer can be linked to the Internet so that I may connect with the myriad of information on the digital superhighway, such participation in the ethereal world of the World Wide Web seems to fall short of the sort of participation defenders of theosis envisage in the case of the union between Christ and the redeemed, having to do with "participating in the divine nature" (2 Pet 1:4) and becoming "gods . . . children of the Most High" (Ps 82:6). The organic analogies in places like Ephesians 5 that present a relation between Christ and his body (the church) more intimate and mysterious than that between spouses indicate something of what it is that is still lacking. In short, we need an account of participation that is more intimate than the most intimate human relationships (according to Ephesians), that is unitive in nature (according to Peter), but that falls short of a loss of the human individual in the divine life. In his work on the indwelling of the Holy Spirit, William Alston points out that models for thinking about the intimate relationship between the Spirit and redeemed human beings need to pay attention to the need for shared reciprocity.[16] This feature is also missing from the hub-computer analogy, which is not a union between agents.

A promising line of research on the relation of participation in this context can be found in a recent (currently unpublished) paper by Carl Mosser. In the course of his work, he suggests several possible models for thinking about participation in the divine life that pick up the biblical motifs and some of the most important postbiblical theological distinctions often found in discussion of the topic.[17]

One of these suggestions turns on understanding the notion of union with the divine in terms of powers-metaphysics. I take it that powers are something like dispositional properties that may be actualized given the right circumstances. Normally such dispositional powers have mutual manifestation partners, for example, the power of solubility that a sugar cube has when it is placed in water (an example Mosser also uses). Sugar has the

[16] William Alston, "The Indwelling of the Holy Spirit," in *Philosophy and the Christian Faith*, ed. Thomas V. Morris (Notre Dame: University of Notre Dame Press, 2006), 121–50.

[17] Mosser, "Metaphysics of Union with God." Mosser also considers the notion of union as instrumental agency whereby human beings may be God's instruments or vice-regents in the created order as a number of recent biblical-theological studies of the image of God in human beings have concluded. But I shall leave this to one side here as a model that I find less conducive to the present work.

dispositional property of being soluble in water. When a sugar cube is placed in a glass of water, the power of solubility that the cube has and the power of being an agent of solubility, which the water has, are mutually manifested with the result that the sugar cube is dissolved. Transpose this sort of thinking to the topic of participation in the divine life. Although human sin may inhibit human beings from manifesting the power of being united to God in Christ, the power of the Holy Spirit makes that possible, acting as a kind of manifestation partner and bringing about union with God in Christ. This seems like one promising way of conceiving how the union relation at the heart of the doctrine of participation works, but it doesn't really do very much to explain the relation itself.

Perhaps the model of union on analogy with the notion of an instrumental union may address this concern. The paradigm of an instrumental union is between an agent and some artifact. A good example of this is chopping a carrot with a knife. The instrument (knife) is utilized to bring about a nonbasic action that could not otherwise be brought about without the knife (chopping the carrot). We have such accidental instrumental unions all the time, from the use of kitchen implements to how we interact with our smartphones.

Now, apply this to the question of participation in the divine life. Given our assumption that God desires union with his human creatures, one way of bringing that about might be to have Christ act as an interface between divinity and humanity in order that human beings can be united to God via the Holy Spirit. However, unlike the examples of the smartphone and the knife, in "extending" himself to unite himself with human beings, God does not reduce humans to mere instruments. That would be to fail in an important respect to treat us as created agents, and I suggest that it would be a significant shortcoming in God if he treated his creatures merely as instruments for the bringing about of his own purposes. Nevertheless, there may be a sense in which the unitive relation brought about by the Holy Spirit in the life of the redeemed individual does extend God's action into the life of that individual, bringing about a mutual awareness and reciprocity (such as William Alston suggests should characterize the indwelling of the Holy Spirit), as well as a unitive relation that is asymmetrical in important respects as the relation between the agent and the artifact (knife, smartphone) is asymmetrical. For here in the theological context, it is God that takes the initiative, God who secures the means by which we may be united to him in Christ by the Spirit, and God who sustains and nourishes the relationship of participation as it develops. We might think of this theological application of instrumental union as a particular instance of a kind of asymmetrical accessing relation of the sort more familiar in discussion of Thomas Morris' two minds Christology.[18] God has complete access to our minds and our desires; we have only partial access to the divine mind and desires. Yet, on this way of thinking, that access may grow and develop as the redeemed human continues to grow in his or her knowledge and understanding of this union with the divine. And, for all we know, this spiritual growth could be everlasting.

The Theory of Final Assumptions

Earlier, in attempting to clarify what the doctrine of theosis commits the theologian to, I said that one misunderstanding of the doctrine was that theosis means becoming divine as God is divine. Instead, as I have construed it, the doctrine is about being united to God in Christ by the Holy Spirit and being conformed to the image of his glorified human nature—that is, a certain cluster of qualities his glorified human nature exemplifies. However, in the recent philosophical-theological literature, Thomas Flint has argued that a "consummation devoutly to be wished" is that redeemed human beings be assumed by Christ so that they are hypostatically united to the divine nature. This, Flint maintains, is one plausible way to think about the existence enjoyed by the redeemed in the life to come. And, although he doesn't put it this way, it may also provide a way of construing the metaphysics of the beatific vision.

His reasoning goes like this: Suppose that incarnation involves the assumption of a concrete particular, a human nature, by a divine person. In assuming a human nature, a divine person "uploads" himself into that nature, taking possession of it. In taking possession of it, he makes it his own—it is his human nature. Normally speaking, the concrete particular that is a human nature would be formed in utero and in due course become a human person distinct from the divine persons of the Trinity. In the case of Christ, the formation of a normal human nature occurs in utero, but it does not become a human person distinct from a divine person, although he has the complete natural endowment of human nature that would, under normal circumstances, simply form a human person at a certain moment of biological development (whenever that may be). The difference in the case of the incarnation is that at the very moment in human biological development at which a human person would normally begin to exist, the Second Person

---

[18] See Thomas V. Morris, *The Logic of God Incarnate* (Ithaca, N.Y.: Cornell University Press, 1986).

of the Trinity assumes the human nature in question. He makes it his own so that it never forms a person independent of the divine persons of the Godhead. In the language of medieval school theology, Christ's human nature never forms a supposit or fundamental substance independent of the divine persons of the Godhead as would normally happen in the case of the biological development of a mere human. This is because the concrete particular of Christ's human nature is assumed before it can become a fundamental substance or supposit. It is personally united to a divine person instead, and it is the divine person "in" Christ that forms the person of Christ—the fundamental substance that is at the root of Christ's being, so to speak.

So much for the metaphysics of the incarnation. Flint takes something like this model, a model that has a long theological history, and asks whether this could tell us something about the final goal of human beings. In particular, he asks whether God the Son could assume not just the human nature of Jesus of Nazareth but also the human natures of all the redeemed in the eschaton. That is, could God the Son take possession of our human natures in addition to his own, bringing our human natures into personal union with his own nature? And could he do that in such a way that we would enjoy the intimate relation of participation with the divine that traditional doctrines of theosis presume, yet without effacing *us* in the process? Flint thinks that such a doctrine of multiple incarnations is metaphysically possible, and maybe even desirable. He calls this *the Theory of Final Assumptions* (hereinafter, TFA).[19]

According to Flint it is metaphysically possible for a divine person to bring multiple human natures into personal union with himself so that these redeemed concrete particulars cease to be persons. He writes, "Why not think that the nature survives the assumption without any corruption of any sort, but that, because of its new state of union with the Son, it no longer qualifies as a person?"[20] This question motivates the central claim of the TFA—namely, that *the ultimate end of all human beings who attain salvation is to be assumed by the Son*. Although redeemed human beings do not become divine as such, they do come to be assumed by a divine person. They

---

[19] Thomas P. Flint, "Molinism and Incarnation," in *Molinism: The Contemporary Debate*, ed. Ken Perszyk (Oxford: Oxford University Press, 2011), 13 (Oxford Online edition, DOI: 10.1093/acprof:oso/9780199590629.001.0001). His TFA is set in a broader context, that of his Molinist account of the incarnation. But the TFA argument can be lifted from that broader context so that it stands alone as an argument for a particular eschatological view of human beings that is independent of his Molinism. That is what I shall do here.

[20] Flint, "Molinism and Incarnation," 13.

are hypostatically united to a divine person. This amounts to the claim that personhood is an accidental property of human beings. Flint speculates that human beings are either persons or assumed by a divine person—that is, belong to a divine person as an assumed human nature.

Ryan Mullins has taken issue with Flint's account, Flint has replied, and Mullins has lodged a rejoinder.[21] In that debate Flint clarifies his position in several respects that are salient. First, he makes it clear that the TFA means redeemed humans in the eschaton do cease to be human persons but do not thereby cease to exist full stop. "Rather," he says, "they continue to exist, but now in an exalted position, as body/soul composites united with the Son in the unfathomably rich and complete way that CHN [Christ's Human Nature] was always united with him."[22] The idea seems to be this: There is a group of entities that are all human beings. These human beings prior to their glorification are all human persons. However, at the moment of glorification, they lose the property of personhood in virtue of being assumed by a divine person. They remain concrete particular individuals, but they cease to be "independent substances of a rational nature," to appropriate the traditional Boethian account of personhood. They are now dependent substances of a rational nature because they belong to—that is, are the assumed human natures of—a divine person.

Now Mullins has other concerns about Flint's position, including a concern about its theological orthodoxy. Although I do not propose to enter into those claims in detail here, some brief comments on Mullins' concerns seem appropriate. First, Mullins thinks that on Flint's view, kicking Crisp in the eschaton implies kicking Jesus because Crisp and Jesus are both assumed human natures that belong to one subject—namely, God the Son. He writes,

> At present, if you kick my body, you will have kicked me. You will not have kicked the Son. I bear the property *having been kicked*. When we reach the eschaton, however, things will be different. If you kick me, you will have kicked the Son. If the Son assumes my human nature, I cease to be a person. Through the *communicatio idiomatum* [that is, the communication of attributes in Christ from one nature to the other, or from both natures to the person], the Son becomes the ultimate bearer of the properties of

---

[21] See R. T. Mullins, "Flint's 'Molinism and the Incarnation' Is Too Radical," *Journal of Analytic Theology* 3 (2015): 1–15; Thomas P. Flint, "Orthodoxy and Incarnation: A Reply to Mullins," *Journal of Analytic Theology* 4 (2016): 180–92; and R. T. Mullins, "Flint's 'Molinism and the Incarnation' Is Still Too Radical—A Rejoinder to Flint," *Journal of Analytic Theology* 5 (2017): 515–32.

[22] Flint, "Orthodoxy and Incarnation," 184.

all the assumed human natures. So if you kick me in heaven, you will have ultimately kicked Christ. If I kick you in return, I will have kicked Christ. Given the *communicatio idiomatum*, Christ will have kicked Christ, and Christ will have responded to this kick by kicking Christ. That seems ludicrous.[23]

On the face of it, this state of affairs does indeed seem odd, but it isn't clear to me that it is ludicrous. Consider the case of Eschatological Crisp and Jesus. These are two distinct human natures that are concrete particulars assumed by God the Son. However, given Flint's account of the metaphysics of the incarnation, the two concrete particulars in question are clearly distinct; they are not identical to one another. True, they are both concrete particulars "owned" by one divine person, and that is a very strange state of affairs—one in which a single divine subject owns two (or more) human natures. But the compositional model of the incarnation favored by Flint does not imply that God the Son is identical with Christ, only that God the Son is a part of Christ. Jesus is composed of his human nature and God the Son. Eschatological Crisp is composed of his human nature and God the Son. But if that is right, then clearly Jesus and Eschatological Crisp are not identical for they do not share all and only the same parts. True, one divine subject owns two human natures, on this way of thinking. Nevertheless, it is not incoherent to think that Eschatological Crisp may kick Jesus, although it is very strange to think he might do so for it does amount to a state of affairs in which one divine subject uses his Eschatological Crisp human nature to act upon his Jesus human nature. An exotic implication of Flint's TFA? No doubt. A ludicrous implication of Flint's TFA? Not obviously.

Second, Mullins thinks that Flint's position is unorthodox because, according to the Fifth Ecumenical Council of Constantinople, the human nature assumed by Christ is made personal by its union with God the Son. It is said to be anhypostatic (without personhood) in abstraction, as it were, from the incarnation, and enhypostatic (made personal) by its union with a divine person. But Flint's position does not necessarily fall foul of this theological distinction. For suppose that the an-enhypostatic nature distinction is right. That just means that Christ's human nature is made personal by its union with God the Son. True, Flint seems to think that Christ's human nature would form a mere human person independent of assumption in possible worlds at which Jesus of Nazareth obtains without the act of

---

[23] Mullins, "Flint's 'Molinism and the Incarnation' Is Too Radical," 5.

incarnation.[24] But the logic of the TFA taken as a stand-alone argument for the conclusion that the redeemed are eventually hypostatically united to God the Son doesn't *require* that concession. A defender of such a stand-alone version of the TFA could affirm the following:

(1) Christ's human nature is formed for God the Son.
(2) Christ's human nature only exists at worlds where God the Son assumes it.
(3) There are no worlds at which the human nature of God the Son exists unassumed and forms a mere human person independent of incarnation.

Whatever the metaphysics of assumption in the case of Christ's human nature turn out to be, the interesting theological question for our purposes is whether *we* could be assumed by God the Son in the eschaton. I don't see why something like Flint's TFA could not be taken up with the an-enhypostatic nature distinction in place so that in the case of Christ his human nature is made personal through union with God the Son (and there are no worlds at which his human nature exists unassumed), but my human nature is rendered nonpersonal by being assumed by God the Son. In fact, that is what we would expect to happen given that in the case of Christ, God the Son assumes an "impersonal" human nature generated for assumption, whereas in the case of Eschatological Crisp (and all other redeemed human beings), an existing human person loses that personhood in being assumed by a divine person, on analogy with the heretical doctrine of adoptionism in Christology.

Now, at first blush it seems odd to think that something like adoptionism obtains in the case of the redeemed though it is a heresy when applied to Christology. But there are good theological reasons for that, reasons having to do with ensuring that there is only one (divine) person in Christ from the get-go in order that the person who is incarnate is a suitable candidate for being the mediator of human salvation. These considerations clearly do not apply to the assumption of my human nature or yours.[25]

---

[24] This has to do with Flint's commitment to a Molinist account of the incarnation, a matter that we need not enter into here. Interested readers are directed to Flint's work on this topic for more information.

[25] Another objection to Flint's view was put to me by Dru Johnson. Let us call it *the multiple incarnations simpliciter objection*. Suppose that at the very moment when all human natures are assumed by God the Son, there is at least one human conceived in utero. This human being is immediately assumed by God the Son along with every other human nature. However, unlike these other human natures, the nature of the entity generated at the very moment of assumption is not a human person, as such, but the natural endowment of a human person. It has not existed long enough to become a human person independent of a

Nevertheless, I am leery of the prospect of being assumed by a divine person, although the reasons for my concern are rather different from Mullins. To see why, let us return to Flint's claim that personhood may be an accidental quality in human beings that human beings can lose without ceasing to exist altogether. That is, let us return to his claim that *human beings cannot exist without either being a person or being assumed by a person*. Note that Flint here makes sufficient metaphysical room, so to speak, for the theologian to affirm the following: The concrete particular that is a human nature is such that it either forms a fundamental substance independent of a divine person, thereby becoming a human person, or it is assumed by a (divine) person. If it is assumed by a divine person, then the human nature in question either never becomes a human person (because assumption occurs at the moment the human nature is generated) or it ceases to be a human person (because it is assumed by a divine person at some moment later than the first moment at which the complete human nature began to exist). So Flint can accommodate the classical orthodox theological notion that all human natures are in principle assumable by a divine person. It is just that he denies the classical theological assumption that in fact this only obtains in the case of one individual—namely, Christ.

My concern with this reasoning is that it is not clear what is left of a human being once personhood is removed through assumption. In the case of Christ, there is only one person present, though he has two natures. There are at least two concrete particulars (his human nature and his divine nature) but not two persons present in Christ on pain of Nestorianism. But that is because, in the case of Christ, assumption takes place from the first moment at which Christ's human nature begins to exist. There is no period in which the human nature of Christ exists independent of a divine person prior to assumption. But what would it mean for an existing human person to cease to be a person while remaining a distinct individual assumed by a divine person? Flint seems to think that assumption by a divine person will enhance the lives of the redeemed in a way analogous to the optimism transhumanists have about enhancing and enlarging human capacities by adding and integrating new technologies into human organisms. Putting it in the parlance of Boethian persons once more (something Flint himself does not do), we

---

divine person. So at the moment of assumption, this human being is hypostatically united to God the Son, who makes it "his" human nature. But because it is not a human person independent of God the Son at the moment of assumption, it becomes his human nature in a way comparable to the assumption of the human nature of Jesus of Nazareth. The upshot: multiple incarnations *simpliciter*!

might say that on Flint's view redeemed humans remain distinct substances of a rational nature but lose the property of being subsistent beings—that is, of being fundamental substances or supposits that are independent of a divine person.

Still, even if we grant this, it is difficult to see how Christology alone will provide the apparatus by means of which we can explain how the redeemed can be assumed entities that remain human beings without being human persons. How am I still present in the eschaton if I am assumed and lose my personhood in the process, being "personalized" by God the Son? We don't want to apply similar reasoning in the case of Christ because it implies adoptionism. How is this any better in the case of the assumption of mere humans who are existing persons? To put it another way, Flint wants to resist adoptionism in the case of Christ. However, in the case of the redeemed, what obtains in the eschaton looks a lot more like a case of the divine assimilation of an existing person than it does assumption as in the case of a theologically orthodox doctrine of incarnation. This is not so much a problem as a theologically curious consequence of Flint's position. But it is one with which I am rather uncomfortable.

These are not knockdown, drag-out reasons for rejecting Flint's position. There is much that is intriguing about his view, not least because it provides a model for understanding the sort of strong language of participation in the divine life that a doctrine of theosis presumes. But in my judgment the conclusion he draws raises more problems than it solves—particularly in terms of trying to provide some reason to think I may continue to exist in an eschatological state where I cease to be a subsistent entity, becoming an assumed human nature of a divine person. This, it seems to me, is tantamount to too much participation in the divine, or what we might think of as a limit case to the sort of doctrine of participation that I set out to analyze. Although I understand Flint's claim that this might be regarded not so much as a loss but as a gain—the loss of my personhood to gain immediate participation in the divine life through assumption—it amounts to a doctrine of participation at the cost of eliminating or effacing creaturely personhood. Few theologians will want to follow Flint in embracing that eschatological upshot to his position.

Conclusion

I have argued that the doctrine of theosis can be understood in such a way that it encapsulates the broad sweep of God's action in reconciling fallen human beings to Godself via the work of Christ by the power of the Holy Spirit. We could summarize much of the foregoing in the following:

THEOSIS: The doctrine according to which redeemed human beings are conformed to the image of Christ in his human nature. By being united to Christ by the power of the Holy Spirit, redeemed human beings begin to exemplify the qualities of the human nature of Christ and grow in their likeness to Christ (in exemplifying the requisite qualities Christ's human nature instantiates). This process of transformation and participation goes on forevermore. It is akin to a mathematical asymptote.

A key notion at work in this way of thinking about the reconciling action of God in Christ is participation in the divine nature. In keeping with some recent work in the area, I have suggested several ways in which the relation of participation may be construed: in terms of a hub-computer analogy, in terms of dispositional properties or powers, and in terms of extended minds.[26] These are conceptual building blocks that might form the basis of a model of participation in the divine life consistent with theosis—first steps along the way, so to speak, that are supposed to be indicative rather than normative. Finally, I have addressed one recent and interesting argument from Tom Flint that supposes it is metaphysically possible, and perhaps desirable, for multiple incarnations to obtain simultaneously by means of the hypostatic union of the redeemed. Although this is a model of participation that is consistent with the view of theosis outlined here, in my view it is too strong because it requires the loss of human personhood in order for union with God to occur. Thus, I suggest that a plausible doctrine of theosis will be one that takes seriously the need to provide an account of participation that is more intimate than the most intimate human relationships (as per Eph 5), that is unitive in nature, but that falls short of a loss of the human individual in the divine life. This is also consistent with several ways of thinking about the atonement, including the union account I have outlined elsewhere. But I shall leave specifying how theosis and atonement are related for another occasion.[27]

---

[26] Recall that the latter two analogues draw upon the very helpful work of Carl Mosser.

[27] For my own account of the atonement, see *Word Enfleshed*. The doctrine of theosis outlined here is a complement to the doctrine of atonement outlined there.

Bodily Resurrection

The Resurrection of Jesus is the central fact of Christian devotion and the ground of all Christian thinking.

Robert Louis Wilken[1]

The reconciling work of Christ has two aspects or phases: his incarnation life and ministry, and his death and resurrection. Thus far we have considered several nodal issues in the incarnation (virginal conception and dyothelitism) and in the nature of salvation (theosis). In this final chapter we turn to the matter of the resurrection of Christ.

According to the British theologian Gareth Jones, the "one crucial question" facing theologians as they consider the resurrection of Christ is, What happened to Jesus' body? "Any essay on the resurrection which fails to consider this question," says Jones, "fails the resurrection."[2] There are certainly theological voices in recent times that echo this sentiment, and for whom

---

[1]   Robert Louis Wilken, *The Spirit of Early Christian Thought: Seeking the Face of God* (New Haven: Yale University Press, 2002), xv.

[2]   Gareth Jones, "The Resurrection in Contemporary Systematic Theology," in *Resurrection Reconsidered*, ed. Gavin D'Costa, (Oxford: Oneworld, 1996), 31. The history of responses to this question in modern theology is taken up by Douglas Farrow in *Ascension and Ecclesia: On the Significance of the Doctrine of the Ascension for Ecclesiology and Christian Cosmology* (Edinburgh: T&T Clark, 1999), ch. 5. See also Farrow, *Ascension Theology* (London: T&T Clark, 2011), the first few chapters of which recapitulate much of his earlier study in a more popular format. Farrow distinguishes between an Irenaean approach to the ascended, cosmic Christ and an Origenist one. The Origenist approach sees the resurrection and ascension in terms of Christ's increasing presence in creation; the Irenaean approach preserves the traditional notion of Christ's real ascension. Jenson's approach appears to buck this categorization, as we shall see.

there is a close connection between the empty tomb and the historicity of the resurrection event. Among recent systematic theologians, Wolfhart Pannenberg is particularly well known for his trenchant defense of the historical resurrection of Christ.[3] The same is true of Thomas F. Torrance, who maintains that "if the resurrection is not an event in history, a happening within the same order of physical existence to which we belong, then atonement and redemption are empty vanities, for they achieve nothing for historical men and women in the world."[4] Similarly forthright views can be found among contemporary philosophical theologians. For instance, Richard Swinburne maintains that the resurrection of Christ would be "a violation of natural laws that only God could bring about."[5] But there are also important modern theological voices that deny this. The two best known are Rudolf Bultmann and Karl Barth. Both of these theologians argue that the resurrection of Christ is not primarily a matter of history—as if we could have photographed it if we traveled back in time to see the garden tomb—but of eschatology. God's kingdom breaks in through Christ's life and work, and his resurrection is further testimony to this. Yet the resurrection of Christ is not itself a historical event but something beyond or above historical processes.[6]

Robert Jenson's discussion of this issue in the first volume of his *Systematic Theology* is an important recent contribution to this discussion.[7] His argument is neither a defense of the historicity of the resurrection like Pannenberg, Torrance, or Swinburne, nor a denial of it like Bultmann and Barth. Instead, he attempts to reframe the doctrine so that the postresurrection body of Christ is *whatever makes Christ available to us*. This leads him to some unusual and potentially fruitful conclusions about the location of the postresurrection body of Christ that are worth considering in detail.

---

[3] See, e.g., Wolfhart Pannenberg, "History and the Reality of the Resurrection," in D'Costa, *Resurrection Reconsidered*, 62–72; *Systematic Theology*, 3 vols., trans. Geoffrey W. Bromiley (Grand Rapids: Eerdmans, 1994), 10.1.c., 2:343–63; and *Jesus—God and Man*, trans. Lewis L. Wilkins and Duane A. Priebe (London: SCM, 1964), ch. 3.

[4] Thomas F. Torrance, *Space, Time and Resurrection* (Grand Rapids: Eerdmans, 1976), 87. Later, in discussing the ascension of Christ, he remarks, "It is *the empty tomb that constitutes the essential empirical correlate in statements about the resurrection of Christ*, the point where the triumph of Christ over the space-time of our fallen world is nevertheless correlated with the space-time of our ongoing existence in this world" (141, emphasis in original).

[5] Richard Swinburne, *The Resurrection of God Incarnate* (Oxford: Oxford University Press, 2003), 187.

[6] For a helpful discussion of this point, see Murray A. Rae, *History and Hermeneutics* (London: T&T Clark, 2005), ch. 4.

[7] Robert W. Jenson, *Systematic Theology*, vol. 1, *The Triune God* (New York: Oxford University Press, 1997).

To that end, in the first section that follows I shall provide an overview of Jenson's argument. Then, in a second section, I shall consider two issues that arise from Jenson's account, pursuant to Jones' question. The first has to do with whether his position implies a doctrine of multiple incarnations. The second has to do with the puzzle of Christ's missing body on Easter Day. The third section attempts to amend one central strand of Jenson's argument so as to address the puzzle about Christ's missing body. Although it goes beyond what Jenson argues for, the hope is that it provides a *Jensonian* dogmatic sketch of Christ's resurrection that provides a more adequate answer to Gareth Jones' question.

Jenson's Account of the Resurrection of Christ

According to Jenson, the gospel is an expansion of the proposition "Jesus, the one who . . . is risen."[8] Yet the resurrection is not an event that any human being has witnessed, or perhaps can witness. What we are faced with are two closely related issues. The first is explaining the empty tomb attested to by the canonical Gospels, beginning with Mark. The second is giving some account of the resurrection, a matter that can be found in some of the earliest material in the New Testament (e.g., 1 Cor 15). Those, like Pannenberg, Torrance, and Swinburne, who think that these two issues are intertwined presume that the empty tomb implies a resurrection of the body. However, those who like Bultmann (and, perhaps, Barth) think that the two issues are quite distinct do not see things this way. They are willing to consider the prospect of a resurrection independent of the issue of an empty tomb—that is, independent of whether Christ's body remained in the tomb after Easter Sunday morning.

Jenson seems sympathetic to the idea of distinguishing the question of the empty tomb from the question of the resurrection of Christ. He remarks that the church proclaims "a *bodily* resurrection, with or without an emptying of the tomb."[9] At first glance, this is a puzzling remark. However, if we consider what Jenson actually says by way of elaboration upon this point, matters should become clearer.

Following Jenson's lead, let us begin by considering the resurrection of Christ independent of the question of the empty tomb. According to Jenson,

---

[8] Jenson, *Systematic Theology*, 1:4, 195.
[9] Jenson, *Systematic Theology*, 1:201.

Paul speaks of Christ's resurrection as an *apocalypsis*, a revelation.[10] Never-theless, the appearance accounts do not describe Christ's resurrection as a return to the same time and space as his disciples, says Jenson.[11] Although Christ appeared to them, he did not remain with them. Instead, Jesus rose into the future that God prepares for us.[12] Indeed, "Christ is risen into the Kingdom, and Christ is risen into God. He is located in the heaven seen by the apocalyptic prophets [like Daniel], and he is located in the triune life."[13] This eschatological kingdom remains, in some sense, a thing of the future, of which the resurrection of Christ is something like a firstfruit or promissory note. Jenson goes on to say that the future kingdom is available to us in the present through our union with the Son in the church: "The Church is the present *availability* of the Kingdom."[14]

From this it seems that Jenson thinks that there is a bodily resurrection of Christ, but this should not be conflated with a mere resuscitation, as if Christ's return to life on Easter Sunday was the reanimation of his corpse, a return to the human existence that he had enjoyed until Good Friday. There is something about Christ's resurrection that signals the fact that his resurrection life is different in kind from the life he lived until his death on Good Friday. So it is not just some token of the eschatological life we will all enjoy in the future. It is not as if Christ's resurrection should be taken as only indicative of the life to come. It *is* that, in one respect, but it is not *merely* that. In other words, Jenson doesn't content himself with the evangel-ical commonplace that Christ's resurrected life is just the intimation of the coming eschatological kingdom of God. He goes well beyond this—as his initial admission about there being a bodily resurrection "with or without an empty tomb" indicates.

In what manner does he go beyond this evangelical commonplace affir-mation of a bodily resurrection as the firstfruits of the life to come? Here we come to what I think is the constructive heart of Jenson's proposal, which will be the focus of attention in the analysis of his position in the next section of this essay.

---

[10] Jenson, *Systematic Theology*, 1:196, citing Gal 1:12, which is referring not to Christ's resurrection directly but to the gospel message that Paul received through revelation. Perhaps his resurrection, being a central part of the gospel message, may be said to be included in what Paul says by synecdoche.

[11] Jenson, *Systematic Theology*, 1:197.

[12] Jenson, *Systematic Theology*, 1:198.

[13] Jenson, *Systematic Theology*, 1:201.

[14] Jenson, *Systematic Theology*, 1:201 (emphasis added).

On a premodern cosmology, such as is presupposed in traditional accounts of the bodily resurrection of Christ, making sense of the location of the risen Christ is unproblematic. Heaven is a place farthest away from the earth, and Christ's body is said to "ascend" and be located there. This is not feasible in a Copernican cosmology. Jenson remarks, "Within any modern cosmology, the assertion that the body is up there some place must rightly provoke mocking proposals to search for it with more powerful telescopes."[15] It is not surprising, then, that many modern believers cannot fit a bodily resurrection into their worldview. For a "body requires its place, and we find it hard to think of any place for this one."[16] Giving up on a Copernican universe is not feasible. So what is the believer in the bodily resurrection of Christ to do? Jenson suggests reconceptualizing heaven as "the created future's presence to God," not as a location in created space-time.[17] This removes the need to explain how Christ's body moves from one location to another (in the period between resurrection and ascension), although it doesn't alleviate the concern about finding a place for Christ's risen body.

The questions that arise regarding the location of Christ's body postresurrection are not just worries raised by changing cosmological paradigms, however. They are part of the fabric of Christian theology given the fact that, for many Christians, Christ is said to be corporeally present in the eucharistic elements and corporeally present at the right hand of the Father in heaven. As Jenson points out, sacramental theology provides a traditional place at which issues of Christ's postresurrection corporeal location are subject to dogmatic scrutiny.

Medieval scholasticism attempted to negotiate this problem by arriving at creative ways to talk about the notion of corporeal presence (a matter that Jenson doesn't explore in detail). *Circumscriptive presence* is a sort of presence that entails extension at a particular place: my body is circumscriptively present in a particular space and place in Pasadena, California, as I write this line. My whole body exists in a certain place and is extended in a certain space; parts of my body occupy parts of that space and are extended in parts of that space, such as my hands or feet. This seems intuitive for medium to large material objects, like bodies. But some medieval theologians argued that this is not true of spiritual substances like souls that may exist wholly in the body and wholly in every part of the body. This they called *definitive presence*.

---

[15] Jenson, *Systematic Theology*, 1:202. This is a point elaborated upon in much more detail by Farrow in *Ascension and Ecclesia*.

[16] Jenson, *Systematic Theology*, 1:202.

[17] Jenson, *Systematic Theology*, 1:201.

Could a material body be wholly present in the whole of a place and wholly present in every part of that place? That is, could a material body exist somewhere definitively rather than circumscriptively? It seems strange to think so, given that bodies have parts that are extended. But perhaps God can do this miraculously—perhaps he has a reason to do so in the case of the eucharistic presence of Christ in the sacramental elements of bread and wine.[18] Then, Christ could be both fully bodily present in heaven (understood in the premodern sense as a place) and in the eucharistic elements (understood in terms of some unspecified doctrine of real, corporeal presence) without compromising the integrity of his body in heaven or in the communion meal. For Christ could be wholly corporeally present in heaven and wholly corporeally present in the eucharistic elements. Jenson comments that in this affirmation, "Theology short-circuited the whole conceptual framework by which it otherwise accounted for the risen Christ's bodily reality."[19]

Is there an alternative way of thinking about Christ's resurrected body that taps into the traditional, sacramental language of real, corporeal presence[20] and that avoids the problems Jenson perceives exist in the medieval debates? Jenson thinks there is. Taking his cue from the Swabian theologians, and especially Johannes Brenz (1499–1570), he reasons that the problem of Christ's corporeal presence in the sacrament is not particularly troublesome if one is already committed to the doctrine of incarnation. Indeed, "What we call the humanity of Christ and the deity of Christ are only actual as one sole

---

[18] My discussion of circumscriptive and definitive presence is indebted to Marilyn McCord Adams' excellent treatment of this topic in *Christ and Horrors: The Coherence of Christology*, Current Issues in Theology 3 (Cambridge: Cambridge University Press, 2006), 299–302. Jenson's very brief mention of the medieval discussion does not go into this detail.

[19] Jenson, *Systematic Theology*, 1:203.

[20] "Real, corporeal presence" is a term of art that should be explained. A real presence doctrine of the Eucharist claims that Christ's body is somehow really present with, in, or by means of the blessed elements. A corporeal presence doctrine goes a step further, asserting that Christ's body is somehow corporeally present with, in, or by means of the blessed elements. There are a variety of real presence views, and a variety of corporeal presence views. All corporeal presence views are also real presence views; but not all real presence views are corporeal presence views. That is, Christ must be really present in the elements if he is corporeally present. Yet he could be really but not corporeally present in the eucharistic elements. For helpful discussion of these matters, see James M. Arcadi, "Recent Philosophical Work on the Doctrine of the Eucharist," *Philosophy Compass* 11 (2016): 402–12. Arcadi develops his own constructive proposal in Arcadi, *An Incarnational Model of the Eucharist*, Current Issues in Theology 10 (Cambridge: Cambridge University Press, 2018), a work that repays study.

person, so that where the deity of the Son is, there must be Jesus' humanity, unabridged as soul and body."[21]

Moreover, Jenson argues, "Christ has risen to be in God's place. God, however, is *in* no place but *is* his own place."[22] He elaborates,

> For God there are only two places: the place that he is and the place he makes for creatures, immediately and inwardly adjacent to him. Thus the creation is for God just one place. And the one creation is heaven and earth together, however otherwise they differ. Therefore the difference between God's being in heaven and his being on earth can only be a difference between styles of presence.[23]

As Jenson is quick to point out, the problem is not *that* Christ is corporeally present in the eucharistic elements but *how* his corporeal presence in the eucharistic elements is different from the manner of his presence elsewhere, in other contexts. The idea seems to be this: There is God, and there is the created order. God is immediately present to the whole creation. He doesn't exist in some location outside creation, from which vantage he rules over that which he has made. Such reasoning perpetuates the mistaken premodern cosmology from which Jenson wants to distance himself. Instead, God exists, and creation exists, and God is omnipresent in the creation. This omnipresence is not equivalent to omni-location or omni-extension, although there may be different modes of divine presence or different ways in which we experience the divine presence, such as in the Word, in salvation, and so on. Now, Jenson believes that Jesus is identical to God the Son, so that Jesus' humanity makes God the Son available to us—corporeally available, that is. Presumably, he is corporeally available as Jesus while simultaneously omnipresent in the created order (which is just a version of the so-called *extra calvinisticum*). But then, what happens to the body of Jesus upon being resurrected and ascending into heaven? Where does his body "go," so to speak, if heaven is not a location but the presence of God, and God is not located in some separate realm but intimately present with every point in space-time?

Following the Swabian theologians, Jenson's answer is that Christ's resurrected body is what makes him available to us now, just as his human body—the body of Jesus of Nazareth—made him available to his earthly disciples. And what makes him available to us now is his corporeal presence in the eucharistic meal, and his presence in the church, which is the body of

---

[21] Jenson, *Systematic Theology*, 1:203.
[22] Jenson, *Systematic Theology*, 1:203–4.
[23] Jenson, *Systematic Theology*, 1:254.

Christ.[24] This, he thinks, is perfectly Pauline. Although Paul (mistakenly?) believed Christ was visibly located in a heavenly realm spatially related to the rest of creation, "the only body of Christ to which Paul ever actually refers is not an entity in this heaven but the Eucharist's loaf and cup and the church assembled around them."[25] He elaborates upon this theme as follows: "For Paul a person's embodiment is his or her *availability* to other persons [as an object] and thereupon to her or himself."[26] This is not a demythologizing of Christ's resurrected body; no metaphor or "ontological evasion" is intended.[27] Christ presented himself to disciples and the following crowds in the body that he bore to the cross, and "the risen Christ gives himself to us to be our object" now in the sacrament and church.[28]

This brings us to the matter of the empty tomb. Not only might we ask Jenson, Where is the body of Christ postresurrection? We may also ask a prior question: Was the tomb empty? (For it might be thought that Christ could be in the tomb as well as in the eucharistic elements so as to preserve the resurrection of his "body" in the church and her sacraments while rejecting the notion of a bodily resurrection from the tomb.) Jenson's cautious response is that the tomb was indeed empty—and for good theological reasons, though not, perhaps, the traditional one that might be expected. Had Christ's body remained in the tomb, he says, it would have become the focus for devotion rather than the eucharistic meal. It would have become a relic, and Christ would have become a saint of sorts—available only via a corpse. This, Jenson judges, would have yielded an entirely different means by which Christ was made available to us, one that would have been highly undesirable. For this reason the tomb must be empty.

Two Issues for Jenson's Account

We turn now to assess Jenson's position, bearing in mind the question raised by Gareth Jones, with which we began. There are two issues that I want to consider. The first is what I shall call *the question of multiple incarnations*. The second we shall call *the puzzle of the empty tomb*.

[24] Jenson, *Systematic Theology*, 1:204–5.
[25] Jenson, *Systematic Theology*, 1:204.
[26] Jenson, *Systematic Theology*, 1:213.
[27] Jenson, *Systematic Theology*, 1:206.
[28] Robert W. Jenson, "Autobiographical Reflections on the Relation of Theology, Science, and Philosophy; or, You Wonder Where the Body Went," in *Essays in Theology of Culture* (Grand Rapids: Eerdmans, 1995), 220.

To begin with, let us focus on the question of multiple incarnations. We have seen that Jenson is committed to the assumption that God is omnipresent in creation. He is also committed to the notion that Christ is identical to God the Son—a matter that is spelled out in one of his more recent essays.[29] In addition, we have seen that he believes that Christ's body is whatever makes him (i.e., the person of Christ) available to us now. On the basis of these assumptions, Jenson reasons that during his earthly life and ministry, God the Son is made available via the body of Jesus of Nazareth. However, *after* his resurrection God the Son is made available via the eucharistic elements in the church. This implies that God the Son is able to make himself available via more than one body, though perhaps not more than one body at any one time. That is, Jenson appears to be committed to the notion that God the Son (perhaps, divine persons generally)[30] can be made available via different bodies at different times.

Now, recall that according to Jenson a body is what makes a person available at a given time: "In Paul's language, someone's 'body' is simply the person him or herself insofar as this person is *available* to other persons and to him or herself, insofar as the person is an *object* for other persons and him or herself."[31] From this general claim about bodies we get the more specific christological claim (the third of the assumptions just given) that *Christ's body is whatever makes him (i.e., the person of Christ) available to us now.* Now, suppose that Jesus is identical to God the Son in virtue of being hypostatically united to God the Son. This seems to be a reasonable inference given Jenson's catholic Christology.[32] Jenson wants to avoid the claim that Jesus

---

[29] See Robert W. Jenson, "Once More, the *Logos asarkos*," *International Journal of Systematic Theology* 13, no. 2 (2011): 130–33. I have discussed it in Oliver D. Crisp, *The Word Enfleshed: Exploring the Person and Work of Christ* (Grand Rapids: Baker Academic, 2016), ch. 2. It also arises in passing as Jenson defends his denial of the "pre"-existence of Christ in *Systematic Theology*, ch. 8. He closes that chapter by reaffirming that "our divine savior is not an extra metaphysical entity, whether the unincarnate *Logos* of the Antiochenes, or 'the Christ' of the more feeble sorts of modern theology. He is Mary's child, the hanged man of Golgotha"—a doctrine that, he says, is "decisive" for his own approach to theology. Jenson, *Systematic Theology*, 1:145.

[30] The relevant metaphysical distinction depends on whether a particular divine person can become incarnate more than once, and the more general claim that any particular divine person of the Godhead can become incarnate more than once.

[31] Jenson, *Systematic Theology*, 1:205.

[32] To be clear: I am not saying that catholic Christology *requires* the claim that Christ is identical to God the Son, just that this is consistent with catholic Christology, and is Jenson's view. For a rather different account of the composition of Christ that does not entail that Christ is identical to God the Son, see Crisp, *Word Enfleshed*, ch. 6.

just happens to be related to God the Son. In his essay "Once More, the *Logos asarkos*," Jenson writes, "We must not posit the Son's antecedent subsistence in such a fashion as to make the incarnation the addition of the human Jesus to a Son who was himself without him." Moreover, "It is not as an individual instance of humanity as such, not as one among many who have the same human nature, that Jesus is the second hypostasis of the Trinity."[33] Rather, "It is Jesus' relation to the Father—and not Jesus as a specimen of humanity—which is the second hypostasis of Trinity. The Father's sending and Jesus' obedience are the second hypostasis in God."[34] In the context of these passages, it seems clear that the copula "is" in the phrase "Jesus is the second hypostasis of the Trinity" should be taken as a statement of numerical identity: Jesus of Nazareth = God the Son. That was our second assumption. So Jenson thinks that Christ is identical to God the Son.

Now, it is not entirely clear from what he says about the relation between bodies and availability whether Jenson thinks that for any given body that makes a particular person available, that body must be identical to the person concerned. That is a fairly strong metaphysical claim. Instead, Jenson could simply think that bodies make persons available; that in the case of Christ, his body makes his person available (while it is living); *and* that in the particular case of Christ, his body is hypostatically united to God the Son such that Jesus = God the Son. In other words, it could be that Jenson thinks the relation that obtains between persons and bodies such that bodies make persons available doesn't entail that *all* persons and the bodies to which they are causally related are identical, although in the case of Christ that is the relevant relation because of the hypostatic union. Jesus is identical to God the Son, and his body does make him available to us, but that doesn't necessarily generalize to all bodies and the persons to which they are related. This weaker construal of Jenson's position is also more defensible—for the hypostatic union involves a unique relation between a (divine) person and his human nature. So, suppose for the sake of argument that this is what Jenson thinks. It raises the further, relevant question: Must *any* body to which the person of God the Son is related be identical with God the Son? Or, to put it another way, must God the Son be *personally united* to any given body that makes him available at particular times and places so that he is identical with that body?

---

[33] Jenson, "Once More," 130 and 133, respectively.
[34] Jenson, "Once More," 133.

This may be a worry for the following reason: if Jenson holds that *any* body to which the person of God the Son is related by means of metaphysical ownership is identical with God the Son, then by Jenson's own admission it looks like God the Son is identical with multiple "bodies." He is identical with the body of Jesus. But, on this construal of Jenson's position, he is also identical with all the myriad eucharistic elements that have been blessed in liturgies down through the centuries. They are also his body in a metaphysically real manner—on the presumption that the connection between the eucharistic elements and God the Son is a real, corporeal one—in which case God the Son is identical with Christ's body and with what we might call the many different sacramental bodies he acquires through the celebration of the Eucharist down through time. This is odd for at least two reasons.

First, to reiterate, it means that God the Son is identical with numerous "bodies." Though this may not be metaphysically impossible (for who is to say how many bodies a divine person may unite himself to?), it is rather strange, to say the least. Second, it means that God the Son may be identical with different sorts of "bodies," including a "bread body" and "wine body" in the eucharistic elements.[35] What is more, this is equivalent to saying that, according to Jenson's account, a doctrine of multiple incarnations is true. This is not an argument against Jenson's view, of course. For one thing, some theologians are sympathetic to the possibility of multiple incarnations, the present author included.[36] Nevertheless, it might be thought to be a metaphysical cost to his position for those suspicious of the doctrine of multiple incarnations.

---

[35] For recent treatments of such views, see Adams, *Christ and Horrors*, ch. 10; and James M. Arcadi, "Impanation, Incarnation, and Enabling Externalism," *Religious Studies* 51 (2015): 75–90.

[36] See Thomas Aquinas, *Summa theologiae*, 3.3.7, *respondeo*:

> What has power for one thing, and no more, has a power limited to one. Now the power of a Divine Person is infinite, nor can it be limited by any created thing. Hence it may not be said that a Divine Person so assumed one human nature as to be unable to assume another. For it would seem to follow from this that the Personality of the Divine Nature was so comprehended by one human nature as to be unable to assume another to its Personality; and this is impossible, for the Uncreated cannot be comprehended by any creature. Hence it is plain that, whether we consider the Divine Person in regard to His power, which is the principle of the union, or in regard to His Personality, which is the term of the union, it has to be said that the Divine Person, over and beyond the human nature which He has assumed, can assume another distinct human nature.

See also discussion of this point in Crisp, *God Incarnate,* ch. 8.

More importantly, perhaps, it has the eucharistic cost of committing Jenson to a particular sort of view regarding the real, corporeal presence of Christ in the sacramental elements. There are a range of metaphysically possible views consistent with real, corporeal presence doctrines of the sacrament. These include transubstantiation (where the substance in question changes to the body and blood of Christ, the accidents remaining the same), consubstantiation (where Christ's body and blood is added in, with, and under the elements), and other, minority reports, such as impanation (where the bread and wine are hypostatically united to Christ as his "bread body" and "wine body," respectively).[37] However, if Jenson means to say that *any* body to which the person of God the Son is related by means of metaphysical ownership is identical with God the Son, then his options are narrower than this. He is committed to a particular view of the real, corporeal presence of Christ in the Eucharist, according to which the elements are identical to Christ in a manner analogous to the personal union of God the Son and his human nature.

Jenson may balk at this, however. (I expect he would balk at this as a Lutheran.) If he does—if, for instance, he wants to hold to a real, corporeal presence doctrine of the Eucharist without commitment to metaphysical ownership of the elements being equivalent to identity with God the Son—then he needs to provide some account of why it is that God the Son is united in one way with his human nature and in another way with the eucharistic elements. Such an explanation would need to provide a principled reason for such a distinction, rather than merely an ad hoc one. It may be that Jenson thinks Christ is made available in different ways to his people via different relations with different "bodies." Perhaps he is hypostatically related to his human nature so that he is identical with it, but his relation to the eucharistic elements is less metaphysically stringent. If so, however, it does suggest that there is a theologically salient difference between Christ's availability during his earthly life and his availability to us now in the church. For it means that Christ's availability to us now is much less immediate than was the case for those who encountered him walking around Palestine. It is the difference between being in direct contact with a person and having some token that provides a connection to that person—something like a talisman or totem. If this line of interpretation is right, then Jenson's insistence on availability as a necessary condition for communion with Christ needs finessing with other conditions that distinguish the different ways in which he is made available at different times and places.

---

[37] For discussion of the various metaphysical options, see Arcadi, "Recent Philosophical Work on the Doctrine of the Eucharist." I have given only the barest indication of several options here.

Let us turn to the second issue introduced at the beginning of this section—namely, the puzzle of the empty tomb. Here the challenges facing Jenson's account may be weightier. The puzzle is that it is not entirely clear why Jenson thinks Christ's human body disappeared from the tomb on Easter Sunday. Although, as we have seen, he does affirm that the tomb was empty on Easter Day, this is because he thinks that Christ's body would have been treated as a relic, not because an empty tomb is somehow required in order for Christ to be resurrected.

Suppose Jenson is right that Christ's body would have become a relic had it remained in the tomb on Easter Day. This provides no explanation of why it is that the tomb was empty on Easter Day. His body could have been removed without miraculous intervention and privately interred somewhere, or even destroyed, in order to avoid fetishizing Christ's corpse. What is more, given Jenson's argument about bodies and availability, it is not clear that the tomb had to be empty in order for Christ to be resurrected. So, to where did Christ's body disappear? Jenson does not offer a clear answer to this question, and this, I suggest, is an important lacuna in his account.[38] However, we may be able to provide an answer, one that explains why the tomb was empty and that stays within the broadly supernaturalistic framework of historic Christian affirmations about the empty tomb. Although it does not accord with everything Jenson affirms about the resurrection of Christ, this proposal does draw on some of the important themes in Jenson's account, amending them in order to give an answer to this important theological question. We turn to this matter in the next section.

Repairing Jenson's Account

I take it that resurrection implies the presence of a body of some sort. The qualification "of some sort" is important, given that the apostle Paul in 1 Corinthians 15 is clear that resurrection bodies are significantly different from our earthly bodies because they are raised as "spiritual bodies" (1 Cor 15:44).[39] Jenson can argue that Paul's "spiritual body" is conceptually opaque

---

[38] To be fair to Jenson, he is hardly the only theologian that does not provide an unambiguous response to this question. This is also true of Torrance in *Space, Time and Resurrection*.

[39] The Greek phrase is *soma pneumatikon*—literally, a spiritual body. Torrance writes, "The resurrection of the body to be a 'spiritual body' no more means that the body is resolved away into spirit than the fact that we are made 'spiritual men' in Christ means that our humanity is dissolved away in him. . . . To be a spiritual body is not to be less a body but more truly and completely body, for by the Spirit physical existence is redeemed from all that

enough for him to be able to claim that there is a resurrection, but that the resurrection of Christ is not primarily about the revivification of the body in which he walked around first-century Palestine. Rather, it is about a spiritual body, a presence made available to us his disciples in some corporeal fashion. In other words, resurrection does not require that the postresurrection body of Christ is numerically the same body as his preresurrection one. He can be understood to be decoupling the notion of resurrection from the notion of numerical sameness of body. This is very interesting. It means that the corpse of Christ is not necessarily metaphysically salient when asking the question, "Where is the body of Christ after his resurrection?" What is salient is that the resurrected Christ is made available to his disciples and the church. Assuming that resurrection implies the presence of a body of some sort, his ongoing availability in the church could be by means of some hunk (or hunks) of matter suitably related to God the Son postresurrection—namely, the eucharistic elements—in which case, on this reading of Jenson, his account of the resurrection ties the resurrected body of Christ to the central liturgical mystery of the Christian faith. Christ indwells his church eucharistically (in some unspecified manner), wherein he is truly corporeally present to believers.

However, it is still not clear from what he has said what God the Son's ongoing relationship to the corpse of Jesus of Nazareth amounts to postresurrection. Is it still *his* human body, a part of *his* human nature? Given that what Jenson says elsewhere about the incarnation implies that Christ is numerically identical to his humanity, because Jesus just is the Second Person of the Trinity, it would seem that his corpse in the tomb is still his human body. (Perhaps it amounts to something like a nonfunctioning limb while in the tomb, on analogy with those who suffer loss of the use of a limb as a result of some trauma.) Well then, what happens to Christ's corpse on Easter Sunday morning? Jenson doesn't say, though he concedes that it is not present in the tomb from his resurrection onward. It seems to me that this concession on the absence of Christ's corpse from the tomb after Easter Sunday morning is a kind of residue from the traditional, pre-Copernican account of the resurrection that is incommensurate with the constructive elements of his own account, and that wants some correction.

There are a number of options open to Jenson that avoid the conclusion that Christ's body must be located somewhere after Easter Sunday morning,

---

corrupts and undermines it, and from all privation of being" (*Space, Time and Resurrection*, 141). That seems right to me.

even if it is not the empty tomb. Here are four options regarding the resurrection of Christ consistent with what Jenson says about the empty tomb of Easter Day:

OPTION 1: At the moment of resurrection, Christ's human corpse is annihilated by God the Father.

OPTION 2: At the moment of resurrection, Christ's human corpse miraculously fissions into its subatomic parts, which are scattered over a particular region of space-time.

OPTION 3: At the moment of resurrection, Christ's human corpse is made a living being once more. He appears to his disciples and, at the moment of ascension, is immediately translated to the first moment of the eschaton, at which point Christ comes to judge the quick and the dead.

OPTION 4: At the moment of resurrection, Christ's human corpse is made a living being once more. He appears to his disciples and, at the moment of ascension, is removed from this space-time continuum to an adjacent one that he occupies until the first moment of the eschaton, at which point Christ is returned to this space-time continuum to judge the quick and the dead.

Some comments on these options: OPTION 1 involves the utter obliteration of Christ's corpse without remainder. Annihilation here is equivalent to utter destruction, or, more precisely, it is equivalent to the utter destruction of the matter-energy of which Christ's corpse is composed.[40] After this event there is no matter that composes Christ's corpse. So the way is open for Jenson's constructive argument about availability and eucharistic elements. This does have the downside that Christ is not incarnate between the moment at which his corpse is annihilated and the blessing of the elements at the next Eucharist. We shall return to this cost presently.

Consider the second option. This is equivalent to what happens to all bodies after somatic death. It is just that, given OPTION 2, there is a metaphysical leap, as it were, from the stage at which the body becomes a corpse to the stage at which it has reached such a level of decomposition that it ceases to have integrity as an organic whole, with its most simple metaphysical parts (the subatomic particles that compose the body) scattered across a particular region of space-time. In other words, it is as if Christ's body is suddenly and miraculously reduced to a cloud of scattered particles imperceptible to the human eye. Like the first option, this second option means that no corpse would appear to be present on Easter Sunday morning. But unlike the first

---

[40] I realize that some readers will balk at the idea that matter may be annihilated in this manner. However, I presume that someone attracted to OPTION 1 is unlikely to think that the cosmos is a closed physical system in which the total amount of energy remains constant.

option, this is not because the corpse is annihilated. Rather, it is because the most basic component parts of the matter that composes it have been scattered. So, on this view, postresurrection God the Son may still be hypostatically united to his human corpse. It is just that this union is not the union of one fundamental substance (the divine person of the Son) with a created substance (his human body and soul rightly configured). It is rather the union of a fundamental substance with something akin to a particle cloud that is the remains of his human corpse, plus his human soul. One upshot of this is that Christ remains incarnate in a rather strained or Pickwickian sense of the term postresurrection, because the matter that composes his human body at the moment of somatic death is still present. It is just that it is no longer intact; it no longer has integrity as a body. (Think of a Lego spaceship that is then dismantled and the parts scattered over the floor of a room. In one sense the Lego spaceship has gone. However, in another sense all its parts are still present. They are just scattered, and no longer compose the spaceship as an integrated whole made up of contiguous parts, rightly related to one another so as to form a composite whole.) From the foregoing it should be clear that this second option does not imply that Christ is no longer incarnate between the moment at which his corpse is annihilated and the blessing of the first eucharistic elements after his resurrection. For between Easter Sunday morning and whenever the next eucharistic meal is enjoyed by his disciples, God the Son is still "united" with the parts of his human body, now scattered. But equally, it does not really explain how God the Son is related to the dispersed elements of his human body postresurrection, let alone how it is that he is related to these elements on the one hand and related to the eucharistic elements postresurrection on the other hand.

Let us turn to the third option. Something like it has recently been mooted as a piece of speculative theology by the biblical scholar Robin Parry. He wonders whether Christ can be said to "ascend" into the future, eschatological age. "In this speculation," he writes "the body of Jesus is not located anywhere in the cosmos *now* because it exists in the future."[41] Like Jenson, Parry acknowledges that this view requires some important qualifications. These include Christ's presence by the Holy Spirit in the Eucharist, and in his body, the church.[42] Like Parry's speculative suggestion, OPTION 3 "translates" the resurrected Christ from the moment of ascension to the eschaton, so that the body of Jesus is not present in our frame of reference from the

[41] Robin A. Parry, *The Biblical Cosmos* (Eugene, Ore.: Cascade, 2014), 187.
[42] Parry, *Biblical Cosmos.*

moment of ascension to his moment of return to inaugurate the eschaton. So on this option the tomb is empty, we treat the resurrection appearances of Christ in the New Testament at face value as reports of a truly resurrected human body, and yet we have an account of what happens to his body at the ascension that is consistent with a Copernican universe. It is translated from one point in space-time to another without interruption to the hypostatic union, but with a temporal "gap" between his ascension and visible return that we would expect given the biblical and creedal affirmations of his ascension and visible return. The sort of gap I have in mind is rather like what happens when you fold a piece of paper in half and pierce it with a pencil. Upon piercing the paper in this way, there are two holes through which the pencil may pass directly from one side of the paper to the other. In a similar way, the suggestion is that Christ's human body may "pass" from one location in space-time to another without interval or interruption.

This piece of dogmatic speculation does not mean we have no access to Christ's body now, however. Taking up Jenson's Swabian-inspired account of the way in which Christ's eucharistic presence may be an analog of his incarnational presence, we can say that Christ is present with us now in the elements of the eucharistic meal. He is now available to his church sacramentally, in the eucharistic elements, which are also united to him in such a way that they become his body for us now, in between the times of his ascension and visible return. This view does have the "costs" associated with Jenson's endorsement of multiple incarnations. For on this view, as with Jenson's account, Christ is hypostatically united to the body of Jesus of Nazareth, and he is also united in an intimate manner—perhaps even *hypostatically united*, though we need not make a judgment on that here—to the blessed eucharistic elements. At the very least, Christ's relation to the eucharistic elements on this view is consistent with a high sacramentalism commensurate with Lutheran theology.

Finally, let us turn to OPTION 4. In many respects it is very similar to OPTION 3. But it has one important advantage. According to OPTION 3, Christ is translated from one point in space-time to another. But this seems unsatisfactory because the translation involved is more like removing Christ at a great distance from where he began. Although one could still have an account of the eucharistic presence of Christ like Jenson, it does mean that any idea of Christ's intercession at the right hand of the Father cannot be given anything like a straightforward or realist interpretation (see Rom 8:34, Heb 1:3). For Christ's human nature, being translated without interval between the ascension to the first moment of the eschaton does not exist in the times between these two intervals. So it makes no sense to say that he is interceding for the saints in the period between his ascension and return at the end of the age.

This is where OPTION 4 has an advantage over OPTION 3. Imagine that our space-time continuum is a kind of growing four-dimensional block. At the leading face of the block are the present temporal events. God could remove Christ's human nature from the block at a certain moment in time, from a certain place (say, the moment at which his human body is hidden from the sight of the apostles at the ascension). He could transpose Christ's human nature to another adjacent block—one that in a sense overlaps the present block but is distinct because it occupies a different set of dimensions to our own. His human nature could continue to exist in this adjacent block, tracking in parallel with the moments that elapse in the spatiotemporal block in which we exist, until at the eschaton his human nature is returned to our block by divine action.

An example will help make this point clearer. Recall that in chapter 4 we used the case of Edwin Abbott's *Flatland* to help explain the mystery of the Trinity. Let us return to Flatland briefly. Now, imagine there is a two-dimensional square figure that can be opened out into a line and then closed up around another plane figure, effectively enclosing the figure contained in the square, thereby sealing it off from other Flatlanders. Suppose this is done with a small circle that is enclosed in the square in this manner. Now imagine that a Spacelander (that is, a three-dimensional being) comes along and removes the circle from the square by moving it up and out of the two-dimensional world of Flatland, into the third spatial dimension "above" Flatland, so to speak. Upon opening up the square, the Flatlanders would be shocked and dismayed to find the small circle gone—as if by magic! Thereupon, having closed the square, the Spacelander returns the small circle to its position within the square. Whereupon, the Flatlanders are astonished a second time when they open the square up to find the small circle contained within it once more! The idea mooted here is that it may be that there are other hyperspace dimensions beyond our own three-dimensional space to which objects may be removed ana or kata (the hyperspace equivalent of up and down in our Flatland story).[43]

---

[43] I've stolen this example from Hud Hudson. Flatland examples crop up several times in his remarkable book *The Metaphysics of Hyperspace* (Oxford: Oxford University Press, 2005). Perhaps the most salient example for our purposes is the case of the Hermit Flatlander on pp. 176–77.

Such a position has been argued for in great detail, and with considerable energy and ingenuity, by the Christian philosopher Hud Hudson. He says this about an OPTION 4–style account of the resurrection that utilizes a hyperspace metaphysics (along the lines just given):

> Let us acknowledge that a body moving ana or kata [that is, the fourth-dimensional equivalent of moving up and down] could leave its clothes or burial robes without taking them off, could vanish from a dinner table without a trace, and could appear in a locked room without passing through its windows, doors, or walls. In short, a body free to move in hyperspace could be positions just inches away, yet remain undetectable for days on end, and could enter and leave our own three[dimensional]-space with exactly the ease and abruptness that is attributed to the risen Christ.[44]

Such speculative metaphysics is a long way from most contemporary systematic theology, but it forms an important part of the contemporary physics of four-dimensional space. Even if this is not the truth of the matter, it does offer one way of construing the metaphysics of the resurrection and ascension of Christ that is consistent with the traditional doctrine of the resurrection, and that provides a manner of construing Christ's intercession for the saints at the right hand of the Father. Thus, even if this turns out to be a metaphysical just-so story, it is a just-so story that may be true for all we know. That is all we need to show that some metaphysical sense can be made of Jenson's claim about the resurrection of Christ.

With this friendly amendment in place, Jenson's position makes good theological sense of the resurrection of Christ, of his ascension, and of his eucharistic presence, and does form the outline of a joined-up whole that yields a distinct and theologically rich contribution to constructive accounts of Christ's resurrection. This does not solve all the worries one might have with respect to Jenson's position. But it does take a constructive step toward a *Jensonian* account of these matters—a kind of dogmatic sketch that a fuller treatment would fill out.

---

[44] Hudson, *Metaphysics of Hyperspace*, 204.

Conclusion

Anglo-American philosophy has typically been concerned with analysis, to such an extent that its other common name is "analytic philosophy." It has been preoccupied with precise definitions of terms, fine distinctions among concepts, and complex arguments for philosophical claims. It is in consequence also marked by a hunt for counter-examples to someone else's definition, further distinctions lying between things someone else has already distinguished, and even more complex arguments showing the invalidity of someone else's complex arguments. . . . Such practices and skills are certainly important to any careful thinking in general and to philosophy in particular. Without them, philosophy is in some danger of turning into what can be (and often is) practiced by anyone at all over a couple of beers.

Eleonore Stump[1]

Eleonore Stump's characterization of contemporary Anglo-American philosophy in her magisterial study *Wandering in Darkness*, captured in the excerpt above, is salient for analytic theologians as well as analytic philosophers. But what she says by way of praising the virtues of the analytic approach is a prelude to some pointed criticism of this particular philosophical method. She goes on to say, "In its emphasis on left-brain mediated pattern-processing, philosophy in the Anglo-American tradition has tended to leave to one side the messy and complicated issues involved in relations among persons." Analytics have preferred instead the thin thought experiments involving the "philosophical crash-test dummies Smith and Jones."[2] What is lacking, in Stump's diagnosis, is a greater willingness to tolerate the messiness of the human condition as exemplified in the great literature and narratives of biblical and postbiblical traditions. Consequently, one

---

[1] Eleonore Stump, *Wandering in Darkness: Narrative and the Problem of Evil* (Oxford: Oxford University Press, 2000), 24.

[2] Stump, *Wandering in Darkness*, 25.

important focus of her work on the problem of suffering and the problem of evil in *Wandering in Darkness* has to do with bringing such biblical narratives to bear upon the task of philosophical analysis. However, the rationale for doing so is not to furnish new subject matter for thought experiments populated by philosophical crash-test dummies. Rather, it is to reflect on the complexities of narratives on the problem of suffering and of evil *as well as* contemporary analytic discussions of these problems. "It is my hope," she writes "that the result will be a true marriage, generating something newly good, and not just a forcible joining together of reluctant bedfellows."[3]

Unsurprisingly, perhaps, the same virtues and limitations beset analytic theology. It is good at certain tasks, but poor at others. Good at analyzing and clarifying, at stripping away ambiguity and distinguishing difficult and subtle concepts; but poor at the "messy relations" among persons that Stump writes about. This is important when it comes to systematic theology because the "systematic" component doesn't just involve the task of analyzing doctrine, but of providing some plausible account of the whole—of telling us how these different parts fit together into one larger, coherent story.

It is the task of this final chapter to provide such a summary account. Given the foregoing analyses of the doctrine of God, of God's intention in creation, of sin, Christ, and salvation culminating in the hope of resurrection, what whole emerges from these doctrinal parts? Perhaps something like these Theological Theses for constructive analytic systematic theology:

Theses for Constructive Analytic Theology

I. The task of analytic systematic theology

Systematic theology is (or, in my view, ought to be) a truth-apt, truth-aimed enterprise that attempts to give a coherent account of Christian doctrine that is realist in nature. That is, it presumes that there is a God who reveals himself to us in the world, in Scripture, and supremely in Christ. And it presumes that God is a mind-independent entity, the creator of all things apart from Godself. Systematic theology may be pursued by paying attention to particular creeds and confessions of the Christian faith. In that case, it is dogmatic theology, for systematic theological reflection on creeds and confessions is concerned principally with dogmas of the faith—doctrines that have some formal, institutional shape. But it may also be pursued in a more constructive direction, where the emphasis is upon giving an account of the

---

[3] Stump, *Wandering in Darkness*, 25.

Christian faith for today, in which case it is constructive theology. These are not mutually exclusive tasks; they can be pursued in conjunction with one another. Analytic systematic theology can be understood in either of these ways or in both, as dogmatic *or* constructive theology, or as dogmatic *and* constructive theology. Like a number of other modes of systematic theology today, it is consistent with SHARED TASK:

SHARED TASK: Commitment to an intellectual undertaking that involves (though it may not comprise) explicating the conceptual content of the Christian tradition (with the expectation that this is normally done from a position within that tradition, as an adherent of that tradition), using particular religious texts that are part of the Christian tradition, including sacred Scripture, as well as human reason, reflection, and praxis (particularly religious practices), as sources for theological judgments.

In light of this, I have argued that when it is practiced as systematic theology, analytic theology is a way of doing systematic theology that utilizes the tools and methods of contemporary analytic philosophy for the purposes of constructive Christian theology, paying attention to the Christian tradition and development of doctrine.

II. Doctrines, dogma, and models

On my way of thinking, a doctrine is (minimally) a comprehensive account of a particular teaching about a given theological topic held by some community of Christians or some particular denomination. As I just indicated above, dogma is a certain sort of doctrine, one that has a canonical form or definition that is part of the conceptual core of the faith and that has normative status, such as the dogma of the Trinity or the dogma of the incarnation. A model is something else. It is a simplified account of more complex data that approximates to the truth of the matter. The data in question usually comprises doctrinal material. So a model of divine simplicity, or the Trinity (such as the ones discussed in chapters 3 and 4, respectively) is an approximation to the truth of the matter that seeks to give an account of the data of revelation in Scripture and of other sources of theological authority, such as the creeds and confessions of the churches. Although (in my view) theological models should be truth-apt and truth-aimed, they are still proxies. For this reason, theological models can be revised or overturned by more accurate, or more comprehensive, or more helpful models that better approximate the truth of the matter as expressed in revelation and tradition.

So although systematic theology is (or ought to be) a truth-apt, truth-aimed enterprise that attempts to give a coherent account of Christian doctrine that is realist in nature, this claim needs some finessing. The notion of "giving an account" of Christian doctrine at which systematic theology aims may mean just giving some version of the doctrine in question—whatever version of the doctrine the particular theologian favors. (For instance, if eucharistic theology were the focus, the Roman Catholic theologian would be giving an account of the doctrine of transubstantiation, and the Lutheran would be giving an account of consubstantiation, and so on.)

But "giving an account" might also involve the production of theological models rather than doctrine as such. What is the difference? I did not really spell this out in the first few chapters of this work. But now, having thought about some of these matters over the course of writing this volume, I would hazard the following remarks: A particular theologian may wish to simply give an account of an existing body of doctrinal and dogmatic material by rehearsing the doctrinal deposit of a particular theological tradition, such as one can find readily available in texts like Ludwig Ott's *Fundamentals of Catholic Dogma*, or Heinrich Heppe's *Reformed Dogmatics*, or Heinrich Schmid's *The Doctrinal Theology of the Evangelical Lutheran Church*.[4] However, the analytic theologian engaged in theological construction is doing something different even if the aim is to shore up a given traditional doctrine. (As examples, consider analytic theologians like Sarah Coakley on the Trinity, or Marilyn McCord Adams on Christology, or, more recently, James Arcadi on the Eucharist.[5]) Often this involves using models as a way of explicating particular doctrinal or dogmatic commitments, as I have done in this work. So models are different from doctrines. They are ways of construing doctrines much like a painting of a sculpture, like Michelangelo's *David* is a way of construing the sculpture. Yet the statue of David is itself a representation of the idea that the artist had of the artwork in the first place. Similarly, models are to doctrines as the painting of David is to the sculpture of David. And doctrines are to divine revelation as the sculpture of David is to the conception of the artwork as the inspiration for it came to the mind of the artist.

---

[4] Ludwig Ott, *Fundamentals of Catholic Dogma*, 4th ed. (Rockford, Ill.: Tan Books, 1960); Henrich Heppe, *Reformed Dogmatics*, ed. Ernst Bizer, trans. G. T. Thomson (1861; repr., London: Collins, 1950); Heinrich Schmid, *The Doctrinal Theology of the Evangelical Lutheran Church*, trans. Charles A. Hay and Henry E. Jacobs (Minneapolis: Augsburg, 1889).

[5] Sarah Coakley, *God, Sexuality, and the Self: An Essay 'On the Trinity'* (Cambridge: Cambridge University Press, 2013); Marilyn McCord Adams, *Christ and Horrors: The Coherence of Christology*, Current Issues in Theology 3 (Cambridge: Cambridge University Press, 2006); James M. Arcadi, *An Incarnational Model of the Eucharist*, Current Issues in Theology 10 (Cambridge: Cambridge University Press, 2018).

We might put it like this: divine revelation (in Scripture, say), is normative for Christian doctrine. This is often expressed in a dogmatic form in the catholic creeds and in confessions of particular ecclesial bodies. Christian doctrine reflects this dogmatic deposit. It attempts to provide Christian teaching for particular communions that takes this dogmatic deposit into account. The work of particular theologians is a further tier of theological reflection on the existing body of material provided by divine revelation and the dogmatic traditions (creeds, councils, confessions), and that (usually) reflects the particular theological traditions to which the theologian belongs. Analytic theologians are no exception to this. So theological models generated by analytic theological work are ways of construing divine revelation, usually understood in light of a dogmatic tradition and a particular theological tradition. That is how I understand the theological task, and how I have pursued it here.[6]

III. Picturing the divine nature

Catholic doctrinal reflection on the biblical traditions yields the conclusion that God reveals himself as both one (in essence) and three (divine persons). This is the clear teaching of the Nicene-Constantinopolitan Symbol, which has been received as dogma by all catholic Christians. Reflection on this dogmatic deposit, and upon Scripture as the source of these creedal claims, has generated several "pictures" of God in the Christian tradition. Classical theism is a metaphysical package of claims about God that comprises a particular view of both God's unity and simplicity on the one hand and his triunity on the other. I summarized it thus:

CHRISTIAN CLASSICAL THEISM: God is one simple, perfect, immutable, impassible, and infinite being who is independent of his creation, existing eternally as one entity and revealed in three persons: the Father, the Son, and the Holy Spirit. God's essence is one, yet each person is the essence. The Father is the essence. The Son is the essence. The Spirit is the essence. The Father, the Son, and the Spirit are also the essence. Nonetheless, there is only one essence and three persons. The persons are distinguished by their relations.

---

[6] See also my earlier discussion of similar issues in Crisp, *God Incarnate: Explorations in Christology* (London: T&T Clark, 2009), ch. 1; and Crisp, *Deviant Calvinism: Broadening the Reformed Tradition* (Minneapolis: Fortress, 2014), ch. 1. Note: not *all* analytic theologians will agree with my way of understanding these matters, but neither is this way of thinking about different sources of theological authority particularly eccentric.

Theistic personalism takes a different view of both "poles" of the doctrine of God, emphasizing a weaker account of divine unity alongside a stronger account of divine triunity than that preferred by classical theists, like this:

THEISTIC PERSONALISM: God is strongly unified, perfect, unchanging in his character, responsive to his creatures, infinite, everlasting, and revealed in three persons: the Father, the Son, and the Holy Spirit. God is one in a generic sense, with each person being a distinct center of will and action that instantiates the divine nature. The divine persons interpenetrate one another in a way commensurate with WEAK PERSON PERICHORESIS.

WEAK PERSON PERICHORESIS: The persons of the Trinity share all their properties in a common divine essence apart from those properties that serve to individuate one of the persons of the Trinity, or express a relation between only two persons of the Trinity.

A via media between these two conceptual pictures is *chastened theism*, which attempts to provide an account of the divine nature that is more cautious in its claims about divine unity and diversity than classical theism, yet without necessarily giving up on a concept of divine simplicity or conceding to social Trinitarianism the claim that there are three centers of divine action and will in the Godhead. The potential benefit of chastened theism can be seen by giving an account of divine simplicity and the Trinity as the two fundamental poles of the Christian doctrine of God.

IV–V. Models of divine simplicity and the Trinity

Traditional accounts of divine simplicity presume that God is without any composition whatsoever. Such strong versions of the doctrine have come under sustained criticism. The parsimonious model of divine simplicity treats the divine nature as a kind of metaphysical simple—an entity that cannot be further divided. It can be summarized like this:

(1) God is a concrete entity. That is, he is not an abstract object, like a number or proposition. He is a concrete thing, like a human being.
(2) God is an immaterial person. That is, he is not merely a metaphysical aggregate or artifact (like a chair or table). He is an agent, a living being, but not a material agent.
(3) God is a necessary being. That is, he exists in all possible worlds.
(4) God is metaphysically simple. That is, he is not composed by more fundamental elements, as is the case with material things (e.g., the fundamental subatomic elements that compose objects like tables and chairs at particular times and places).
(5) God is essentially metaphysically simple. That is, it is not the case that he

just happens to be metaphysically simple (i.e., accidentally or contingently). He cannot fail to be metaphysically simple; it is part of his nature to be metaphysically simple.

(6) God has distinct attributes that he exemplifies.[7]

Nevertheless, such an entity may have different states and different properties. Although the parsimonious account is significantly weaker than traditional versions of the doctrine of divine simplicity, it may be useful as a proxy that can do theological work without the costs associated with the traditional doctrines—costs having to do with the much stronger claim that God is without any composition whatsoever.

Similarly, existing accounts of the Trinity run into problems as they attempt to explicate the notion of triunity. I have set out a model of the Trinity that I called *chastened Trinitarian mysterianism*, which is a kind of Trinitarian counterpart to chastened theism. This required the following assumptions consistent with earlier claims about doctrinal models and the Trinity:

MODEL: A simplified conceptual framework or description by means of which complex sets of data, systems, and processes may be organized and understood.

MYSTERY: A truth that is intelligible in principle but that may not be entirely intelligible to human beings in their current state of cognitive development.

TRINITY: The conjunction of dogmatic propositions concerning the divine nature, expressing the claim that God is one in essence and subsists in three persons, that are found in the dogmatic deposit of the ecumenical creeds, especially the Nicene-Constantinopolitan Symbol, and that reflect (a particular way of understanding) the teaching of Scripture and the apostolic faith. The dogmatic core of this conjunction of claims is as follows:

(T1) there is exactly one God;
(T2) there are exactly three coeternal divine persons "in" God: the Father, the Son, and the Holy Spirit;
(T3) the Father, the Son, and the Holy Spirit are not identical;

---

[7] As I have labored to make clear, this, being a model, is only a proxy. So, for example, it may be theologically useful to speak of distinct divine attributes that God exemplifies even if, in fact, one does not think that God stands in a relation of exemplification to properties as universals or as abstract objects that exist outside the divine nature, so to speak. For those who are theistic conceptualists, like Augustine or Anselm, this is an important issue—and I am sympathetic to such views. For discussion of this important matter, see William Lane Craig, *God over All: Divine Aseity and the Problem of Platonism* (Oxford: Oxford University Press, 2016); and Paul M. Gould, ed. *Beyond the Control of God? Six Views on the Problem of God and Abstract Objects* (London: Bloomsbury, 2014).

(T4) the Father, the Son, and the Holy Spirit are consubstantial.

TRANSCENDENCE: God is transcendent in virtue of being the creator of all things.

With this in mind, the model was expressed like this:

(1) The triunity of the divine nature is an instance of MYSTERY because God is transcendent (as per TRANSCENDENCE).

(2) Human beings cannot apprehend the triunity of God absent divine revelation.

(3) In revealing himself to us, God accommodates himself to the epistemic limitations of human beings. (Presumably, this includes allowing for the noetic effects of sin.)

(4) TRINITY is a revealed dogma (that is, a doctrine that has a particular canonical form).

(5) TRINITY provides a dogmatic framework for understanding the divine nature that is theologically minimal.

(6) TRINITY does not *explain* how God is triune; it does not in-and-of-itself offer a particular MODEL of the Godhead; it is metaphysically underdetermined. (For this reason it is consistent with more than one dogmatic extrapolation, including a range of Trinitarian doctrines and MODELS.)

(7) The terms "person" and "essence," and their cognates that demarcate the way in which God is three and the way in which God is one in TRINITY, are referring terms that are placeholders; we do not have a clear conceptual grip on their semantic content. (This is consistent with the claim that we may have a partial, piecemeal, or analogous sense of these terms.)

(8) TRINITY is consistent with MYSTERY.

This model prescinds from providing some account of triunity, though it is consistent with the notion that at least some claims about the divine nature are univocal, such as that God is in some fundamental manner one and in some fundamental manner three. How God is both of these things simultaneously is mysterious, not because the chastened Trinitarian mysterian has a high tolerance for contradiction or paradox, but because it is beyond our ken. One could take such Trinitarian mysterianism as a kind of metamodel or theory about models of the Trinity. In this case it is not necessarily inconsistent with other existing models of the Trinity, though they would be understood in light of this theory about models of the Trinity.

These two models, of divine unity and the divine triunity, provide two examples of how the chastened theist may generate useful theological models for thinking about the divine nature.

VI. God's eternal purposes in creation and incarnation

It seems to me that God's purpose in creation is fundamentally about enabling human creatures to participate in the divine life.[8] In chapters 5–6 I argued against three theses in modern non–analytic systematic theology regarding the relationship between God, time, and creation. These were the Hegelian Thesis, the Hellenization Thesis, and the Eschatological Identity Thesis. Although I maintain that these ways of thinking about the divine nature, time, and creation are mistaken, at least some of those engaged in developing these views have the right intuitions—they just develop arguments on the basis of such intuitions that end up going in the wrong direction. In chapter 6 I turned from doctrinal criticism to construction, setting out a positive alternative to these accounts, building on and extending my work in *The Word Enfleshed* (although the argument of chapter 6 can be read independent of that earlier work). This is a species of incarnation anyway argument, the view that even if human beings had not fallen into sin, God would have provided an incarnation in those possible worlds that contain human creatures. In keeping with my previous work, I have called the version of the argument developed in chapter 6 the *christological union account,* because the central idea is a fitting means by which God is able to provide an interface between divinity and humanity so that human beings may participate in the divine life. Thus, the account of incarnation anyway developed here is a counterpart to the doctrine of theosis discussed in chapter 10.

VII. Original sin

From discussion of God's aim or end in creation, chapter 7 segued to outline a particular account of original sin. This I called the *moderate Reformed doctrine of original sin.* In outline it can be put like this:

(1) All human beings after the first primal sin (barring Christ) possess original sin.
(2) Original sin is an inherited corruption of nature, a condition that every fallen human being possesses from the first moment of generation.
(3) Fallen humans are not culpable for being generated with this morally vitiated condition.
(4) Fallen humans are not culpable for the primal sin, either. That is, they do

---

[8] See Crisp, *The Word Enfleshed.* This represents a modification to my earlier views, moving from a more obviously Edwardsian view (i.e., a view in some important respects like that of Jonathan Edwards) to a more Thomistic view (i.e., a view in some important respects like that of Thomas Aquinas).

not bear original guilt (i.e., the guilt of the sin of some putative first human pair or human community being imputed to them along with original sin).

(5) This morally vitiated condition normally inevitably yields actual sin. That is, a person born with this defect will normally inevitably commit actual sin on at least one occasion provided that person lives long enough to be able to commit such sin. (The caveat "normally" indicates that there are limit cases that are exceptions to this claim, including the limit cases discussed above, e.g., infants that die before maturity and the severely mentally impaired.)

(6) Fallen human beings are culpable for their actual sin and condemned for it, in the absence of atonement.

(7) Possession of original sin leads to death and separation from God irrespective of actual sin.

This view is moderate because it follows a minority report in the Reformed tradition that draws on the work of the Magisterial Reformer Huldrych Zwingli (although, as I indicated in that chapter, there is evidence that Calvin's position is not unlike this in important respects). Zwingli denies that human beings bear original guilt—something that seems to be reflected in some of the early Reformed confessions as well. Instead, he thought of original sin as a kind of moral corruption or disease that is passed down the generations, rather like we would now think of a congenital disorder in human biology. In my earlier work I defended a more standard Reformed doctrine that includes the notion of original guilt. This is the notion that, in virtue of being concreated with original sin, fallen human beings also bear original guilt—the guilt for the first or primal sin of Adam. This now seems to me to be both philosophically indefensible (for the culpability aspect of guilt cannot transfer in this way) and biblically and historically dubious (a kind of theological accretion that adheres to the doctrine of original sin but that should be cut away from it). The moderate Reformed account does not suffer from these defects and may be more ecumenically advantageous as well. It also does not take a position on the origin of human sin (whether in some emerging early hominid population or via some first human pair).

VIII. Incarnation and salvation

This account of original sin informs what was said about the two phases of Christ's reconciling work—that is, his incarnation and theosis—in chapters 8–10. Human beings need salvation from the moral corruption that they bear and that is passed down the generations like an inherited disease. They also need saving from the guilt that they accrue on the basis of actual sins—sins performed at least in part because of the moral corruption with which they are generated. We focused on three nodal issues in the reconciling work of Christ. These were the virgin birth (really, the virginal conception of Christ) which was the focus of chapter 8; the doctrine of dyothelitism, which was the focus of chapter 9; and the notion of theosis as a way of conceiving the nature of salvation as participation in the divine life, in chapter 10—this last being the counterpart to the incarnation anyway argument of chapter 6.

Chapters 8 and 9 were defensive rather than constructive in nature, and built upon my previously published body of work in Christology. They were attempts to meet recent criticisms of these two traditional creedal and confessional dogmas rather than to present new arguments for these two doctrines. With respect to the virginal conception of Christ, I argued against Andrew Lincoln that although God could have brought about the incarnation without a virgin birth, it is a fitting means of incarnation and indicates that Christ was set apart from birth as a divine agent. (Compare the special circumstances of John the Baptist's birth or, in the Old Testament, of the birth of Isaac.) In the case of dyothelitism, I defended the creedal and confessional dogma against the neomonothelitism of Moreland, Craig, and DeWeese, alongside the partial defense of their views by Jordan Wessling. Here, too, it seems to me that there is sufficient theological warrant to retain the catholic teaching.

Chapter 10 was constructive rather than merely defensive. I argued that the right way to think about theosis was along these lines:

THEOSIS: The doctrine according to which redeemed human beings are conformed to the image of Christ in his human nature. By being united to Christ by the power of the Holy Spirit, redeemed human beings begin to exemplify the qualities of the human nature of Christ and grow in their likeness to Christ (in exemplifying the requisite qualities Christ's human nature instantiates). This process of transformation and participation goes on forevermore. It is akin to a mathematical asymptote.

Although I did not offer an account of the nature of atonement, this way of thinking about the nature of salvation is, I think, commensurate with the *union account of atonement* that I have given elsewhere.[9] This can be outlined as follows:

---

[9] In *Word Enfleshed*. Of course, it is consistent with more than one account of the nature of atonement. But for my purposes, all that is necessary is that this is consistent with the union account of atonement. The union account depends in large measure upon a particular understanding of Pauline Christology and the patristic theology of Athanasius and Irenaeus. I give a more thorough account of these things in *Approaching the Atonement: The Reconciling Work of Christ* (Downers Grove, Ill.: IVP Academic, 2019).

(1) God brings about an entity comprising Adam (from the fall onward) and all of post-fall humanity, barring Christ. This is called fallen humanity.

(2) Fallen humanity is a real entity that exists across time, like the different stages of the life of one tree from acorn to mature oak.

(3) I possess Adam's sin because I am a "part" of fallen humanity along with Adam, on analogy with the parts of my body and the whole of my body.

(4) Adam's sin is passed on to the later "parts" of this whole extended across time because he is the first human, just as the disease infecting the acorn (the first stage of the life of the oak) affects all the later stages of the life of the oak tree.

(5) Christ is the Second Adam. He is the first member of a new humanity, one that is cleansed from sin and reconciled to God.

(6) Christ, together with those he comes to save, are members of a second real entity, called redeemed humanity.

(7) As the hub between divinity and humanity, Christ is the intersection between God and humanity and a fitting means by which humans may be reconciled to God. As the God-human, he is able to act on behalf of both God and humanity, communicating between them.

(8) Christ has a priority over other "parts" of redeemed humanity, although he exists later in time than some of them. For instance, he lives later than Abraham, although his work as the Second Adam reconciles Abraham to God (Heb 11:8-16, 39-40).

(9) Hence, those living prior to Christ can be proleptically incorporated into Christ's work as the Second Adam.

(10) Christ is not guilty of sin, yet he takes on himself the penal consequences of the other members of redeemed humanity that are guilty of sin (and, therefore, also members of fallen humanity) because they are "parts" of the same entity extended across time (2 Cor 5:21).

(11) Christ's work atones for human sin, removing the obstacle of sin and reconciling members of fallen humanity to God.

(12) Through union with Christ by the power of the Holy Spirit, members of redeemed humanity begin a process of transformation into the likeness of God, becoming partakers of the divine nature.

(13) This process of transformation goes on forevermore. It is like a mathematical asymptote in that the human members of redeemed humanity draw ever closer to God in this process, yet without ever becoming God or losing themselves in God.

IX. Resurrection

The final chapter dealt with the doctrine of Christ's resurrection, in conversation, as it were, with the constructive theological proposal of Robert Jenson. I offered a friendly amendment to Jenson's view that depends on the metaphysics of hyperspace recently developed by Hud Hudson. If we think of the resurrection of Christ along the lines Hudson suggests, then Christ's resurrected body could move beyond our current three-dimensional space at the ascension, ana, and return at the first moment of the eschaton, kata. (This, as I pointed out in the chapter, is rather like the idea that Christ's human body is moved "above" our three-dimensional space on analogy with the way in which a two-dimensional figure could be moved "above" the plane of Flatland by a three-dimensional being.) This, I reasoned, is an elegant solution to the perennial problem of the missing body of Christ that may also be true for all we know.

The Upshot

Defense and construction, engagement with tradition and doctrinal criticism—these are important characteristics of all systematic theology. Nevertheless, I hope at the end of this work that the virtues of an analytic theological approach to some of the traditional loci of theology are apparent. Eleonore Stump is right about the limits of the analytic approach and the way in which we too need to learn from those committed to rather different methodological virtues. Yet analytic theology is particularly well suited to the work of world building. That is the task with which we have been engaged in this volume. For analytic theology as I understand it is nothing if not ectypal, attempting to approximate our human theologizing to the divine archetype so that—*mirabile dictu!*—we might be able to think God's thoughts after him.

Bibliography

Abbott, Edwin A. *Flatland: A Romance in Many Dimensions*. London: Seeley, 1884.

Abraham, William J. *Canon and Criterion in Christian Theology: From the Fathers to Feminism*. Oxford: Oxford University Press, 1998.

———. "Systematic Theology as Analytic Theology." In Crisp and Rea, *Analytic Theology*, 54–69.

Abraham, William J., Jason E. Vickers, and Natalie B. Van Kirk, eds. *Canonical Theism: A Proposal for Theology and the Church*. Grand Rapids: Eerdmans, 2008.

Adams, Marilyn McCord. *Christ and Horrors: The Coherence of Christology*. Current Issues in Theology 3. Cambridge: Cambridge University Press, 2006.

Allen, R. Michael. "Calvin's Christ: A Dogmatic Matrix for Discussion of Christ's Human Nature." *International Journal of Systematic Theology* 9, no. 4 (2007): 382–97.

———. "Divine Attributes." In *Christian Dogmatics: Reformed Theology for the Church Catholic*, edited by Michael Allen and Scott R. Swain, 57–77. Grand Rapids: Baker Academic, 2015.

Alston, William. "The Indwelling of the Holy Spirit." In *Philosophy and the Christian Faith*, edited by Thomas V. Morris, 121–50. Notre Dame: University of Notre Dame Press, 2006.

Anatolios, Khaled. *Retrieving Nicaea: The Development and Meaning of Trinitarian Doctrine*. Grand Rapids: Baker Academic, 2011.

Anderson, James. *Paradox in Christian Theology: An Analysis of Its Presence, Character, and Epistemic Status*. Milton Keynes: Paternoster, 2007.

Anselm of Canterbury. *Anselm: Basic Writings*. Edited and translated by Thomas Williams. Indianapolis: Hackett, 2007.

Aquinas, Thomas. *Summa contra gentiles*. Vol. 1, *God*, translated and with introduction and notes by Anton Pegis. 1955. Reprint, Notre Dame: University of Notre Dame Press, 1975.

———. *Summa contra gentiles*. Vol. 2, *Creation*, translated and with introduction and notes by J. F. Anderson. 1955. Reprint, Note Dame: University of Notre Dame Press, 1975.

———. *Summa Theologica* [*Summa Theologiae*]. Translated by the Fathers of the English Dominican Province. London: Burns, Oates, and Washbourne, 1911. Repr., Westminster, Md.: Christian Classics, 1981.

Arcadi, James M. *An Incarnational Model of the Eucharist*. Current Issues in Theology 10. Cambridge: Cambridge University Press, 2018.

———. "Impanation, Incarnation, and Enabling Externalism." *Religious Studies* 51 (2015): 75–90.

———. "Recent Philosophical Work on the Doctrine of the Eucharist." *Philosophy Compass* 11 (2016): 402–12.

Armstrong, D. M. *A World of States of Affairs*. Cambridge: Cambridge University Press, 1997.

Athanasius. *On the Incarnation*. Translated by John Behr. Yonkers: Saint Vladimir's Seminary Press, 2011.

Augustine, Aurelius. *Confessions*. Translated by Henry Chadwick. Oxford: Oxford University Press, 1991.

Ayres, Lewis. *Nicaea and Its Legacy: An Approach to Fourth-Century Trinitarian Theology*. Oxford: Oxford University Press, 2004.

Barbour, Ian G. *Religion and Science: Historical and Contemporary Issues*. San Francisco: HarperCollins, 1997.

Barrett, Jordan P. *Divine Simplicity: A Biblical and Trinitarian Account*. Emerging Scholars Series. Minneapolis: Fortress, 2017.

Barrett, Matthew, and Ardel B. Caneday, eds. *Four Views on the Historical Adam*. Grand Rapids: Zondervan Academic, 2014.

Barth, Karl. *Church Dogmatics* II/2. Edited by T. F. Torrance and Geoffrey W. Bromiley. London: T&T Clark, 1957.

Bauckham, Richard. *The Bible in the Contemporary World: Hermeneutical Ventures*. Grand Rapids: Eerdmans, 2015.

———. "Eschatology." In *The Oxford Handbook of Systematic Theology*, edited by John Webster, Kathryn Tanner, and Iain Torrance, 306–22. Oxford: Oxford University Press, 2009.

Berry, R. J. "The Virgin Birth of Christ." *Science and Christian Belief* 8 (1996): 101–10.

Boethius, Anicius Manlius Severinus. *The Consolation of Philosophy*. In *Theological Tractates*, translated by H. F. Stewart. Loeb Classical Library. 1918. Reprint, Cambridge, Mass.: Harvard University Press, 1973.

Borg, Marcus, and N. T. Wright. *The Meaning of Jesus: Two Visions*. San Francisco: HarperCollins, 2000.

Bradshaw, Timothy. *Pannenberg: A Guide for the Perplexed*. London: T&T Clark, 2009.

Brower, Jeffrey E. "Simplicity and Aseity." In *The Oxford Handbook of Philosophical Theology*, edited by Thomas P. Flint and Michael C. Rea, 105–28. Oxford: Oxford University Press, 2009.

Busch, Eberhard. *Karl Barth: His Life from Letters and Autobiographical Texts*. Translated by John Bowden. London: SCM, 1975.

Caldwell, Robert W., III. *Communion in the Spirit: The Holy Spirit as the Bond of Union in the Theology of Jonathan Edwards*. Milton Keynes: Paternoster Press, 2006.

Calvin, John. *The Epistle of Paul the Apostle to the Hebrews and the First and Second Epistles of Saint. Peter*. Edited by David W. Torrance and Thomas F. Torrance. Translated by William B. Johnston. Edinburgh: Oliver & Boyd, 1963.

———. *Institutes of the Christian Religion*. Edited by John T. McNeill. Translated by Ford Lewis Battles. Library of Christian Classics 20–21. 1559. Reprint, Philadephia: Westminster, 1960.

Coakley, Sarah. *God, Sexuality, and the Self: An Essay 'On the Trinity.'* Cambridge: Cambridge University Press, 2013.

———. "On Why *Analytic Theology* Is Not a Club." *Journal of the American Academy of Religion* 81, no. 3 (2013): 601–8.

Collins, Robin. "Evolution and Original Sin." In Keith B. Miller, ed. *Perspectives on an Evolving Creation*, 469–501. Grand Rapids: Eerdmans, 2003.

Cooper, John W. *Panentheism: The Other God of the Philosophers—From Plato to the Present*. Grand Rapids: Baker Academic, 2006.

Copleston, Frederick. *A History of Philosophy*. Vol. 2, *Medieval Philosophy*. London: Continuum, 2003.

Craig, William Lane. *God over All: Divine Aseity and the Problem of Platonism*. Oxford: Oxford University Press, 2016.

Crisp, Oliver D. *An American Augustinian: Sin and Salvation in the Dogmatic Theology of William G. T. Shedd*. Milton Keynes: Paternoster; Eugene, Ore.: Wipf and Stock, 2007.

———. "Analytic Theology." *Expository Times* 122, no. 10 (2011): 469–77.

———. *Approaching the Atonement: The Reconciling Work of Christ*. Downers Grove, Ill.: IVP Academic, forthcoming.

———. *Deviant Calvinism: Broadening the Reformed Tradition*. Minneapolis: Fortress, 2014.

———. *Divinity and Humanity: The Incarnation Reconsidered*. Cambridge: Cambridge University Press, 2007.

———. *God Incarnate: Explorations in Christology*. London: T&T Clark, 2009.

———. *Jonathan Edwards among the Theologians*. Grand Rapids: Eerdmans, 2016.

———. "Methodological Issues in Approaching the Atonement." In *T&T Clark Companion to Atonement*, edited by Adam J. Johnson, 315–33. London: T&T Clark, 20173.

————. "On Analytical Theology." In Crisp and Rea, *Analytic Theology*, 33–53.

————. "Retrieving Zwingli's Doctrine of Original Sin." *Journal of Reformed Theology* 10, no. 4 (2016): 1–21.

————. *Revisioning Christology: Theology in the Reformed Tradition*. Aldershot: Ashgate, 2011.

————. "Sin." In *Christian Dogmatics: Reformed Theology for the Church Catholic*, edited by Michael Allen and Scott R. Swain, 194–215. Grand Rapids: Baker Academic, 2016.

————. *The Word Enfleshed: Exploring the Person and Work of Christ*. Grand Rapids: Baker Academic, 2016.

Crisp, Oliver D., and Michael C. Rea, eds. *Analytic Theology: New Essays in the Philosophy of Theology*. Oxford: Oxford University Press, 2009.

Crisp, Oliver D., and Fred Sanders, eds. *Advancing the Trinity: Explorations in Constructive Dogmatics*. Grand Rapids: Zondervan Academic, 2014.

————, eds. *The Task of Dogmatics: Explorations in Theological Method*. Grand Rapids: Zondervan Academic, 2017.

Cross, Richard. "Two Models of the Trinity?" *Heythrop Journal* 43 (2002): 275–94.

Davies, Brian. *An Introduction to the Philosophy of Religion*. 3rd ed. 1982. Reprint, Oxford: Oxford University Press, 2004.

————. "Simplicity." In *The Cambridge Companion to Christian Philosophical Theology*, edited by Charles Taliferro and Chad Meister, 31–45. Cambridge: Cambridge University Press, 2010.

Dempsey, Michael T., ed. *Trinity and Election in Contemporary Theology*. Grand Rapids: Eerdmans, 2011.

Deutsch, Harry. "Relative Identity." *Stanford Encyclopedia of Philosophy* (2007). https://plato.stanford.edu/entries/identity-relative/.

DeWeese, Garrett J. *God and the Nature of Time*. Aldershot: Ashgate, 2004.

————. "One Person, Two Natures: Two Metaphysical Models of the Incarnation." In *Jesus in Trinitarian Perspective*, edited by Fred Sanders and Klaus Issler, 114–56. Nashville: Broadman & Holman Academic, 2007.

Diller, Kevin. *Theology's Epistemological Dilemma: How Karl Barth and Alvin Plantinga Provide a Unified Response*. Strategic Initiatives in Evangelical Theology. Downers Grove, Ill.: IVP Academic, 2014.

Dolezal, James E. *All That Is in God: Evangelical Theology and the Challenge of Classical Christian Theism*. Grand Rapids: Reformation Heritage, 2017.

————. *God without Parts: Divine Simplicity and the Metaphysics of God's Absoluteness*. Eugene, Ore.: Pickwick, 2011.

Domning, Daryl P., and Monika K. Hellwig. *Original Selfishness: Original Sin in the Light of Evolution*. Ashgate Science and Religion Series. Farnham: Ashgate, 2006.

Donceel, Joseph. "Immediate Animation and Delayed Hominization." *Theological Studies* 31 (1970): 76–105.

Duby, Steven J. *Divine Simplicity: A Dogmatic Account*. London: T&T Clark, 2015.

Edwards, Jonathan. *Ethical Writings,* edited by Paul Ramsey. Vol 8 of *The Works of Jonathan Edwards, edited by Perry Miller.* New Haven: Yale University Press, 1989.

Emery, Gilles, and Matthew Levering, eds. *The Oxford Handbook of the Trinity.* Oxford: Oxford University Press, 2011.

Farris, Joshua R., and Charles Taliaferro, eds. *The Routledge Companion to Theological Anthropology.* London: Routledge, 2015.

Farrow, Douglas. *Ascension and Ecclesia: On the Significance of the Doctrine of the Ascension for Ecclesiology and Christian Cosmology.* Edinburgh: T&T Clark, 1999.

———. *Ascension Theology.* London: T&T Clark, 2011.

Flint, Thomas P. "Molinism and Incarnation." In *Molinism: The Contemporary Debate,* edited by Ken Perszyk, 187–207. Oxford: Oxford University Press, 2011.

———. "Orthodoxy and Incarnation: A Reply to Mullins." *Journal of Analytic Theology* 4 (2016): 180–92.

———. "Should Concretists Part with Mereological Models of the Incarnation?" In Marmadoro and Hill, *Metaphysics of the Incarnation,* 67–87.

Ford, Norman M. *When Did I Begin?* Cambridge: Cambridge University Press, 1988.

Freddoso, Alfred J. "Human Nature, Potency, and the Incarnation." *Faith and Philosophy* 3 (1986): 27–53.

Gäb, Sebastian. "The Paradox of Ineffability." *International Journal of Philosophy and Theology* 78, no. 3 (2017): 289–300.

Ganssle, Gregory, ed. *God and Time: Four Views.* Downers Grove, Ill.: IVP, 2001.

Gavrilyuk, Paul L. "The Retrieval of Deification: How a Once-Despised Archaism Became an Ecumenical Desideratum." *Modern Theology* 25 (2009): 647–59.

Gerrish, B. A. *Christian Faith: Dogmatics in Outline.* Louisville: Westminster John Knox, 2015.

Giles, Kevin. *The Eternal Generation of the Son: Maintaining Orthodoxy in Trinitarian Theology.* Downers Grove, Ill.: IVP Academic, 2012.

Gould, Paul M., ed. *Beyond the Control of God? Six Views on the Problem of God and Abstract Objects.* London: Bloomsbury, 2014.

Gunton, Colin E. *Act and Being: Toward a Theology of the Divine Attributes.* Grand Rapids: Eerdmans, 2002.

———. "The Indispensability of Theological Understanding: Theology in the University." In *Essentials of Christian Community: Essays for Daniel W. Hardy,* edited by David Ford and David L. Stamps, 266–77. Edinburgh: T&T Clark, 1996.

Haarsma, Deborah, and Loren Haarsma. *Origins: Christian Perspectives on Creation, Evolution, and Intelligent Design.* Rev. ed. Grand Rapids: Faith Alive Christian Resources, 2011.

Habets, Myk. "The Doctrine of Election in Evangelical Calvinism: T. F. Torrance as a Case Study." *Irish Theological Quarterly* 73, nos. 3–4 (2008): 334–54.

——. "'Reformed Theosis?' A Response to Gannon Murphy." *Theology Today* 65 (2009): 489–98.

——, ed. *Third Article Theology: A Pneumatological Dogmatics*. Minneapolis: Fortress, 2015.

Hallonsten, Gösta. "Theosis in Recent Research." In *Partakers of the Divine Nature: The History and Development of Deification in the Christian Traditions*, edited by Michael J. Christiansen and Jeffrey A. Witting, 281–93. Grand Rapids: Baker, 2007.

Harnack, Adolf von. *What Is Christianity?* Translated by Thomas Bailey Saunders. 2nd ed. New York: G. P. Putnam's Sons, 1901.

Hasker, William. "Eternity and Providence." In *The Cambridge Companion to Philosophical Theology, edited by* Charles Taliaferro and Chad Meister, 81–93. Cambridge: Cambridge University Press, 2010.

——. *God, Time, and Knowledge*. Ithaca, N.Y.: Cornell University Press, 1989.

——. *Metaphysics and the Tripersonal God*. Oxford Studies in Analytic Theology. Oxford: Oxford University Press, 2014.

Helm, Paul. *Eternal God: A Study of God without Time*. 2nd ed. 1988. Reprint, Oxford: Oxford University Press, 2010.

——. "Karl Barth and the Visibility of God." In *Engaging with Barth: Contemporary Evangelical Critiques*, edited by David Gibson and Daniel Strange, 273–99. New York: T&T Clark, 2008.

Heppe, Heinrich. *Reformed Dogmatics*. Edited by Ernst Bizer. Translated by G. T. Thomson. 1861. Reprint, London: Collins, 1950.

Hinlicky, Paul R. *Divine Simplicity: Christ the Crisis of Metaphysics*. Grand Rapids: Baker Academic, 2016.

Holmes, Stephen R. *The Quest for the Trinity: The Doctrine of God in Scripture, History and Modernity*. Downers Grove, Ill.: IVP Academic, 2012.

Horton, Michael S. *Covenant and Salvation: Union with Christ*. Louisville: Westminster John Knox Press, 2007.

Howard-Snyder, Daniel. "Panmetaphoricism." *Religious Studies* 53, no. 1 (2015): 25–49.

——. "Trinity," (Revised Version). *Routledge Encyclopedia of Philosophy Online* (2015). https://www.rep.routledge.com/articles/thematic/trinity/v-2.

Hudson, Hud. *The Fall and Hypertime*. Oxford: Oxford University Press, 2014.

——. *The Metaphysics of Hyperspace*. Oxford: Oxford University Press, 2005.

Immink, F. G. *Divine Simplicity*. Kampen: Kok, 1987.

Insole, Christopher. "Anthropomorphism and the Apophatic God." *Modern Theology* 17, no. 4 (2001): 475–83.

Jacobs, Jonathan D. "The Ineffable, Inconceivable, and Incomprehensible God: Fundamentality and Apophatic Theology." In *Oxford Studies in Philosophy of Religion*, vol. 6, edited by Jonathan L. Kvanvig, 158–76. Oxford: Oxford University Press, 2015.

Jenson, Robert W. *Essays in Theology of Culture*. Grand Rapids: Eerdmans, 1995.

————. "Once More, the *Logos asarkos*." *International Journal of Systematic Theology* 13, no. 2 (2011): 130–33.

————. *Systematic Theology*. Vol. 1, *The Triune God*. New York: Oxford University Press, 1997.

Johnson, Elizabeth. "The Incomprehensibility of God and the Image of God as Male and Female." *Theological Studies* 45, no. 3 (1984): 441–65.

Jones, David Albert. *The Soul of the Embryo: An Enquiry into the Status of the Human Embryo in the Christian Tradition*. London: Continuum, 2004.

Jones, Gareth. "The Resurrection in Contemporary Systematic Theology." In *Resurrection Reconsidered*, edited by Gavin D'Costa, 31–47. Oxford: Oneworld, 1996.

Kärkkäinen, Veli-Matti. *Trinity and Revelation*. Vol. 2 of *A Constructive Christian Theology for the Pluralistic World*. Grand Rapids: Eerdmans, 2014.

Kaufman, Gordon D. *In the Face of Mystery: A Constructive Theology*. Cambridge, Mass.: Harvard University Press, 1993.

Kretzmann, Norman. *The Metaphysics of Creation: Aquinas's Natural Theology in "Summa contra gentiles II."* Oxford: Oxford University Press, 1998.

Kvanvig, Jonathan L. "Divine Transcendence." *Religious Studies* 20, no. 3 (1984): 377–87.

Leftow, Brian. "Anti-social Trinitarianism." In McCall and Rea, *Philosophical and Theological Essays on the Trinity*, 52–88.

————. "The Humanity of God." In Marmadoro and Hill, *Metaphysics of the Incarnation*, 20–44.

————. *Time and Eternity*. Ithaca, N.Y.: Cornell University Press, 1991.

————. "A Timeless God Incarnate." In *The Incarnation*, edited by Stephen T. Davis, Daniel Kendall, and Gerald O'Collins, 273–99. New York: Oxford University Press, 2002.

————. "Why Perfect Being Theology?" *International Journal for Philosophy of Religion* 69 (2011): 103–18.

Leget, Carlo. "Eschatology." In *The Theology of Thomas Aquinas*, edited by Rik van Nieuwenhove and Joseph Wawrykow, 365–85. Notre Dame: University of Notre Dame Press, 2005.

Levering, Matthew. *Engaging the Doctrine of Creation: Cosmos, Creatures, and the Wise and Good Creator*. Grand Rapids: Baker Academic, 2017.

Lewis, C. S. *Fern Seeds and Elephants, and Other Essays on Christianity*. London: Fontana, 1975.

Lincoln, Andrew T. *Born of a Virgin? Reconceiving Jesus in the Bible, Tradition, and Theology*. Grand Rapids: Eerdmans, 2013.

————. "'Born of the Virgin Mary': Creedal Affirmation and Critical Reading." In *Christology and Scripture: Interdisciplinary Perspectives*, edited by Andrew T. Lincoln and Angus Paddison, 84–103. London: T&T Clark, 2008.

Loke, Andrew Tern. *A Kryptic Model of the Incarnation*. Farnham, Surrey, UK: Ashgate, 2014. Reprint, London: Routledge, 2016.

————. "On Dyothelitism Versus Monothelitism: The Divine Preconscious Model." *Heythrop Journal* 57, no. 1 (2016): 135–41.

Long, Stephen D. *The Perfectly Simple Triune God: Aquinas and His Legacy*. Minneapolis: Fortress, 2016.

Lowe, E. J. *The Four Category Ontology: A Metaphysical Foundation for Natural Science*. Oxford: Oxford University Press, 2006.

MacIntyre, Alasdair. *Whose Justice? Which Rationality?* Notre Dame: University of Notre Dame Press, 1989.

Marion, Jean-Luc. "In the Name: How to Avoid Speaking of 'Negative Theology.'" In *God, the Gift, and Postmodernism*, edited by John D. Caputo and Michael Scanlon, 42–53. Bloomington: Indiana University Press, 1999.

Marmadoro, Anna, and Jonathan Hill, eds. *The Metaphysics of the Incarnation*. Oxford: Oxford University Press, 2011.

McCall, Thomas H. *An Invitation to Analytic Christian Theology*. Downers Grove, Ill.: IVP Academic, 2015.

————. "Trinity Doctrine, Plain and Simple." In *Advancing Trinitarian Theology: Explorations in Constructive Dogmatics*, edited by Oliver D. Crisp and Fred Sanders, 42–59. Grand Rapids: Zondervan Academic, 2014.

————. *Which Trinity? Whose Monotheism? Philosophical and Systematic Theologians on the Metaphysics of Trinitarian Theology*. Grand Rapids: Eerdmans, 2010.

McCall, Thomas H., and Michael C. Rea, eds. *Philosophical and Theological Essays on the Trinity*. Oxford: Oxford University Press, 2009.

McCormack, Bruce L. "The Actuality of God: Karl Barth in Conversation with Open Theism." In *Engaging the Doctrine of God: Contemporary Protestant Perspectives, edited by Bruce L. McCormack,* 185–242. Grand Rapids: Baker Academic, 2008.

————. "In Memoriam: Robert Jenson (1930–2017)." *International Journal of Systematic Theology* 20, no. 1 (2018): 3–7.

————. *Orthodox and Modern: Studies in the Theology of Karl Barth*. Grand Rapids: Baker Academic, 2009.

————. "Union with Christ in Calvin's Theology: Grounds for a Divinization Theory?" In *Tributes to John Calvin: A Celebration of His Quincentenary*, edited by David W. Hall, 504–29. Phillipsburg, N.J.: Presbyterian & Reformed, 2010.

McDonald, Suzanne. *Re-imaging Election: Divine Election as Representing God to Others, and Others to God*. Grand Rapids: Eerdmans, 2012.

McFarland, Ian A. *In Adam's Fall: A Meditation on the Christian Doctrine of Original Sin*. Oxford: Wiley-Blackwell, 2010.

McMartin, Jason. "The Theandric Union as *Imago Dei* and *Capax Dei*." In *Christology Ancient and Modern: Explorations in Constructive Dogmatics*, edited by Oliver D. Crisp and Fred Sanders, 136–50. Grand Rapids: Zondervan Academic, 2013.

Miller, Keith B., ed. *Perspectives on an Evolving Creation*. Grand Rapids: Eerdmans, 2003.

Moltmann, Jürgen. *The Trinity and the Kingdom: The Doctrine of God*. Translated by Olive Wyon. 1980. Reprint, London: SCM, 1981.

Moreland, J. P., and William Lane Craig. *Philosophical Foundations for a Christian Worldview*. Downers Grove, Ill.: IVP, 2003.

Morris, Thomas V. *The Logic of God Incarnate*. Ithaca, N.Y.: Cornell University Press, 1986.

———. *Our Idea of God: An Introduction to Philosophical Theology*. Downers Grove, Ill.: IVP, 1991.

Mosser, Carl. "The Metaphysics of Union with God." Unpublished paper presented at Fuller Theological Seminary, May 4, 2017.

Mostert, Christiaan. *God and the Future: Wolfhart Pannenberg's Eschatological Doctrine of God*. London: T&T Clark, 2002.

Muller, Richard A. *Post-Reformation Reformed Dogmatics*, vol. 3. Grand Rapids: Baker Academic, 2003.

Mullins, R. T. "The Difficulty with Demarcating Panentheism." *Sophia* 55 (2016): 325–46.

———. "Flint's 'Molinism and the Incarnation' Is Still Too Radical—A Rejoinder to Flint." *Journal of Analytic Theology* 5 (2017): 515–32.

———. "Flint's 'Molinism and the Incarnation' Is Too Radical." *Journal of Analytic Theology* 3 (2015): 1–15.

———. *In Search of the Timeless God*. Oxford Studies in Analytic Theology. Oxford: Oxford University Press, 2016.

———. "Simply Impossible: The Case against Divine Simplicity." *Journal of Reformed Theology* 7, no. 2 (2013): 181–203.

Murphy, Gannon. "Reformed Theosis?" *Theology Today* 65 (2008): 191–212.

Nazianzus, Gregory. *The Fifth Theological Oration: On the Holy Spirit (Oration 31)*. In *Cyril of Jerusalem, Gregory Nazianzen*, 318–28. Vol. 7 of NPNF Second Series, edited by Philip Schaff and Henry Wace. Edinburgh: T&T Clark, 1893.

———. *On God and Christ: The Five Theological Orations and Two Letters to Cledonius*. Translated by Frederick Williams and Lionel Wickham. Yonkers: Saint Vladimir's Seminary Press, 2002.

Nemeş, Steven. "On the Priority of Tradition: An Exercise in Analytic Theology." *Open Theology* 3 (2017): 274–92.

Olson, Roger E. "Deification in Contemporary Theology." *Theology Today* 64 (2007): 186–200.

———. "Trinity and Eschatology: The Historical Being of God in Jürgen Moltmann and Wolfhart Pannenberg." *Scottish Journal of Theology* 36 (1983): 213–27.

———. "Wolfhart Pannenberg's Doctrine of the Trinity." *Scottish Journal of Theology* 43, no. 2 (1990): 175–206.

Ott, Ludwig. *Fundamentals of Catholic Dogma*. 4th ed. Rockford, Ill.: TAN Books, 1960.

Otto, Randall. "Moltmann and the Anti-monotheism Movement." *International Journal of Systematic Theology* 3, no. 3 (2001): 293–308.

Pannenberg, Wolfhart. "The God of History: The Trinitarian God and the Truth of History." Translated by M. B. Jackson. *The Cumberland Seminarian* 19, nos. 2–3 (1981): 28–41. Originally published as "Der Gott der Geschichte: der trinitarische Gott und die Warheit der Geschichte." *Kerygma and Dogma* 23 (1977): 76–92.

———. "The God of Hope." In *Basic Questions in Theology: Collected Essays*, vol. 2. Minneapolis: Fortress, 1971.

———. "History and the Reality of the Resurrection." In *Resurrection Reconsidered*, edited by Gavin D'Costa, 62–72. Oxford: Oneworld, 1996.

———. *Jesus—God and Man*. Translated by Lewis L. Wilkins and Duane A. Priebe. London: SCM, 1964.

———. *Systematic Theology*. 3 Vols. Translated by Geoffrey Bromiley. Grand Rapids: Eerdmans, 1991–98.

Parry, Robin A. *The Biblical Cosmos*. Eugene, Ore.: Cascade, 2014.

Pawl, Tim. *In Defense of Conciliar Christology: A Philosophical Essay*. Oxford Studies in Analytic Theology. Oxford: Oxford University Press, 2016.

Peacocke, Arthur. "DNA of our DNA." In *The Birth of Jesus, Biblical and Theological Reflections*, edited by George J. Brooke, 59–70. Edinburgh: T&T Clark, 2000.

———. *Theology for a Scientific Age: Being and Becoming—Natural, Divine and Human*. Oxford: Blackwell, 1993.

Percival, Henry R., ed. *The Seven Ecumenical Councils of the Undivided Church: Their Canons and Dogmatic Decrees*. New York: Edwin S. Gorham, 1901.

Perspectives on Science and Christian Faith 62, no. 3 (2010). http://www.asa3.org/ASA/PSCF/2010/PSCF9-10dyn.html.

Phan, Peter C., ed. *The Cambridge Companion to the Trinity*. Cambridge: Cambridge University Press, 2011.

Pike, Nelson. *God and Timelessness*. London: Routledge and Kegan Paul, 1970.

Plantinga, Alvin. *Does God Have a Nature?* Milwaukee: Marquette University Press, 1980.

———. "On Heresy, Mind, and Truth." *Faith and Philosophy* 16, no. 2 (1999): 182–93.

Pseudo-Dionysius. *Pseudo-Dionysius: The Complete Works*. Edited by Colm Lubheid. Mahwah, N.J.: Paulist, 1987.

Rea, Michael C. "Hiddenness and Transcendence." In *Hidden Divinity and Religious Belief: New Perspectives*, edited by Adam Green and Eleonore Stump, 210–25. Cambridge University Press, 2015.

———. "Relative Identity and the Doctrine of the Trinity." In McCall and Rea, *Philosophical and Theological Essays on the Trinity*, 249–62.

———. "The Trinity." In *The Oxford Handbook of Philosophical Theology*, edited by Thomas P. Flint and Michael C. Rea, 403–29. Oxford: Oxford University Press, 2009.

Rae, Murray A. *History and Hermeneutics*. London: T&T Clark, 2005.

Richards, Jay Wesley. *The Untamed God: A Philosophical Exploration of Divine Perfection, Simplicity and Immutability*. Downers Grove, Ill.: IVP, 2003.

Rogers, Katherin A. *Anselm on Freedom*. Oxford: Oxford University Press, 2008.

———. *Perfect Being Theology*. Edinburgh: Edinburgh University Press, 2000.

Romanides, John S. *The Ancestral Sin*. Ridgewood, N.J.: Zephyr, 2002.

Rowe, William L. *Can God be Free?* Oxford: Oxford University Press, 2006.

Sanders, Fred. *The Triune God*. New Studies in Dogmatics. Grand Rapids: Zondervan Academic, 2016.

Schaff, Philip, ed. *The Creeds of Christendom: With a History and Critical Notes*. Vol. 3, *The Evangelical Protestant Creeds*, revised by David Schaff. 6th ed. 1931. Reprint, Grand Rapids: Baker, 1983.

———. *History of the Christian Church*. Vol. 8, *Modern Christianity. The Swiss Reformation*. 3rd ed. 1910. Reprint, Grand Rapids: Eerdmans, 1976.

Schmid, Heinrich. *The Doctrinal Theology of the Evangelical Lutheran Church*. Translated by Charles A. Hay and Henry E. Jacobs. Minneapolis: Augsburg Publishing, 1889.

Sexton, Jason, ed. *Two Views on the Trinity*. Counterpoints Series. Grand Rapids: Zondervan Academic, 2014.

Shedd, William G. T. *Dogmatic Theology*. Edited by Alan Gomes. 3rd ed. 1888. Reprint, Philipsburg, N.J.: Presbyterian and Reformed, 2003.

Sider, Ted. *Writing the Book of the World*. Oxford: Oxford University Press, 2011.

Staniforth, Maxwell, and Andrew Louth, trans. *Early Christian Writings: The Apostolic Fathers*. 1968. Reprint, Harmondsworth: Penguin Books, 1987.

Steinmetz, David C. "Uncovering a Second Narrative: Detective Fiction and the Construction of Historical Method." In *The Art of Reading Scripture*, edited by Ellen F. Davis and Richard B. Hays, 54–65. Grand Rapids: Eerdmans, 2003.

Strobel, Kyle. "Jonathan Edwards's Reformed Doctrine of Theosis." *Harvard Theological Review* 109, no. 3 (2016): 371–99.

Stump, Eleonore. *Aquinas*. London: Routledge, 2003.

———. "Aquinas on the Metaphysics of the Incarnation." In *The Incarnation*, edited by Stephen T. Davis, Daniel Kendall, and Gerald O'Collins, 197–220. Oxford: Oxford University Press, 2002.

———. "Dante's Hell, Aquinas's Moral Theory, and the Love of God." *Canadian Journal of Philosophy* 16 (1986): 181–98.

———. *The God of the Bible and the God of the Philosophers*. The Aquinas Lecture 2016. Milwaukee: Marquette University Press, 2016.

———. "The Problem of Evil: Analytic Philosophy and Narrative." In Crisp and Rea, *Analytic Theology*, 251–64.

———. "Simplicity." In *A Companion to Philosophy of Religion*, edited by Philip L. Quinn and Charles Taliaferro, 250–56. Oxford: Blackwell, 1997.

———. *Wandering in Darkness: Narrative and the Problem of Evil*. Oxford: Oxford University Press, 2000.

Stump, Eleonore, and Norman Kretzmann. "Eternity." *Journal of Philosophy* 78, no. 8 (1981): 429–58.

Swain, Scott R. *The God of the Gospel: Robert Jenson's Trinitarian Theology*. Downers Grove, Ill.: IVP Academic, 2013.

Swinburne, Richard. *The Christian God*. Oxford: Oxford University Press, 1994.

———. *The Coherence of Theism*. Rev. ed. 1977. Reprint, Oxford: Oxford University Press, 1993.

———. *The Resurrection of God Incarnate*. Oxford: Oxford University Press, 2003.

Tanner, Kathryn. *Christ the Key*. Cambridge: Cambridge University Press, 2009.

———. "The Trinity as Christian Teaching." In Emery and Levering, *Oxford Handbook of the Trinity*, 349–58.

Tanner, Norman P., S.J., ed. *Decrees of the Ecumenical Councils*. 2 vols. Washington, D.C.: Georgetown University Press, 1990.

Tappert, Theodore G., trans. and ed. *The Book of Concord: The Confessions of the Evangelical Lutheran Church*. Philadelphia: Fortress, 1959.

Torrance, Alan J. "Is There a Distinctive Human Nature? Approaching the Question from a Christian Epistemic Base." *Zygon* 47, no. 4 (2012): 903–17.

Torrance, Thomas F. *Space, Time and Resurrection*. Grand Rapids: Eerdmans, 1976.

Tuggy, Dale. "Metaphysics and Logic of the Trinity." *Oxford Handbooks Online* (Dec. 2016). https://doi.org/10.1093/oxfordhb/9780199935314.013.27.

———. "On Positive Mysterianism." *International Journal for Philosophy of Religion* 69, no. 3 (2011): 205–26.

———. "Trinity." *Stanford Encyclopedia of Philosophy* (March 2016). http://plato .stanford.edu/entries/trinity/.

———. "The Unfinished Business of Trinitarian Theorizing." *Religious Studies* 39, no. 2 (2003): 165–83.

Unger, Peter. *All the Power in the World*. Oxford: Oxford University Press, 2005.

van Driel, Edwin Christian. *Incarnation Anyway: Arguments for Supralapsarian Christology*. American Academy of Religion Series. New York: Oxford University Press, 2008.

Vanhoozer, Kevin J. *Remythologizing Theology: Divine Action, Passion, and Authorship*. Cambridge Studies in Christian Doctrine 18. Cambridge: Cambridge University Press, 2010.

Visser, Sandra, and Thomas Williams. *Anselm*. Great Medieval Thinkers. Oxford: Oxford University Press, 2008.

Wainwright, William J. "Jonathan Edwards, William Rowe, and the Necessity of Creation." In *Faith, Freedom, and Rationality*, edited by Jeff Jordan and Daniel Howard-Snyder, 119–33. Lanham, Md.: Rowman & Littlefield, 1996.

Ware, Timothy [Kallistos]. *The Orthodox Church*. New ed. 1963. Reprint, London: Penguin, 1997.

Webster, John B. "Principles of Systematic Theology." *International Journal of Systematic Theology* 11, no. 1 (2009), 56–71.

————. "Theological Theology." In *Confessing God: Essays in Christian Dogmatics II*, 11–32. London: T&T Clark, 20052.

————. "What Makes Theology Theological?" *Journal of Analytic Theology* 3 (2015): 17–28.

Wessling, Jordan. "Christology and Conciliar Authority: On the Viability of Monothelitism for Protestant Theology." In *Christology Ancient and Modern: Explorations in Constructive Dogmatics*, edited by Oliver D. Crisp and Fred Sanders, 151–70. Grand Rapids: Zondervan Academic, 2013.

Westcott, Brooke Foss. *Christus Consummator: Some Aspects of the Person and Work of Christ in Relation to Modern Thought*. 2nd ed. London: Macmillan, 1887.

————. "The Gospel of Creation." In *The Epistles of St John: The Greek Text with Notes and Essays*, 283–328. 3rd ed. London: Macmillan, 1892.

Wilken, Robert Louis. *The Spirit of Early Christian Thought: Seeking the Face of God*. New Haven: Yale University Press, 2002.

Williams, N. P. *The Ideas of the Fall and Original Sin*. London: Longmans, 1927.

Wilson, E. O. *On Human Nature*. Cambridge, Mass.: Harvard University Press, 1978.

Wolterstorff, Nicholas. "Divine Simplicity." In *Philosophy of Religion*, 531–52. *Philosophical Perspectives 5*, edited by James Tomberlin. Atascadero, Calif.: Ridgeview, 19912.

————. "God Everlasting." In *God and the Good: Essays in Honor of Henry Stob*, edited by Clifton Orlebeke and Lewis Smedes, 181–203. Grand Rapids: Eerdmans, 1975.

————. "How Philosophical Theology Became Possible within the Analytic Tradition of Philosophy." In Crisp and Rea, *Analytic Theology*, 155–68.

————. "To Theologians: From One Who Cares about Theology but Is Not One of You." *Theological Education* 40, no. 2 (2005), 79–92.

Wood, William. "Modeling Mystery." *Scientia et Fides* 4, no. 1 (2016): 39–59.

————. "Trajectories, Traditions, and Tools in Analytic Theology." *Journal of Analytic Theology* 4 (2016): 254–66.

Yadav, Sameer. "Mystical Experience and the Apophatic Attitude." *Journal of Analytic Theology* 4 (2016): 18-43.

Zwingli, Huldrych. "Account of the Faith to Charles V." In *On Providence and Other Essays,* edited by Samuel Macauley Jackson, 33–61. 1922. Reprint, Durham, N.C.: Labyrinth, 1983.

Index